I Was Not the Blossom

Growing With Your Students in a

Nurturing Classroom

Eric Stemle

Note: While this is a work of non-fiction, some of its names have been changed by the author.

Cover Design by Paul Stemle

Printed in the United State of America

For Teresa, Paul, and Ellen

Table of Contents

Tilling

W alk down the halls of an American high school, take a look inside the doors and windows as you pass. Where is your attention drawn? Quite often it is to the place where nearly all of the eyes inside are trained, on the one person not seated. Look further around the room, and you will likely see desks arranged in an orderly fashion, one that makes it easy for their inhabitants to see both the person standing and the technology set up to convey information, be it a white board, a projection screen, or a television. While you might also pass by classrooms with chairs and tables arranged to promote conversations or stationed with computers to allow for individualized learning, there is more than a good chance that most of the rooms you observe will be designed to focus their students' attention on one person.

The teacher.

It's a system that has served public schools and universities longer than anyone who is reading this can remember, and not only was it the primary way in which I was taught, but it was also the way I felt most comfortable teaching in the early years of my career. The classroom was my theater, and when the bell rang to start each class, I took the stage. I was a performer, a salesman, a purveyor of arcane knowledge. I enjoyed having those eyes on me, those ears receptive to the wisdom I was sharing, but when they weren't, when my students were distracted or just not interested in what I was saying, I became a taskmaster, a disciplinarian who concentrated less on instructing and more on keeping my students riveted to my delivery. After a while, however, I tired of being the focal point at the front of the room, and by reflecting, I realized that it was never supposed to be about me. And while I loved all aspects of the language arts, it really wasn't about the English course curriculum, either. Here I was all that time, thinking I was in the spotlight, when another metaphor was much more apropos.

My classroom was a garden. That was it! Hardly an original notion, but one that called to me all the same. I was a gardener, preparing the soil, planting seeds, nurturing, weeding, and in time each year, I was surrounded by brilliant colors and dazzling fragrances. Of course! Any visitor could see what remarkable flowers I was producing, could appreciate all the time I spent, the tender care that I provided to bring out such an amazing array of blooms. A gardener!

But no.

That wasn't quite right, either, because if that was my role, then I was still separating myself from my students, still keeping a distance as I had as an actor on that stage. If I was going to think of our classroom as a flower bed, then I didn't want to be merely a caretaker. I wanted to be part of what grew there. All well and good, but just what part of the flowers was I, exactly? I knew I wasn't the leaves, taking in light, facilitating photosynthesis. That's what my students did when they absorbed information and converted it into knowledge. I wasn't the petals, either, using their beauty to attract bees that took away their pollen. That was my kids when they expressed their learning, when they shared ideas and created new understandings around the room. Eventually, the answer came to me, and it turned out to be really quite simple, for I was not the leaf, and I was not the blossom.

I was the stem.

And there it was. I was a conduit, rooted in the soil and delivering water and nutrients to the petals, much as I shared my knowledge with my students. I was also a support, helping to hold the blossoms up so that they could reach for the sun, could join with those who would help them share their learning. My role as the stem was perhaps more important than any information I ever imparted about reading and interpreting, writing and presenting, because it kept my kids going when the winds of doubt threatened, encouraged them to grow higher and more beautiful than any seeds ever had. That's what I wanted people to see when they visited our classroom. If they looked closely, they might see my influence, but it mattered more to me that my students were the stars. After all, they were the reason I worked so hard for all those years.

Forty-one years it was, though when I first stepped on the Michigan State University campus as a freshman in the fall of 1971, I never imagined that I would be leaving with a degree in education. I had experienced a certain amount of anxiety in high school, more nights than I care to admit spent silently crying into my pillow because I had not a clue as to what I would do for a living after I graduated. My friends talked about medicine, law, and engineering, but I didn't see any of those in my future. I tried to figure out what I was good at. I wasn't mechanical, and I struggled in biology and chemistry and geometry. It came down to the fact that I could read, and I could write. Oh, and I could cover first base and sink jump shots against a zone. I didn't see any of those skills readily transferring to a satisfying career.

Or could they? At the end of my freshman year, emboldened by my dreams of becoming a professional writer, I declared myself a journalism major. After taking a few introductory courses, however, I came to the sad realization that a lot of MSU students had similar aspirations, and I was unprepared for the competition that J-School was providing me. A year later I switched my major to English and adjusted my sights on a career of writing fiction, but a conversation with an advisor from my new department abruptly doused those ideas. Following her pragmatic suggestion, I soon became a member not only of the College of Arts and Letters, but also of the College of Education.

I was surprised by how much I enjoyed my early experiences in the latter. In my first two years at the university, I had endured a string of classes and credits, term papers and exams, but now I was involved in what I saw as a purposeful curriculum. I had found a new path for my studies and an opportunity to redefine myself on that road. Suddenly, I was working harder on my assignments than I ever remembered doing, and I discovered a geyser of creativity that had lain dormant for far too long. For the first time since grade school, I felt special as a student, ready to make a difference somehow. So it was that in the fall of 1976, I

3

entered the teaching profession, a practice that lasted over four decades. I went from being a disinterested student in high school to being a teacher who loved the idea of going there every morning. What brought about that change?

The answer lies in this book. What follows in these pages is a compendium of one year of blogging about my classroom. I had started posting a few years earlier with the express purpose of informing my students' parents of what their daughters and sons were doing in our class, and I had also invited my fellow teachers to follow along in hope that my writing would generate a conversation about our common as well as our differing methods. To my dismay, I soon saw that I was basically writing to myself. Occasionally, one of my colleagues would mention that he had read a post, but no one was leaving comments on my site, and the monologue seemed to be nothing more than my reflections being shot out into the ether. A friend suggested that I try posting on a broader platform, and after initially dismissing her advice, I decided to migrate my blog to Facebook. Starting with my first day with my students, I publicly recorded the experiences that we shared for that entire year.

The response to my sharing surprised me. My first post brought over one hundred comments, and while some came from friends and other teachers, a great majority came from former students, many then in their forties with families and careers of their own. It was remarkable to see not only what they were doing with their lives but to also learn what they remembered from our time together. What a gift, I thought, to be back in conversation with old friends. Some told me that reading my entries was like being in our class all over again, and I wanted to tell them, "If you only realized how much more I know about teaching than I did then." Deep down, though, I understood that despite all of the changes that I made over the span of my career, some things about my teaching never changed. That is one thread you will read throughout this book.

Another theme you'll see in these pages is the nature of our country's approach to teaching over the years. The process of education in the United States has been compared to a pendulum, and its momentum for the past thirty years or so has drifted toward the science of instruction, the idea that good teaching can be created by formula. Educational leaders have operated on the belief that given the right curriculum, the right professional development, and the right evaluation system, school districts can produce a competent instructor out of anyone who has the desire to succeed in the field. As the pendulum continues to swing inexorably in that direction, it moves us away from the art of teaching, those aspects of the practice that include, among other things, building relationships, fostering a nurturing classroom climate, and providing inspiration for our students.

The pendular arm of the educational system is long and heavy, and for those of us who revere the affective side of teaching, it will probably take a long time for it to swing back and eventually find its equilibrium. Why do we have to wait, however? At the moment, America's teachers are being tasked with assessing their students' learning, generating data from those assessments, and using that statistical analysis to plan their lessons, and while that has been the focus of the educational establishment for a number of years, school doesn't have to be a zero-sum game. Teachers have always known that they are most effective when they combine mechanics with imagination. The science of teaching might indeed provide the easel, the canvas, the paints, and the brush, but it is with the art of teaching—the observant eye, the attentive ear, the open heart—that we paint.

As you read this book, you will follow the arc of one year in my career as a teacher. The final year. Along the way, I'll provide you with context and stories and opinions on what John Steinbeck called "the greatest of the arts." More than anything, though, I will open the door to my teaching to you. After four decades of working with young people in the confines of a small circle of desks, after discovering what few if any of my own teachers ever seemed to know about motivating a student like I was in high school, my dream now is to extend my teaching to a different set of hearts and minds, to those just entering the teaching world. To realize that dream, I am passing along my thoughts and feelings about what we need to do to bring balance back to our schools. It's true that for our children to learn in remarkable ways, schools will always need structure and accountability, but they will also need the magic that happens when a teacher helps students recognize their own powers, helps them develop those abilities beyond what they had previously thought possible.

Welcome to our classroom as it was in that last year of my teaching. Whether you are currently a student enrolled in a college of education who is now beginning to think of school from a teacher's perspective or a certified faculty member just starting to gain experience, this book is designed to help you better understand the nature of your profession and to celebrate with you as a fellow artist. And while the conversation that follows is directed particularly at my younger colleagues, I welcome other readers to listen in as well. Maybe you're a parent who wants to know more about the inner workings of your daughter or son's classroom. Perhaps you're a school board member or an administrator looking for secrets to helping your teachers become more effective in relating to their students. No matter your perspective or purpose, I hope that you will come to know our classroom as I knew it, a vibrant and organic place where I sought every day to encourage and challenge and inspire my students. A room that I loved that was filled with students who I loved even more. I may no longer have the key to that place, but its door will always be open to my heart and to the hearts of all of those young people who grew and blossomed and made it beautiful.

And with that, it's time you got to experience our garden. Come in and meet my flowers. . . .

P*lanting*

All right, so maybe I was a gardener, too. Before I could be the stem, could support and nourish my students, it was also up to me to prepare an environment in which we could all grow. Grow as independent flowers and flourish as an array as well. As each class came together in the fall, I had already made ready the soil that would foster them. The tools I employed were my years of experience in the classroom and the training that I received in both my university classes and in a variety of professional development programs throughout my career. Those implements enabled me to smooth the way, to remove any stones or other impediments that could hinder the maturation of my young charges. I then devoted the first few weeks of the school year to careful planting, knowing that seeds need two things after they are placed in the soil if they are to grow successfully. The first is warmth, and in our classroom that involved surrounding my students with a certain amount of security from day one. That meant creating norms and situations that ensured that my kids would feel safe in their new surroundings, that they would begin to develop trust in me as that gardener who would protect them when they took risks. The second need is water, and in our case that came in the form of the early language arts content that I sprinkled on each seed. The essence of that water had to be novel and intriguing in order to stimulate each mind to open itself to possibility. Once the seeds were safely planted and cared for, we all began the business of growing, and from then on, whenever I was in that garden, I expressed two natures. In one, I was the gardener, assuming the responsibility of caring for each

7

flower and keeping in mind the welfare of the garden as a whole. In the other, I was the stem, a part of the emergence of both, though that's something that my students were probably unaware of in those early days of the academic year. They had known gardeners all throughout their school years, but before long they would come to realize that this one was a part of them as well.

What Steinbeck Said: Post #1
Monday, August 29, 2016
The Room Where It Happens

For the past few years, I have blogged after each day of teaching. I have described my lessons and the thinking behind them, and while my original intended audience was my colleagues and the parents of my students, today I have decided to post my entry here to make it available to old friends as well. I hope you enjoy it.

First, an explanation of the blog's title. A poster hangs on my classroom wall across the way from a large, framed portrait of John Steinbeck. It reads: "I have come to believe that a great teacher is a great artist and that there are as few as there are other great artists. Teaching might even be the greatest of the arts since the medium is the human mind and spirit." To that end, this blog is dedicated to the development of great artists. May we all benefit from our discoveries and our collaborations as we learn what it means to be great teachers. In other words, how can we live up to Steinbeck's vision for our profession?

Whether or not we are certified, we are all teachers, my friends, and we can all contribute to the learning of young people. Thanks for sharing ideas with me!

Today marked the beginning of my forty-first year of teaching, and as always, I considered it the most important day of the year in our classroom. This was our first time together as classmates, and I began it as is my custom by standing at my door, greeting each arrival with a smile and a handshake and a welcome into our circle. First days can be about a lot of things. Rules. Expectations. Materials. In Room 218, the first day is about us. Who are we as we gather as individuals? Who will we become as a class of thinkers, of writers, of artists? We took our first steps in discovering answers to those questions today.

Each summer I decide on a theme for my classes, a message that will run throughout everything we do during the year. Two years ago it was The Senior Dimension, *a variation on Edwin Abbot's* Flatland, *a brilliant satire based on a two-dimensional world. I exhorted my students to see beyond school as we normally perceive it. Last year the focus was on* Master and Apprentice, *and I guided my kids through the attainment and polishing of their language skills.*

Today, I introduced still another approach.

Early in the class period I told my students the story of a scene from the Broadway musical, Hamilton. *Aaron Burr feels that he's been left out of a dinner meeting attended by Thomas Jefferson, James Madison, and the title character. The result of the meeting is a proposal to move the nation's capital from New York to Washington. Burr questions Hamilton after the meeting, chastising him for selling out New York City. Hamilton replies that he has gotten what he wanted all along: New York will be the financial center of the new country. He explains that he wants to build something that will last beyond his lifetime.*

"What do you want, Burr?" he asks repeatedly.

His rival sings his answer: "I wanna be in the room where it happens, the room where it happens. I wanna be in the room where it happens, the room where it happens."

I sang those words to my students today. I explained the societal importance of closed doors and brokered deals. I talked about the importance of being present with power. I told them that it's not about privilege but rather about membership. Then I pointed to a sign above our windows: "The Room Where It Happens." Admission to this room has to be earned because my students have to qualify in order to register for our class. Today, years of effort came to fruition as they entered Room 218. Now that all that intellectual and creative power has been assembled, we are ready to do some remarkable learning together. It all began today.

What do you remember about first days when you were in school? Were you excited to be back, looking forward to a new adventure? Or were you in mourning for the dying of summer and a return to the year-long grind? First days are often more about what we feel than they are about what we see and hear. On the second day of school each year I began each period by asking my students what they had done in their other classes the day before. They invariably groaned in unison and told me, "Rules!" They had heard all about the requirements of those classes, they had read through syllabi that laid out procedures and expectations and consequences. Mostly what they had done was sit and look and listen.

Sound familiar? I know that was my experience as a student. Each Tuesday after Labor Day, I came into classes full of wonder as to what each one would hold. Which of my friends would be in there with me? What I would be learning for the year? Was this a class that was going to change my life? Sometimes it seemed that it would be, and I couldn't wait to come back there for the second day. Then again, a lot of times I felt let down. Here is what you have to do. Here is what will happen if you don't. You know, rules. When I found myself in a room where the teacher seemed more preoccupied with keeping us all in line than with inspiring our young minds, I gave enough effort to satisfy the course's demands, but I didn't always do my best in living up to my part of the teaching-learning bargain. Just didn't feel it. Yet, when I was fortunate to be with teachers who seemed tuned in to the needs and interests of their students, I found myself enthralled by the lure of possibility because for those teachers, the focus was less on what I had to do or wasn't allowed to do and more on what I was free to do. Remember teachers like that?

It took me a while to get to that point as a teacher myself. In my early years, I strived to be creative, to teach like those who had captured my heart from the very first moment, but those connections often took a little while to make with my own students. Something was holding me back on those first days. Sure, I joked a bit to get a laugh or two out of those twenty-five strangers lined up before me, but fear had a strong grip on me in two ways. For one, I was afraid that if I didn't explain the rules from the outset, I would quickly lose control of my classroom. Like any other inexperienced teacher, I was all too often tested by students who were looking for an easy way to get through the class or for a way to take some control of the situation, and I was afraid that if I did not start by enforcing the law in my classroom, I would soon be at the mercy of an unruly mob. A second fear that I had was that I would be viewed as weird by my students if I allowed the joy that I felt about starting another year to give way to exuberance in the sight of those new witnesses. Better to play it cool, to temper my enthusiasm until we all knew each other better. Besides, I planned on smiling long before Christmas came.

Reputation helps a teacher loosen up on that first day. Well, that and tenure. Once I felt that my principals, my colleagues, and my incoming students had a sense that I was an effective instructor, that I knew what I was doing, I felt much more comfortable letting my playful side show. To sing, even. On that first day of my last year of teaching, invoking my inner Leslie Odom, Jr., I cared not so much about what my students saw as I shuffled about the room, not so much about what they heard as I sang Lin-Manuel Miranda's words and melody. What I really cared about was how my kids felt about that moment, what they would feel each time they entered our room.

You may have grown up, as I did, in a school district that welcomed students in early September. Maybe your schools started, as mine eventually came to do, in late August in order to afford more vacation time during the year. It took a while for me to appreciate the significance of the earlier start, even though it borrowed from those precious days of summer to bring us back indoors to begin the task of learning. Eventually, I came to see August not just as a month but as an adjective. Its name is derived from the Latin *augustus*, meaning "consecrated, venerable." For me, it did indeed become a sacred time, one that deserved my most sincere respect. That is why I greeted each of my students with a handshake on that first day and why I devoted the first few of our days together not to diving into the language arts curriculum but instead to taking a plunge into the culture that we would develop over the course of our nine months as a class. That's why I modeled risk-taking from the outset, why I sang to my students and danced inside our circle. That's why I hung a sign above one of our windows that

11

anyone passing by could read that announced that this was a unique place for learning.

While in my students' minds that first day may have been nothing more than walking into a room on the second floor of our building, for me, it was always much more than that. It was the beginning of a magical season of growth that I created with my students every year, a metamorphosis that I dreamed of every summer. My new kids would see a teacher inviting them into a circle of desks inside four walls. I saw it much differently. From the moment they stepped into our space for the first time, I wanted my kids to understand that no matter what was going on in the halls, no matter what what happening in other classes, no matter what was occurring outside of our school, our room was special. How I created that sense differed from year to year. One time I borrowed a concept from Joseph Campbell, who described his first experience in a sacred place in NewYork:

I walk off 52nd Street and Fifth Avenue into Saint Patrick's Cathedral. I have left a very busy city and one of the most fiercely economically inspired cities on the planet. I walk into that cathedral, and everything around me speaks of spiritual mystery. The mystery of the cross; what's that all about there? The stained glass windows which bring another atmosphere in. My consciousness has been brought up onto another level altogether, and I am on a different platform. And then I walk out and I'm back in this one again. Now, can I hold something from that?

A different platform. A raised level of consciousness. Inspired by Campbell's transcendence of the mundane, I borrowed a wall ornament of about thirty colored strings from our daughter's bedroom and hung it above our classroom door. With the help of push pins, I separated each string so that the arrangement created a curtain of sorts. In order to enter our room on that first day, kids had to push through that veil, and once they were inside the room, I greeted each with a handshake and a personal introduction. Some looked excited, others a bit nervous. A few tried to slip past without making eye contact at all, but that moment when we touched hands and regarded each other face to face served the first purpose of the year. Whether or not they were conscious of the import of that act, entering Room 218 was transformative. By the time they arrived for our second meeting, I had taken down the physical barrier, but I hoped that the memory remained. I wanted my students to realize that when they came into our classroom, they would be, in a sense, entering a place organic. Our class would not be a destination for eighty-five minutes every other day. Rather, it would be where we all came to develop both as individuals and as a class. Each time they crossed that threshold, I wanted them to understand that because of them, our garden had grown just a little bit from what it had been the time before.

As for the rest of our first day together, I had planned the lesson knowing that my students' initial impressions of me and of our environment would be crucial, and the last thing I wanted on that first day was for my kids to leave at the bell thinking that our class was going to be like every other one they had taken in high school. Perhaps that's why I took the chance that what I considered different about my approach might come off more as odd to my new students. When I was a middle school teacher, that had been no problem because if my seventh graders told me, "You are weird, Mr. Stemle," then I knew that I had scored in their world. Being called strange by twelve and thirteen-year-olds was a high compliment. Hearing a senior whisper to a classmate, "Well, that was bizarre" didn't carry the same cachet. Nonetheless, the longer I taught, the more likely it was that my new kids each fall were either siblings or friends of my previous students, and those who had heard about my classroom were willing to endure a few quirks at the outset for the promise of a singular experience later on. Plus, teenagers are no different than anyone else. They are pleased with novelty, they are enchanted by mystery, even if they might not want to admit it.

By the time the ending bell sounded on that first day, we were ready to begin creating an effective learning culture. As I introduced myself and a glimpse of my vision for the year, my classes learned that they were going to work hard all year, but they were also going to have a good time. Through their introductions of themselves, I learned much, much more. On that very first day, I had an early idea of who spoke fluently and confidently, and who appeared shy and maybe tongue-tied. I got a clue as to who had a sense of humor and who seemed anxious. I never told my students that I was checking for those behaviors as I listened to them speak for the first time, but that assessment would prove invaluable as I sought to help them move from a collection of random individuals to a tight-knit group. There was much for us to learn about each other in the coming days, but the seeds had been sown.

As you make your way through that final year with me, through each blog post and each commentary, you'll find that this first reflection is one of the longer ones in the book. Perhaps that is because it deals with the most important class period of any year, and in sharing a few memories of my opening days, I hope I have reminded you of the importance of a little extra planning for that initial meeting with your students. After all, you'll have all summer to get ready for day one, and how you present yourself and your course to your kids in those early minutes will in many ways determine just how well you will all grow together.

What Steinbeck Said: Post #2
Wednesday, August 31, 2016
Toward Eloquence

*O*n Monday I welcomed my students to "the room where it happens." *Today, I gave them an overview of what can and probably will happen in our room. We talked about three basic motifs that will guide our learning:* quality, aesthetics, *and* integration. *And indeed, each day we will do useful and purposeful work to the best of our abilities. We will seek the beauty in the arts that we study but also look for the beauty in each other. Most importantly, we will embrace the beauty within ourselves. As I spoke those last words today, I looked deeply into my students' eyes. I know that some of them struggle to truly love themselves, and I told them that in order for us to teach each other and to learn with each other, we will need to create and sustain a loving and nurturing environment. That's why our first* Word of the Day *each* *year is* sanguine. *As I shared that opening word with my kids today, I was simply labeling the cheerfulness and optimism and hope that they dared to carry into Room 218. Without that hope, without that good cheer, nothing will happen.*

I also introduced a fourth motif today, an addition to this year's course of study. Eloquentia Perfecta *dates to the classic works of Aristotle and Cicero. The Latin label was coined by Jesuit scholars in 1599, and while the Jesuits sought to add good works and faith to the secular practices of the ancient rhetoricians—as Steven Mailloux describes it, "uniting the language arts with wisdom and virtue"—our class will focus on "communicating in a way so that people are willing to listen to what [we] have to say." What will that mean in simple terms? It means that we will employ logic to guide our thinking, and we will develop our skills in expressing our thoughts persuasively both in writing and in speech. Today I told my kids that I dream of them coming to the end of their senior project presentations and hearing their judges sighing and begging for more. I dream of their professors smiling when they come to their papers in a stack because they know that they are about to be both informed and entertained.*

In the coming months, we will integrate those ideas. We will strive toward quality in our writings and in our presentations and discussions. In the end, we will find true beauty in what we create as a class.

Is there any wonder that I'm so excited to start another year?

Hoping that I had somehow touched my students' hearts on that first day, I designed the second to appeal to their minds. If the first day had been one to give them a sense of who we were going to be as a class, then the second was one to stoke their imaginations as to what they could learn in the coming year. Before we examined our syllabus, a document born more of accountability than vision, I gathered my kids in a circle on the carpet inside our larger circle of desks and employed a cardboard ring to help them see the flow of our learning for the year. I had divided the ring into twelve sections to represent the cycle of months in a calendar year, and as I talked with them about our readings and essays and projects, I placed little icons in each month's wedge to help them visualize what lay before us. For them, it was a different way of looking at the assignments to come. For my part, I felt more like a landscape architect sharing a map of the garden we had already planted. A syllabus told us what would be due and when. A map showed us features that would eventually emerge. Again, it was a matter of feel.

For some, this preview of the course was daunting. Students in two different classes stayed after that second meeting to tell me they weren't sure that they were up to the expectations.

"I don't think I belong in this class," one girl told me. "I've never been good at English, and this all looks like it will be hard."

"Tell you what," I said to her. "Why don't you give it a few days? I agree with you, this class is hard, as a college class should be, but that's why I'm here. I'll give you as much help as you need if you decide to stay."

"Really?"

I grinned. "Really. If you want to give it a try, I'm willing to be here for you all the way through. Why don't you think it over and let me know, OK?"

Quite often, it was those students with the greatest doubts about their ability to succeed in our class who ended up giving the greatest effort. Maybe it was a matter of gratitude, maybe it was the motivation to show me and themselves that they were worthy of taking an advanced course, but I know that none of those students would have had the courage to approach me about dropping the class if we had not somehow connected on those first two days. It was quite simple. For forty-one years, those first two days meant that I was not just inviting my students into my classroom. It meant that I was inviting them into my *life*.

That's the commitment you are going to have to make if you want to become a great teacher. When you do wind up making a connection with your students, then your influence will extend beyond the walls of your classroom, beyond the limits of time imposed by a bell schedule. Your kids will take you home with them each afternoon, will talk about you and your teaching with their friends and with their families. That will open the door to deep relationships, and when those develop, your students will feel empowered to strive for their own greatness. Just understand one thing. When you make a commitment to give your heart to your kids in class, you'll be taking them home with you as well. That can be a burden at times, a pure joy at others, and if you're not ready to accept both, well, there's still time to reconsider your career choice.

But why would you throw away the opportunity to touch so many lives?

What Steinbeck Said: Post #3
Friday, September 2, 2016
Groundwork

*D*ay 3 gave us an introduction to conceptual thinking. While each year my students arrive blessed with the ability to infer and to interpret symbolism, it still takes them a while to see things at subtler levels. On Friday we began digging down to those substrata by viewing a YouTube video produced by the band Walk Off the Earth. As I introduced their cover version of Gotye's "Somebody That I Used to Know," I asked my kids to watch and listen for principles of cooperation. The clip is entertaining, but my larger purpose for screening it was to help us focus on what effective teams do to achieve. On a different level, I wanted my students to begin seeing and hearing more attentively and in turn to start applying what they observe to their own learning.

At the conclusion of the video, I paused the image and with a SMART board stylus, I labeled each performer by name: Joel Cassady, Mike Taylor, Sarah Blackwood, Gianni Nicassio, and Ryan Marshall. I did this because I want my kids to get in the habit of identifying characters by name in their writing and in our discussions. So often, we'll say, "The girl" or "the father," and as I will show my classes in a few weeks, such references often discount the meaning that authors ascribe to their characters with their choices of names.

When I asked my kids to share aspects of cooperation they had witnessed in the video, they proved to be keen observers. "They really must feel comfortable with each other because they have to touch each other in order to play the guitar," said a boy in my second period class. "I noticed how they looked down when they weren't singing," said one in my third. Another student, a guitarist *himself, pointed out that three of the members were playing what would amount to three parts. Ryan played bass, Gianni lead, and Sarah rhythm. Other kids pointed out that Joel was playing percussion while Mike, well, Mike seemed to be basically holding up the neck of the instrument. The kids got a kick out of him.*

The discussions took a more interesting turn when I asked my classes to compare the band's performance to our own upcoming work as teammates. Now we started having some fun. We talked about dividing the parts of a task, about contributing according to our strengths, about creating an incredible synergy by being able to work closely and creatively together. In the span of fifteen minutes, we opened the door to thinking about our learning conceptually. Our first step inside that door led us to interpreting a Robert Frost poem. This coming week, it will take us to sea with Hemingway. You're welcome to sail along!

Paul Simon and Art Garfunkel knew each other in elementary school in Queens. Paul McCartney and John Lennon first became acquainted at a church party in Liverpool. Dean Martin and Jerry Lewis met in a nightclub in New York City. Like many creative teams, each of those three had its genesis in a chance meeting, eventually developed into a remarkable artistic entity, and in the end dissolved. Yet, what all three accomplished in their short times together was remarkable, the result of a happy accident for the rest of us. While I was all in favor of serendipity as a teacher, I didn't have much time to wait for chance to intervene and bring my students together into dynamic groups that created amazing learning. If I wanted my cooperative teams to function effectively early in the year, I had to help them bond, and I had to show them what it took to be a great team.

Ever been thrown into a random group and asked to come up with a product in a short amount of time? Exasperating, isn't it? So much of your early work together is spent trying to figure out how to play off each other, so much energy is spent trying to organize the task. We're told from childhood that "two heads are better than one," but that aphorism leaves out a lot of the sweat equity that a successful partnership invests in order to become a successful venture. Whether they be teachers or business project managers, leaders who put people together and assign them a task without also helping them to learn how to work with each other often grow as frustrated as their students and employees do when results don't match expectations. You just can't take two musicians, introduce them to each other, and say, "OK, I'm giving you two weeks to become Rodgers and Hammerstein."

If you are going to ask kids to collaborate, then not only will you have to do a lot of preparation with them, but you'll also need to monitor their progress closely. That means that rather than sitting at your desk grading papers while your class does teamwork, you'll be walking around the room, checking with each group from time to time to see how they're doing. It means you'll be willing to arbitrate little disagreements and to encourage kids to play nice. It also means that you will help them work through the mechanics of completing a complex assignment as a unit. None of that work as a teacher will come easy, but it will be essential that you find a way to lead in a cooperative learning setting. By the end of my career, I had learned a lot about creating successful teams, and I knew that if we were going to work together to create a deeper understanding of our language, of literary themes, of the writing process, then we had to start learning to collaborate in those first few days of school. From that very first week of the year, we needed to formulate an idea of what cooperative learning would involve in our classroom. Watching the Walk Off the Earth video was a start because it gave us a chance to identify elements of teamwork, let us see what it could look and sound like. Playing Balloon Bounce, a structure I had learned from Spencer and Laurie Kagan, let us feel what teamwork can do.

On the second day of class I had formed random teams, my only guidelines being to create as many four-student groups as possible and to maintain gender balance whenever I could. On that third day, before my kids actually took on an academic task together, I gave each of them a balloon to blow up and tie off. Then I chose a team as my demonstration group and showed the class how the game was played. It began with the team forming a circle by holding hands and then taking one of their balloons and doing whatever was needed to keep it aloft without letting go of each other's hands. I let the demo group try doing that for about twenty seconds before turning the rest of the teams loose to try. Once they

19

got pretty good at keeping one balloon off the carpet, I called time out and challenged them to try two. The ultimate goal was to keep all of their balloons in the air, something that was a lot harder than you might think.

First of all, Balloon Bounce was noisy. Kids yelled suggestions (commands) at each other as they struggled to reach balloons that tended to float beyond their handheld perimeter, and occasionally an overinflated balloon unexpectedly popped, but the din that ensued in the room was primarily the sound of unbounded laughter and cheers when a teammate made an athletic move to lift a wayward balloon with a stretched foot or a header. The activity took maybe three minutes, and while it served the purpose of loosening up new teammates, my other intention with playing the game was to help us look much deeper at the concept of collaboration.

We began that examination by brainstorming about what we had done to be successful in the activity. Kids said that they had moved together, that they had used a lot of body parts to bounce the balloons, that they hadn't gotten frustrated when a balloon hit the floor. After that list was complete, we converted each item to a learning tool. "Moving together" translated to being in-sync with the task. "Using a lot of body parts" became using multiple resources to accomplish a goal. We decided that one way to avoid frustration was to laugh when we failed and to try again. Before the next class period, I turned that new list into a poster on our wall to remind us of what we needed to remember whenever we came together to learn as teams.

I could have told my classes that list in just a few seconds, but by giving them twenty minutes to experience the elements of collaboration, we created a model that we would follow for the rest of the year. In a sense, we learned how to play one guitar together. We may not have been Lennon and McCartney at that moment, but we were certainly starting to feel the beat.

What Steinbeck Said: Post #4
Wednesday, September 7, 2016
Of Human Bonding

O*ver the weekend I continued to build relationships with my students. No, we didn't meet at school, and I didn't invite the lot to a barbecue at the house. Rather, I conversed with my kids by reading their notebooks and commenting throughout. I wrote a remark for each* Word of the Day *sentence, I asked them questions in the margins of their entries where they introduced themselves or described their writing history. I looked for openings to be witty with them, and wherever I could, I encouraged them, reassured them when they confessed their weaknesses, showed my appreciation when they shared their talents and their accomplishments. At the end of each entry, I helped them look ahead to their inevitable success in our class. Put in lots of exclamation points, a smiley face here and there.*

I love to watch my students read through those comments when they pick up their notebooks at the beginning of the week. I pretend to busy myself with taking attendance or straightening my desk, but I try to slip a glance around the room to watch them grin and giggle as they flip through the pages. It's a private thing, the notebook. I am sure that some kids share my comments with their friends, and that's fine, but so much of our growth as learners will depend on the trust that we build together in these early days. The time and affection that I invest in these first few weeks will provide great dividends as the year progresses. It takes a lot of time outside of the classroom, but I get such a kick out of our pen and pencil talks.

There was more bonding today in my classes, though a freshman-senior orientation trip took nearly all of my kids to the mountains for the day. I took advantage of the situation by getting to better know the handful of students who stayed behind. To complete our model literary interpretation from Friday, we formed teams and created skits to demonstrate a theme from Robert Frost's "Out, Out." While the players were presenting to each other, I observed on a different level. I watched to see which of my kids were risk-takers, which were openly

21

appreciative of their classmates' performances. I listened as they prepared their scripts to see who took the lead and who seemed reluctant to try new things. Following the skits, we played a spelling game, and while I ostensibly did the judging, I also watched to see who was competitive, who got frustrated, who lost graciously. I noted those kids who looked up or straight ahead when they were thinking about a spelling because they are most likely visual learners. I saw a few who looked down when they were thinking, a pretty good indication that they are kinesthetic learners who may struggle to spell correctly. We had a great time playing a simple game, and no one learned more than I did.

My classes will be full on Friday, and I'll find ways to get closer to all of the students who we missed today while they were off serving our school. It will be wonderful to hear their stories and to welcome them back to the circle, but at the same time, there will be a few students in each period that I will know just a little bit better because of today.

A young actress struggles to learn her lines, and after working through a series of rehearsals, she is finally ready to take the stage and deliver what has been scripted for her. In time, that learning process will become easier for her, but at this point she is still a good ways from being able to improvise with a troupe before an audience. To do that well will require more experience and a keener understanding of dramatic theory. Teachers are no different. If you have yet to begin your practice, then rest assured that, in rather quick order, you will become adept at designing a lesson plan. Part of that mastery will involve your ability to gauge the amount of time that each part of your lesson will take to accomplish, and as long as everything goes to plan, you will gradually develop an even sharper sense of how to set your students up for success during that class period. As a young teacher, I was able to carry out my lesson plans well as long as circumstances were favorable. Ah, but then, I was always better at hitting a fastball than a curve. It took me years to develop the flexibility I needed when a class was shortened without warning or when a filmstrip projector's bulb burned out.

What I had planned for Day Four's lesson became inoperable when I counted heads at the opening bell. How could we do teamwork when most of each group's members were absent? In my early days, I would have punted and given the few students who showed up a study hall. As I gained experience, however, I grew more and more skillful in my use of pedagogy, and I also learned how to improvise. On that day with so many of my students missing, I decided that if we couldn't accomplish what I had intended, we could at least put our time to good use. Instead of waiting until the whole class was back to put together skits, I let those who were present form ad hoc teams. I would have preferred that each of my kids had an opportunity to perform for the class, but I decided that those who were with me deserved the chance to have a meaningful day in class. The others wouldn't even know what they had missed. As for the spelling game, while it didn't hold much academic merit, it did remind my students that one of our goals for each day was to have fun.

No day was ever wasted in our classroom, and whether my kids were truly aware of that fact as they left at the closing bell, I was creating a bassline that I hoped would stick in their minds: "Every time that I come to class, I will have an opportunity to learn." The same will apply to you as a teacher. Every time you're with students, whether physically at school or in a virtual way as you interact with their work at home, you will have a chance to form a stronger bond with them, and that connection will start on your very first day together.

As for those instances when it seems there aren't enough students present to do anything meaningful as a class, put yourself in the desk of one of those students who does come into the room to learn that day. Imagine how that child will feel if you tell her that she's on her own for the next hour. Oh, some may relish the time to read what they want or to take a break from paying attention for a while, but even if there is only one who is disappointed, can you really look him in the eye and say it's not really your fault? Seriously? Imagine arriving at a restaurant and finding no other customers. Then imagine the hostess telling you that the chef has decided not to serve that evening because there are not enough diners to make it worth his effort. Do you really want your students leaving your classroom hungry because things "beyond your control" prevented you from teaching? There is absolutely no reason to throw away an opportunity to get to know your students better, to give them a chance to learn something. While it might be discouraging when things don't go exactly right, you will eventually develop the ability to make the best of those unforeseen problems. And while your kids might not seem to appreciate your diligence at first, after a while they will come to count on your perseverance. Even if they never do tell you directly, they will want to know that they can depend on you to keep their class from dissolving into what they perceive as a waste of time. Believe me, no matter what they say about school, deep down, they will want to learn, and they will want you to lead them to that possibility, even if you have to make up a few lines on the fly.

What Steinbeck Said: Post #5
Friday, September 9, 2016
More Than Trees

I n recent years, teachers have focused on providing students with learning targets and success criteria prior to a lesson. The idea is to give kids a clear idea of what they are about to accomplish, and in theory, it makes sense. As a student, if I know the expected outcome and the plan for getting there, I am more likely to achieve the intended result. We compare such a lesson design to mapping out a trip or following a recipe. Not only do teachers have a responsibility to plan that learning, but we are also encouraged to collect data along the way to inform ourselves as well as our students of their progress toward the goal. It's all about precision and purpose. There's just one thing. In an effort to carry out this approach, we as teachers often miss opportunities to help our students expand their learning.

Let's think about that metaphorically. If we consider a course's curriculum as a forest, then each lesson involves showing our students a particular tree and then guiding them to reaching it. The path is clear and the objective easy to understand. Yet, so often we find ourselves narrowing our vision to that tree and that tree only. If we lead the kids to finding that target, then we have accomplished our goal for the day. The problem is, there is so much more for us to find in the forest. There is so much more than trees.

On Friday, the tree I selected for my students was the analysis of a novel's setting. Working with setting is a three-step process: we identify the time period of the novel, we identify its physical location, and then we try to predict how that time and place might affect the plot. For this lesson, our path to the tree was easy to follow. As we began our reading of The Old Man and the Sea, *we looked for clues to suggest the time and the place. My students can do that. I know that's so because they've been practicing that strategy in English classes for years. I'm guessing some of my kids could find that tree with their eyes closed.*

There's so much more than trees, though. On Friday, I led my students to the edge of the forest, and I told them that we would find a sturdy trunk by period's end. Yet, as we prepared to enter the woods, I encouraged them to find their own way to the tree.

"Please take out your Chromebooks," I said, "and while I read, go ahead and search to figure out anything you don't understand. Look up words you don't know or other information to help you determine what the setting is."

With that, I read aloud the novel's first paragraph. When I finished, I gave my kids an additional minute to continue their research. Then it was time to share.

"So, what did you look up?"

One student noted Hemingway's mention of the Gulf Stream and found a map that showed its course. Another one looked up the meaning of the Spanish word salao. *The author defines it as "the worst form of unlucky," but the definition my kids found said it meant "salty." We talked about the discrepancy but came to no conclusion. We discussed what a gaff and a skiff are, and we shared photographs of each. I then asked my classes to find the symbolic meaning of the number forty. Hemingway writes that the old man had gone fishing with the boy for forty days without catching a fish. We learned from our searches that* forty *can mean "a long period of trial or waiting." We further discussed its origins in the Bible.*

To that point, we had learned that the action most likely takes place in a Spanish-speaking section of the Gulf Stream, most likely the Caribbean. We had also learned what tools and equipment the old man has at his disposal, and we had observed that Hemingway employs Biblical symbolism to describe his protagonist's situation. We then went further and talked about possible purposes for the author to employ such source material, and I asked my kids why a reportedly casual Catholic might bother to include religious allusions. We decided that Hemingway uses details that many readers can relate to, and we predicted that this would not be his only use of such symbolism. All of this from one paragraph, a computer on each desk, and the freedom to explore.

Did my students find the tree? Sure, they did. They also took their own paths and discovered other parts of the forest along the way. Even with a destination, there is so much else for us to find when we venture into the woods.

Our opening work with *The Old Man and the Sea* marked a slight departure from my customary way of introducing a novel to my students. For as long as I could remember, I had read aloud the first chapter of our books, stopping at various points to ask questions or indicate subtle clues about the story's setting that I assumed my kids might not catch. It was an important step in their understanding of the layered nature of a work of art, and I was always happy to devote some of our precious time to get a firm grounding before we traveled through a piece such as Hemingway's small gem. Now, in what would turn out to be my final trip with Papa and his protagonist, Santiago, I decided to share that preparation with my students. Perhaps it was in keeping with my continual search for a better way, or maybe I was trying to find a practical use for the computers that our school had provided for all of its students. Maybe it was just consistent with my habit of listening to the distant beat of a different drummer. For whatever reason, when I changed my approach, I was pleased to see the variety in the quick research that my kids performed in the span of three minutes.

We had now spent five days together in our classroom, a week's time in a traditional school schedule, two in our school's rotating block. In that short time we had introduced ourselves to each other and previewed the growth that lay ahead by looking at the map that our syllabus provided. We had also begun experiencing the year in microcosm by incorporating key elements such as cooperative learning and literary interpretation into short lessons so as to create a learning context that encouraged risk-taking within a nurturing environment. I knew that many of my colleagues across the disciplines had already delved deeply into their first units, employing a brisk pace in order to push their students toward achievement. That approach seemed to work effectively for a lot of teachers, but at that point in the year, I felt more comfortable taking my time so that my kids felt secure about the challenges they were about to take on. In time, our tempo would quicken and our assignments would grow more rigorous, but at that point we were just feeling our way through the forest, trying to find the next tree.

How you decide to introduce units in your classroom will, of course, be up to you. Your school or your department might have established protocols for you to follow, and those may involve communicating to your students the upcoming instruction's targets and success criteria derived from your current curriculum or a publisher's materials. You might be encouraged to use learning prompts such as "I Can" statements so that your kids will have an idea of what they will know or be able to do by the time each lesson comes to an end. As much as I could, I followed such requests made my administrators, but I never wanted to settle for mechanical approaches. Instead, I made sure to place my own stamp upon the beginning and closing of each class period and of each unit. Till the very end, I looked for creative ways to capture my students' interest, whether through humor or mystery or personal engagement. No matter what your goal or target is, it will always be up to you to find your own way through the forest.

Eric Stemle

*T*oday we began our exploration into Eloquentia Perfecta, *the search for persuasive, entertaining, and memorable communication. This will be a year-long pursuit, though I thoroughly hope that my students will continue to refine their writing and speaking skills long after they leave this class. As a foundation for our practice, I showed them a TED Talk by Julian Treasure entitled, "How to Speak So People Want to Listen." First of all, what a fabulous name the man has. Mr. Treasure! Anyway, as you can see by watching the clip, Julian lays a firm foundation for what we should and should not do in order to gain and hold the attention of one listener or of a roomful. He shares with us his "Seven Deadly Sins of Speaking," and as we finished that section of his talk, I paused the video and interpreted his suggestions in terms of our classroom. Some of his sins such as "gossip" and "lying" are not really germane to our functioning in the circle, but "judging" and "dogmatism" are. If we are going to develop as a society of learners in that circle, then we are going to have to learn to express our ideas without denigrating or dismissing the ideas of our classmates. After two and a half weeks, we seem well on our way to being able to do that, but with the help of Treasure and other authorities on public speaking, we can make that sharing much more purposeful and intentional. Today, I wasn't too concerned that my kids had a firm grasp on Julian's dos and don'ts because those suggestions will soon be a part of our classroom walls, and we will dive more deeply into their practice in good time. For the moment, I want my students to see the landscape for presenting, to begin to realize that good speakers are made, not born.*

While my kids paid attention to Treasure, I paid attention to them. Not as individuals as I did last week, but more to their behavior as a group. They appeared to follow the talk well enough, but they never seemed to laugh when his live audience did. That's all right. They don't laugh at all of my jokes, either. When I paused the video to talk to them about "upspeak," our tendency to rise in pitch at the end of a phrase or a sentence—what we once called "valley girl speech"—they smiled a bit, but I wondered if they were simply having a hard time trying to process all of that information as it related to them as individual speakers. Examining our own personal dialectical features can be a bit disconcerting, and while I tried to make it clear to my kids that I am not expecting them to change the way they talk on a regular basis, I am going to guide them toward eloquence so that they can develop the capacity to communicate in formal situations. Being able to speak to occasion will be a precious tool for them as they go on to college and to careers.

"Don't worry," I said before we continued with the video. "I'm going to do everything I can to help you become great presenters, and I will do it with love and gentleness." I'm not sure they totally believed that last part, but who can blame them? They really don't know me yet.

They will.

Igh school students can be a rather insecure lot. They worry about what their classmates think of their looks, and they fret about making mistakes on the football field or the choir risers. Nothing seems to rattle kids more than to speak in front of their peers. Oh, they put on a fairly brave face when asked to address the group, whether it be in a discussion or a solo presentation, but ask nearly any teenager what he or she hates most about school—well, besides homework—and you'll hear, "getting up to speak." That's OK. Adults will tell you the same. For most of my career, I fell into coachspeak when my kids confessed that they were scared to present to the class. I'd smile and tell them, "I know it's hard, but you can do it!" If that didn't work, I'd smile more broadly and say, "I believe in you!" I'm not sure that my words ever had much effect, maybe like prescribing chicken soup for a broken arm, and while my encouragement may have thawed my frozen speakers just a bit, it did nothing to help them solve their problems with presenting.

Our school's adoption of a senior project requirement for graduation changed all that. It didn't take me too long to decide that accepting mediocre presentations was not going to help my kids. I always knew that speaking was an issue for most of my students, and, not wanting to traumatize their tender psyches, I rarely criticized a performance. The results weren't helpful. The kids who were weak as speakers knew they were weak, and my positive-only comments did little to assuage their fears. If anything, they created distrust and resentment. With all good intentions, I must have come off as condescending to some of my kids. Here's a secret: teenagers don't want to be patronized. Sure, they may seem to appreciate a certain amount of mercy when they mess up, but if you send them the message that their poor performances are OK, then you are also telling them that you don't expect them to ever improve, that in your mind, they aren't capable of doing any better. A well-designed rubric can prove invaluable in helping you provide your students with specific feedback on their performance, information that focuses on the degree to which they have met each expectation for a speech or an essay. And even if your kids score low at first, they will benefit from being able to see just what it will take to eventually meet those standards. We'll talk more about the role of rubrics later.

The presentation game changed for me and for my seniors when we all realized that they had to improve their presentation skills if they were going to earn their diplomas. Before the project presentation requirement, most kids knew that they could slide by with the occasional public speaking demand in a class because, for the most part, how well they spoke had little to do with their overall grade or their credit for the course. Ah, but now that the school board had dictated that a failing project meant no certificate, no walking across the stage with their grandparents watching, the seniors' level of concern rose dramatically. Nothing like that sort of hurdle to motivate a kid to improve.

With that realization, I knew I had to get serious about presentations as well. I had long been meticulous about my students' writing, and I had broken down the elements of an essay to a microscopic level, but now I was faced with the task of helping my students understand the intricacies of public speaking. We had to go beyond eye contact and vocal projection. If we were going to truly practice *Eloquentia Perfecta*, then we first had to figure out what perfect eloquence was. Over the course of the year we would do just that, but on this early day in September, there was no better way to prime my kids for an education on speaking than to introduce them to an unknown Treasure.

I'm sure that at some point early in your career, you are going to lament the fact that your students aren't as prepared as you would like them to be. I totally understand. All teachers would like their kids to come into their classes in the fall fully in control of all the curriculum presented to them up to that point, but that will simply never be the case because, with the exception of a few truly outstanding students, your kids are going to have gaps in their learning. They'll be strong in some areas, weak in others. They might even swear to you that they have never in their lives heard what you claim they should have known before coming into your classroom. None of that matters. What does matter is that you find a way to bring your students up to speed so that they can learn effectively in your class. That might seem like an infringement on your instructional time, but if you don't address those shortcomings, some problems will continue to compound. The answer is simple. If you want your students to do what you perceive that they can't, you will have to teach them how to do it. That is what you signed up for, right?

What Steinbeck Said: Post #7
Thursday, September 15, 2016
Just a Little Nervous

*Y*ou expect us to be able to write like that?"

"Well," I replied, "maybe not on this first paper, but by May, sure."

My answer to a student's question brought a few gasps and more than a few anxious chuckles from the class today. We had just reviewed a sample essay that I had prepared for them, and when I explained that this was a first draft, I could see some discomfort and perhaps a bit of incredulity creeping around the circle. It wasn't so much that my example was beyond their writing capabilities, though some did seem alarmed that I was expecting them to produce a paper at that level. Rather, their real concern was that as I reviewed the piece with them and scored it on our rubric, I gave myself few advanced marks on the standards.

In fact, in some places, I evaluated my work at a "partially proficient" level. I've been through this with classes for years, and even if many of my kids remain silent, I have a good idea that they're worried that the standard for good writing is high in our class. Well, they're right.

As I went on to explain, a college course maintains rigorous expectations for performance. Yes, we have done a lot in the first three weeks to build a culture for ourselves, to have fun, get to know each other, and ease into our studies. Now it's time to get after it, and while I have already developed a great affection for my kids, I also know that they're going to have to work hard to achieve at the level of success to which they are accustomed.

"Remember," I told them, "I will not be the judge of your performance. The rubric will be. I am here to help you satisfy the demands of that instrument, to exceed them, even. Hey, I'm on your side. We're going to have a lot of fun getting this done."

At this point, many of my students probably see that message as just a bit disingenuous. It's just Mr. Stemle trying to reassure us and all, but he doesn't know how we write yet. I can't blame them for being somewhat suspicious of my encouragement—they have not been to the end of the road as I have. They haven't been to the mountaintop. They don't know it yet, but they are going to become great writers.

Get your boots on kids—it's time to start hiking!

I didn't always think of our class as a garden. Sometimes other analogies came to mind. I also saw our experience as a nine-month journey, and we spent those early days preparing for the beginning of the long walk. We had learned some things about who we would be traveling with, and we had already begun to work together in teams. On their own, the kids were reading our first novel, and we would discuss it soon. Now, they were about to take on their first formal writing assignment, and in terms of the hiking metaphor, I had just presented each with a new pair of boots in the form of our composition rubric. While this was not a new form of evaluation for them, there was a new emphasis on performance, and in this lesson, I gave my classes a preview of the level of achievement that they would have to reach in order to earn the grades they coveted. Did I say nervous?

You know how your feet feel when you first lace up a new pair of shoes? They're firm, maybe a little tight. As you take a few steps to check out the fit, you feel taller, just a bit uncomfortable. It's all because the soles are immaculate, as strong and supportive as they will ever be. You know that in time your feet will mold themselves to the inner soles, and as the outer ones wear a bit, your stride will feel more comfortable. On that first walk around the room, however, there is a certain amount of uncertainty as to whether those are the shoes for you.

As we reviewed the model essay that I had written for the lesson, I was not only showing my kids where they were headed with their writing, but in the form of the rubric, I was giving them the proper footwear to enable them to traverse rocky paths and wet conditions. Some, of course, felt differently. What I saw as support, they viewed as rigidity. What I envisioned as a view of the end, they saw as an unattainable goal. Of course, I didn't help the situation when I told them that what they had looked at was a first draft that I had dashed off in ten minutes. I reminded them of the advantages I had with my writing that they did not possess at that point in their lives. Not only did I have a high school diploma, a bachelor's degree, and a master's degree, I also had over forty-five years of life experience beyond theirs. Of course, I was better at writing than they were. Still, that was no reason to believe that they would never get to the point that I was. That's why they enrolled in our class.

In its essence, our rubric consisted of twenty benchmarks calibrated to help my students and me evaluate the elements of organization, idea development, style, and punctuation. While we walked through the performance indicators in light of my model essay, I knew that the rubric felt tight and inflexible to my kids. Some came to see me the next day with the worry that they would never reach proficient or advanced levels on their papers, but I assured them that the rubric would at some point feel better to them. How do you know if those new shoes are right for you until you've walked around a bit, exercised in them? I knew that after a few essays, the kids would come to see the rubric as equipment that would not only protect them as they trod the difficult paths ahead but also

33

support them when they weren't sure about their next steps.

That day's lesson was all about proper preparation. First we put on a pair of wool socks for comfort and protection from irritation. Call them a student's attitude and willingness to try new things. Next came a sturdy pair of shoes, the foundation that provided traction and support. For my students, that was the curriculum that they would be walking around in all year. Finally, we pulled and secured the laces. They served the same purpose as the rubrics we would use to keep us tight in our navigation of that curriculum. It's true that we come barefoot into this world, and my students had come much the same way into our classroom. On that early day in the year, I gave them some important gear as they embarked upon the odyssey of their academic lives. The trip was going to be rigorous enough—no need to get any blisters along the way.

If you plan to have high expectations for your students, then you'll need to prepare yourself for some early trepidation on their part and maybe some resistance from them as well. That's why it's so important that you start building relationships with your kids from the moment you meet them. If your goal is to scare away students who might be hard to motivate or who will have a hard time grasping the demands of your course, then, by all means, tell them on that first day how hard it will be to pass your class, but if you want to give those enrolled a legitimate chance to succeed, then help them equip themselves with what they'll need for the experience and then do everything you can to support them along the way. In time they just might surprise you, and there is little that is more rewarding in teaching than witnessing young people achieving what they weren't sure they could. You may even find yourself saying the same thing about yourself.

What Steinbeck Said: Post #8
Monday, September 19, 2016
The Eyes Have It

I took a knee today. Actually, I took two. While my classes engaged in "learning time" for the last forty minutes of the period, choosing to read The Old Man and the Sea *or to create the first draft of their process paper, I moved around the inside of our circle, kneeling in front of each student and asking where each was with the essay. As with just about anything I do in our classroom, this activity served multiple purposes. The first was easy enough. With a Friday due date for the draft, I was checking to see if kids had started writing or had at least done some prewriting. Experience told me that I would encounter a few who had yet to identify a topic, and conferring with them would help me guide them toward taking that initial step.*

Of more importance was the chance to connect with each student in a way that I haven't thus far in the semester. Up to this point, I have sat next to some kids in the circle, and I have stood in front or behind all of their desks to pass out or collect materials. For the most part, though, my kids have viewed me from a distance, much as we all have viewed most of our teachers, especially those we had in high school and college. What I did today changed all of that. I knelt before them, eye to eye, my face approximately eighteen inches from theirs. Psychologists tell us that a foot and a half is right on the boundary between "intimate" and "personal" distance. If I had I moved back about three feet, I would have created a "social" distance from my students—polite and comfortable, but not ideal for communicating deep thoughts and feelings. Had I moved just a few inches closer, let's say by leaning over a student's desk, I would have invaded that intimate space, and for many kids at this point in the year, that would have been uncomfortable. Positioned as I was, I created an opportunity for us to speak on a personal level without worrying about being too close.

Proximity aside, I accomplished two more things by kneeling before my kids. For one, I adopted the posture of a servant, and that was appropriate because I want my students to see that I do not stand over them as an authority but rather crouch before them to serve. For another, being at eye level helped me connect with each kid on an energy level. We could see the color of each other's eyes, could speak in soft tones, could share a moment that only those sitting in the immediate vicinity could hear. No matter whether a student had completed her draft or had yet to choose his topic, I smiled, I encouraged. I offered some suggestions for developing the structure of the draft, and I did so with the enthusiasm of a reader who couldn't wait to see the finished product. If kids planned on writing about a cooking process, I told them I wanted to be able to smell and taste the dish. If they were thinking of describing a performance such as shooting a free throw, I asked them to put me in the gym, to let me smell the popcorn, hear the cheering.

Writing has been described as a lonely act. It can be. In our classroom, it isn't. In our class, writing is co-creative, and as the year progresses, my students and I will work together to produce remarkable writing. Ultimately, they will receive the credit that they will richly deserve. I will receive the honor of being part of the process. If today is any indication, my kids are willing to dream and to follow their dreams in words on a page. How do I know? I saw it in their eyes.

C hange can come on tiptoe,
Love is where it starts,
It resides, often hides, deep within our hearts."
"Ordinary Miracles"
Music by Marvin Hamlisch
Lyrics by Alan and Marilyn Bergman

You probably won't hear it coming, the change that teaching will bring into your life. You'll be working hard to get through to your students, you'll be dealing with the day-to-day issues that will make you wonder whether you are actually making a difference for them, when a realization will hit you from behind: you love teaching. You love your students. I don't mean in the generic way that we often hear teachers talk about why they put so much effort into their jobs. "I teach because I love kids!" Rather, I mean that you will suddenly understand the power of intimacy in your relationship with your students, with the profession itself. It took me a while to grasp each of those.

I'm sure that you will be warned about getting too close to your students. Some of your principals and colleagues will remind you that your primary purpose is to convey information and to assess how well your students assimilate what you teach them. Both are certainly critical to a successful classroom, but you'll be more effective in working with your kids if you keep them as your focus and not look over your shoulder to see who's watching you. Of course, if you don't turn around from time to time, then you won't see that change coming. That's not necessarily a bad thing.

I thought I was giving my heart to my students in the early years of my career. I enjoyed being with them, even when they pushed my patience. I enjoyed teaching, even though there were times when I wondered if I could possibly grade all of the papers that lay piled on my desk, but still, there were times when I wondered whether I would ever become the artist I had dreamed of being, the writer others enjoyed reading. One day it became clear. I was an artist. Teaching was the book I had been writing all along.

For you it might be quite different. You might step into the classroom and from your first day know that you have found your purpose in life. You might love teaching every minute of your career, and if you do, you will truly be a blessing to your students. The thing is, I thought that I loved it all along. Perhaps what happened was that, without warning, I fell *in love* with teaching. When that happened, I started seeing my practice in a different way. I was no longer playing the part of teacher, but rather I was me, Eric, teaching. I started interacting with my students as my authentic self rather than as someone who carried out a teacher's role. The instructor, the manager, the cheerleader, the judge.

What was the difference? Well, for one thing, because I was more comfortable revealing my inner self to my students, that social distance that we had maintained, both physically and emotionally, started to narrow. It was more than just me kneeling down in front of their desks. It was what I wrote in their notebooks for only their eyes to see. It was the few minutes we spent together after school talking about essay drafts or books they'd just finished reading. It was me sitting in the audience watching them perform in a concert or a play, me calling their names as the public address announcer at their games. In the end, it was me growing closer to them in their hearts and they growing closer in mine.

Funny thing about the intimacy that teachers feel with their students, what students in a nurturing classroom feel with each other. It's not something that you can observe by dropping in once or twice a semester. You can't really learn about it by talking with students, either, because I'm not sure they can honestly explain the experience in words. I know I can't. It's just something you'll feel someday when that change tiptoes up and embraces you from behind. Just know that when that happens, you will be changed forever, and your teaching will never be the same. A not so ordinary miracle, I suppose.

What Steinbeck Said: Post #9
Wednesday, September 21, 2016
A One, A Two. . .

I *do many different things for my students both in and out of the classroom. There are times that I provide information, and there are other times when I coach and guide, encourage and push kids to achieve more than they really believe they can. Sometimes I counsel them, listening to their doubts and problems, helping them make decisions. Today I conducted, and the piece I chose to orchestrate was* The Old Man and the Sea. *I had given my kids the score a few weeks ago and asked them to be ready to play by today. It's a short read, but as I advised them when I handed out the book, it's a lot like the sea itself. We might not notice a lot happening on the surface, but our task is to dive deep, to see what we can fathom.*

Not surprisingly, each class presented a different experience for me as I directed them. In my first class, I had to use my baton more frequently to cue my kids. We brainstormed some insights and questions to discuss, but when I asked them to decide where the discussion should go, they sat silent. I waited for about thirty seconds, and when no one called for the koosh ball, our method for determining who had the floor to speak, I picked a topic from our list to discuss. Sometimes during the discussion, I asked follow-up questions, other times I added a bit of interpretation regarding baseball or the Bible, two major features of the novel. Despite some struggles, overall, the conversation went well. We worked together to go deeper than the surface, and I believe the kids surprised themselves with what they discovered with and without my guidance.

My second class took off with the downbeat. Several students had done some research about the text, and they couldn't wait to share what they had learned about the novel's allusions and its symbolism. A few explained that both Santiago and his protégé Manolin can be considered Christ-figures, and once that chord was struck, a few other kids threw in their own riffs on that possibility. I listened a great deal in that discussion, intervening only a few times to ask for clarification or to help the class see connections.

Along came my last class, and like my second period, they were hot from the beginning. At times they couldn't wait for the brainstorming to end, jumping in with analysis before we had created our menu of topics. Again, I did a minimum of participating, speaking up only to make sure we were still in tune. It was an impressive discussion, especially so early in the year.

Whenever we engage in a circle discussion, our classroom becomes a music hall. Today provided an overture for a season of varied and delightful pieces. Some will be classical in nature, and I'll direct quite a bit with those, using my skills to draw out quiet students, to temper the tones of those who might dominate the conversation without a little help from the podium. Others will be more like jazz, with a sound structure established early and then followed by improvisation and exploration by the players. In those discussions, I will keep a beat, but the music's flow will be determined by the students. Some, and these pieces will be rare, will be jam sessions. Someone will lay down a groove, someone else with add a melody, and others will build a harmony along the way. Those discussions are the most fun for me as all I do is sit in awe of the beautiful music that my students create. You know, we didn't quite jam today, but I do believe I heard a few grace notes, found a few kids willing to take the lead.

We'll rest for a day, and then the second movement begins on Friday. I'm

Eric Stemle

tapping my foot already. . .

T here is an art to asking questions. Anyone who has been through a job
interview knows that. It's more than preparing a list and following it,
more than looking for answers that satisfy a predicted response. Ever
been in a situation where you were convinced that the person posing the
questions was more interested in getting to the next item than in listening to your
response? I felt that way as a student from time to time, especially in college. It
seemed that some of my professors were mainly interested in whether we could
ascertain what they believed an interpretation should be. Nothing was quite so
frustrating as seeing a grimace on my teacher's face when my answer did not
match his or her expectation. Perhaps that's why we have the term teacher-
pleaser to describe students who work hard to give their teachers what they think
they want.

Don't get me wrong, I liked being pleased as a teacher, but the older and
more experienced I got, the less that pleasure came from my students doing what
I wanted or expected. I grew to more enjoy watching my kids find their own
paths, and I came to see myself more often facilitating in discussions, helping
kids check their support and reasoning for their opinions, keeping track of who
was participating and who might need to be cued for an entrance. I conducted
more intuitively, like a Leonard Bernstein who flowed with the emotion of the
score rather than a stern concert master who glared at mistakes and demanded
excellence. I once watched a recording of Bernstein conducting the Berlin
Philharmonic in playing Beethoven's Ninth Symphony. The maestro began in his
usual way, finding an early flow and keeping the tempo going. By the end of the
fourth movement, instruments swelling, voices rising to an incredible level, he
basically quit directing, and, arms down at his sides, merely leaned his head
back, eyes closed, a smile gracing his lips as he bounced in rhythm to the majesty
of the music. He was no longer leading the piece—he was the piece. Each time I
opened a discussion with my students, I carried that vision of Bernstein
somewhere in the back of my mind. If, by the end of the period, I felt myself
anywhere near the rapture that Lenny seemed to feel in that Berlin moment, then

40

I knew my students had found their way.

When you lead discussions early in your career, you'll learn that each session is unique. Even when I was scripting questions as a young teacher, asking each class the same list in order, I was surprised at the variation from one class period to the next. There were a number of factors, of course. The personality of each group differed, and whether or not the class had strong leaders willing to engage their classmates made a huge difference. I once thought that the time of day was important, but not every one of my first period classes was sleepy, and not all of my classes at the end of the day were worn out and restless. The one constant was me and my ability to guide my students to draw interpretations that might not have seemed clear to them as they read. In my final year, as my classes entered into their first full-fledged discussion of the year, trying to find a deeper meaning in *The Old Man and the Sea*, I was cognizant of the interpretations that my new students were sharing, but at the same time, I took an opportunity every so often to take our performance to a metacognitive level and point out the mechanics of our conversation. I asked them to look around the circle and count those who had contributed to that point in the discussion, and then I asked how we could bring more voices into play. I also pointed out that listeners were just as important as speakers because it was by their expressions, their postures, and their gestures that they encouraged classmates to step up. Looking at phones or gazing out the window, whispering to a neighbor or simply appearing bored all tended to undermine confidences. It takes a strong self-concept to address an audience that seems uninterested, and on this September day, I wanted my students to understand how they could make it easier for their colleagues to express themselves. This, however, was far from an altruistic gesture. The more students who offered insights, the richer the whole class became in its ability to analyze and interpret. Think of the difference between one violin and an orchestra, one voice and a choir. On that day, discussing Hemingway, we began moving toward becoming an ensemble, an organism capable of growing more powerful and more complex. My job was simple: create the conditions for that growth and let it go. Lenny would have been proud.

41

Eric Stemle

F*ear is poison in a classroom. It holds us back from taking risks, it limits us in striving to achieve. If I accomplish nothing else in these first few weeks of class, it is to drive out fear. How can we do our best if we are afraid of failure? If we are hesitant to try something new? If we are terrified that someone might find out that we're not perfect? It isn't an easy task, this exorcism. I can't just say, "Hey, everything's going to be OK." Kids bring their doubts and their insecurities and their worries into the circle just as much as they bring their backpacks and their phones.*

Today's uncertainty revolved around sharing the first drafts of our process papers. While we had conferred about the status of those pieces on Monday, those were low-pressure conversations because my kids didn't really have to have an essay started at that point. We talked easily about choosing a topic or developing an idea. By today, however, they were to have submitted their drafts online to share with a partner. It was clear that some of us were a little uptight.

Each year, it's the same. No matter how often I tell them that this is just the first of three drafts, no matter how much I try to assuage their worries by explaining that they have two more drafts left on which to improve, seven more essays to practice on, they still fret. Sometimes this worry comes in the form of complaining that they don't know what to do. Other times it results in writer's block. They stare at a blank screen, apparently waiting for inspiration to strike. As much as anything, I think that kids just really want to impress me with this first effort. They want me to see them as good writers, and they're afraid that if they don't produce a remarkable first draft, then I'll be disappointed in them.

Stop. Right there. Let's understand something from the start, everybody: I do not traffic in disappointment. I do not feel let down if a student fails to reach a certain level of achievement. Instead, I view each performance as an opportunity for growth. Haven't started yet? Let's talk about options. Thesis undeveloped? Let's talk about how to marry the main idea to its impact. Point of view inconsistent throughout the essay? Pick one and really own it. If you're writing in second person, have a fun conversation with your reader. Writing in first person? Take me inside your thinking and your feeling. Eventually, kids learn that I am the eternal optimist, that I love nothing more than to help them see possibilities. Today, as my kids read each other's drafts and evaluated their own, I conferred with them once again. This time, I carried my laptop and read the documents they had shared with me. I found a way to focus on at least one aspect of each student's piece, and I made sure that they all knew that I couldn't wait to read their second drafts on Tuesday.

When that night arrives, and I open Google Classroom to read each of those efforts, I will learn which of my students have improved their essays and which continue to struggle. I'm sure that I'll even find some who have yet to put a word on the page. I'll take each writer where she or he is, and together we'll continue the journey toward eloquence. Am I worried about getting there? 'Fraid not.

N ot everything that can be counted counts, and not everything that counts can be counted."
—Albert Einstein

That is certainly one of my favorite quotes. In an era where students and parents are hyper-conscious about grade point averages and their effect on college admissions, where school administrators are understandably anxious about data collection and test score performance and their effect on school ratings, it seems that we have lost perspective on what really matters in the classroom. To be fair, I will grant that from time to time the powers that be will profess that learning is the ultimate goal of any lesson or unit or course of study, but really, when the folks in charge talk bottom line, it's numbers that drive the system. They just never drove mine.

I used to love to have a discussion or a class reading of a play, pretty much any activity, actually, and at its end, with a circle full of shining eyes and bright smiles, ask my kids, "How do you think we might assess what just happened here on a standardized test?" Of course, they knew that such a thing was preposterous, and I didn't dwell on the matter, but so much of what we did together in our classroom, stuff that really counted in the development of students' critical thinking abilities and their aesthetic appreciation, was in no way measurable. And when those same kids returned to see me over their Christmas breaks a year or two later, it wasn't commas and topic sentences they wanted to reminisce about. They didn't wax lyrical about the difference between metaphor and simile. No, they talked instead about the culture of our classroom. They talked about feelings that they had while learning together, the laughter they shared that had stayed with them. As I look through my Facebook blog, I see comments from students I taught in the eighties, and their memories still remain.

Memories of things that cannot be counted.

My task early in the year would have been easier had my September students understood that dynamic. How could they, though? They were products of a results-driven system, and as such, they put pressure on themselves to not just succeed but to succeed from the get-go. To never fail, even in the most insignificant tasks such as a first draft of an essay. In many cases, that pressure led to stress and that stress to fear. Eventually, some kids found that even if they could get started on an essay—and many of them couldn't, it seemed—they had a most difficult time finishing the initial draft, for to say that something is complete is to certify it ready to be judged. Rather than risk the pain of a harsh evaluation, many of my students were willing to own up to being lazy or forgetful. Most likely they were neither.

On that first of drafts of that first of essays, I did all that I knew how to do to help my kids get past their paralyzing fear of assessment and failure. All that I could really do at that point was to be understanding and encouraging and nurturing. Perhaps some of my kids couldn't quite trust that I was genuine in telling them that where they were with their writing was just fine with me, but I had faith that deep down, all of them wanted to believe that I was. In that third week of school, that was a belief that could sustain us as our garden grew.

I'm not telling you that it will be easy to be patient when your students don't complete assignments. On the contrary, you will be frustrated for a while, and in the meantime, you'll be subject to your own fears. You'll be afraid that if you don't threaten your kids, they'll just continue to play you and never put forth the effort required for improving their skills. You'll worry that your colleagues and principals will see you as weak, incapable of disciplining your classes. We all go through that phase in our practice when we care more about what others think about our teaching than we do in understanding the self-esteem issues that our students bring with them into our classrooms every day, but in time, your own confidence will grow. When you move from September to June a few times, you'll see that the problems that arrive in the fall are mostly solved by spring. You'll learn that if you believe in yourself and in your students, the flowering of their success will eventually appear. Of course, that blossoming won't be the same for every kid, and some may not seem to bloom much at all, giving up or simply failing to improve, but those failures will tend to lessen in number the longer you teach, the more you grow with your students. In the end, you'll find experience to be a ray of sunshine that will dispel your fears.

What Steinbeck Said: Post #11
Tuesday, September 27, 2016
Runneth Over

I had one of those feelings before school started today. I reviewed my lesson plan, estimating how much time each section would require if we executed it properly. To my dismay, no matter how many times I checked my math, I had simply set up more learning than we had time to accomplish. I had twenty ounces of teaching and a twelve-ounce glass to pour it into. That's a recipe for a mess.

Immediately, I dropped a written reflection on our second draft of the process paper. It's useful to ask kids to check their progress on the paper at each stage, but I had a sense, an accurate one as it turned out, that most of my writers had yet to finish their drafts, and so that made the decision to skip the writing easy. As for the rest of the time, I knew it was going to be a squeeze.

For my first two periods, I found myself struggling to find a rhythm. A model presentation on Edwin Hopper, a major American artist, was fun, and we did some fine critical thinking as we examined his work, but our next section, our initial foray into the world of parts of speech, was pretty sloppy. I tried to combine two lessons into one as I explained simple and perfect verb tenses, but I am pretty sure that I confused my students in those first two hours more than I enlightened them. Bless their hearts, they stuck with me and gave a good effort in understanding material that they haven't formally touched for years. They could have used another ten minutes or so to ask questions and make connections, but I felt the need to push on. We finished those two periods by continuing our discussions of The Old Man and the Sea. *It had been almost a week since we had last talked about the book because of a shortened class schedule on Friday, and I must say that the water was choppy for a while. The material was cold, lifeless, and though I urged my kids to take charge of the conversation, I found myself directing more than I like to. Again, there didn't seem to be enough time to ease into a free-flowing discussion. I decided that things had to change after lunch.*

As the prime mover in my classroom, my mood and energy affect my students greatly. During the morning classes, I made sure to remain upbeat, but for my own sake, I wanted to feel effective as a teacher before I closed the door at the end of the day. To that end, I took made a few adjustments for my fourth period. For one, I did a much better job of explaining verbs, of giving directions for my kids' notebook practice. When it came time to discuss Hemingway, I tried something novel. "It's been a week since we discussed this book," I began. "What we talked about then isn't fresh in our minds now, is it? Let's do something about that." I asked my kids to inhale deeply and imagine that their memories of that discussion had moved into their lungs. I then went around the circle with a Styrofoam bowl in hand. I asked them to blow their memories into the bowl. Naturally, they looked at me with genuine doubt regarding my sanity, but each did as I requested, and nearly all of them giggled after they did. I blew as well, and then I popped the container into our microwave for all of five seconds. When I took it out, I held the bowl above my head and announced, "Our discussion from last week is now piping hot and ready to enjoy once more!"

Corny? Of course. Effective? Absolutely. We dived right back into the sea, and in a few short minutes, we made some quite remarkable discoveries about the depth of the novel, about the mastery of Papa Hemingway. Me? I left school feeling as if I had made a difference for at least one of my classes today.

On Thursday, I'll bring a bigger glass.

Y ou will have those days. It won't matter how well you prepare for your lesson, it won't matter how engaged your students are, the wheels will just start to wobble early on in the class period, and it won't get much better the rest of the way. My first such experience occurred on the first day that I went solo during student teaching. My instruction that day was actually fairly good. I have no recollection of what I taught, but I do remember feeling satisfied that things had gone well, only to look at the clock and realize that there were twenty-two minutes remaining until the bell. No backup plan in place, no handy bag of tricks to sponge up those precious seconds and keep my students interested and in their seats if not actually learning. I'm sure that at that moment, my freshmen at Coloma High School were wondering just who this guy was that they had been matched with for the next ten weeks and whether every day was going to be that disorganized. That afternoon, driving back to my apartment, I vowed to never underplan again.

In time, I did develop the ability to switch to Plan B, and I did acquire strategies for creating more learning opportunities when there was time left to use. Moreover, I learned how to save even more time by being more efficient in distributing materials. I divided ninety-minute periods into segments that kept my students more attentive, and when I was unhappy watching them doing nothing while they waited for others to finish an assignment or a test, I started aligning those portions of the periods so that students always had something else to work on whenever they completed a task.

All of those moves made our classroom more productive, and my kids prospered in an environment that allowed them to learn effectively, but such untidy days happen to the most veteran of teachers. And those days seemed harder if I had a principal who viewed school from a factory model perspective. Because those administrators believed that, given the proper input, throughput, and output, I could roll out successful products—widgets or otherwise—they had a hard time seeing why my classroom didn't always operate smoothly when they dropped in to evaluate my teaching. I mean, it was simple, right? In their eyes, teaching wasn't much different from supervising an assembly line of learning, but you won't be working with inanimate materials when you walk into the classroom every day. You won't be in an art studio where you can paint over a mistake or a movie set where you can do multiple takes. Your teaching won't be a machine that can be switched off, recalibrated, and turned on again. Rather, it will be a live performance, and all you will be able to do is control what you can control and that won't include student attitudes, interruptions, or technical difficulties. On the other hand, because teaching and learning include an element of unpredictability, there will be the wonderful promise of surprise that walks into your classroom with you every day. Because you won't know just what is going to transpire from bell to bell, you will be blessed with daily opportunities to be creative, flexible. It will be the dream of a great day of teaching that will lead you back to that collection of young minds hoping to be inspired. That's something to look forward to.

What Steinbeck Said: Post #12
Thursday, September 29, 2016
The Strawberry Fields Process

L ike most of America that night, I was introduced to John Lennon and the Beatles on February 9, 1964, when they performed on The Ed Sullivan Show. *I was in fifth grade, and I sat mesmerized before the black and white images and the raucous sounds that emanated from our family's RCA television. Three years later, a different-looking Lennon recorded a demo tape of a new song at Abbey Road Studios in London. One man, one microphone, one acoustic guitar. What John played that day eventually turned into "Strawberry Fields Forever." Today I played that demo for my students, along with Take One and Take Seven. Each version is quite different from the other two. The song progresses from a scratchy vocal with uncertain lyrics to a more substantially orchestrated piece and finally to what basically amounts to the released cut with a multi-tracked vocal, a raised key, and the addition of some percussion and keyboards. As I played each iteration, I asked my students to analyze what they heard, what changes they'd detected. As it turned out, they demonstrated keen ears, though they didn't always agree on which version they preferred.*

I concluded the activity by comparing the Beatles' recording practice to our own writing process. Ideally, my writers will start with a simple draft, will enhance it with a revision, and will then produce a polished essay by editing and revising a final time. That's not always the case with my kids, however, and I discussed the possibilities with them. Some students want their first drafts to sound like a song on their headphones, and when they run into difficulty, they find themselves stuck, victims of writer's block. Others want to avoid drafting altogether, and they submit their only attempt at a paper as a finished product. I assured each class today that I have a very good ear for demo tape essays. The Beatles, like most bands, often recorded thirty or more takes of a song before deciding they had something worth publishing. "That's our challenge," I told my kids. "Can we approach the music industry standard?" I hold no illusions that my students will write papers of professional quality this year, but I do believe that they can produce great writing if they take the refinement approach that Lennon and his mates adopted so many years ago.

We applied that same idea to our discussion to end the period. We had only twenty minutes available to wrap up our analysis of The Old Man and the Sea, *and still, we went deep. We began our interpretation last week with an enthusiastic but somewhat random discussion of several topics. On Tuesday, we refined that process by concentrating on character motivations. Today, we narrowed the focus even further by examining symbols and their relationship to theme. I went to the board and wrote a few equations for my class to consider: Santiago = _____, marlin = _____, boat = _____, sharks = _____.*

"If you add up what's on the left side of each equation," I said, "you have what happens in the book. What we'll add to the right side will be what the book is about."

49

I started the process by completing the first equation: Santiago = me. If Hemingway presents his protagonist as a representation of each of us, then what do the other items represent? What followed was a remarkable discussion of symbol, and we concluded it by combining those symbols into themes for the novel. It was a brief conversation, but it was more polished than our previous discussions of the book.

Suitable for iTunes? Well, not yet. We did, however, lay down some pretty tasty tracks today. We may still be messing around in the studio, but if you happen to be passing by Room 218 in the coming months, you just might hear some memorable music wafting into the hallway: "College English Forever!"

I am a slow walker, but I never walk back."
                                    —*Abraham Lincoln*

While I started each class period by examining a quotation with my students, quite often in service of the learning that was to follow, I also found those quotes helpful when I reflected each evening on the effectiveness of our learning on that day. The words above describe my teaching style perfectly. I was never one to rush through a lesson or a unit in order to satisfy a curricular calendar. My goal was to foster learning, not to make it through a plan. As Madeline Hunter said in her book, *Mastery Teaching*, "Don't just cover material. If you do, use a shovel and cover the material with dirt, and lay it to rest, for it will be dead as far as memory is concerned." I loved having the freedom to adjust the pace of my teaching to suit the needs of my students. I was forever trying to find ways to help kids put their learning into their memories, to acquire concepts that framed that learning. I knew that if my students could grasp how things fit together, then they would be empowered to learn much more on their own. That campaign grew frustrating at times when I couldn't seem to find a way to communicate those concepts effectively, but like Mr. Lincoln, I never went back down a road. I was in continual pursuit of a viable path.

The first time I used the "Strawberry Fields" model with a class, I was searching for a way to help my struggling students relax on their first drafts and work much harder on their second. I had encountered that problem for a number of years, and I had never quite found the words that got through to my kids. I continually urged them to let their ideas flow early on, to let go of the need to be perfect with their wording, their reasoning. I pleaded with them to not be satisfied with whatever they scratched out in their first drafts as they moved on to revising, and yet I knew that I was up against our tendency to coast once we feel that we have accomplished something. One night, listening to the second Beatles Anthology album while planning for the next day's classes, inspiration decided to pay a visit. Who knows? Maybe it was the ghost of Lennon. Anyway, as I began listening to the second disk in the set, the three versions of his song, I suddenly heard a solution. With that, an idea was born that gave me hope that there just might be a way to help my kids better understand the value of the writing process.

The exercise took less than ten minutes, and even though I hadn't included it in my original plan for the week, I decided that we could take a little detour in hope of finding that more productive way. It turned out to be a wise investment. From time to time for the rest of the year, I returned to the "Strawberry Fields" analogy to remind my kids of the nature of the creative process. And because one year's students rarely differed all that much from another's in their approach to learning, I thereafter included the interlude in my plans. In fact, it became something I looked forward to, not just because it proved an effective tool for helping kids see the big picture, but because, well, I like listening to the Beatles.

There is an incredible energy generated when a teacher finds another way. It creates a renewal, a recharging, and that power eventually affects the students. It wasn't just that my demonstration gave my kids a way to think about drafting and revising and editing. It was more than that. It gave me a boost because I felt that I was taking charge of my teaching, that I was not always beholden to my planning. The energy that I felt when I did something novel on that day long ago carried over to the rest of the class period, the remainder of the day. And on that day at the end of my last September, it energized our study of symbol as well. I'm not sure exactly how it impacted my students, but if nothing else, it sent them a signal that they could never be sure about when Mr. Stemle was going to do something a little bit different. To make a difference, we have to embrace being seen as different.

As you develop your classroom culture, you will make choices every day that will distinguish your students' experience from any other in the school. You won't have to play The Beatles in order to do that. You won't have to play music at all. You'll simply have to use your imagination to find ways to engage your students in the learning. When you find those ways, you'll also tap into that renewable energy source that will keep you going from day to day. My question is, will you limit that energy's potential by settling for standardized instruction? And another question. Will you have the courage to do what's best for your kids?

What Steinbeck Said: Post #13
Monday, October 3, 2016
The Beauty of Ambiguity

*W*e began our class today with a quote from Ralph Waldo Emerson: *"Nothing great was ever achieved without enthusiasm." This was a perfect lead-in to our first project of the year, an extension of our study of* The Old Man and the Sea *called* Endless Voyage. *How else can we begin any significant undertaking in our class unless we have embraced it totally? Of course, my kids don't understand Emerson's point just now. They know that they accomplish greatness when they have enthusiasm, when they follow their passions to that end, but they haven't learned as yet that they can create that energy to pursue any task. As a result, they find success only when their interest matches their assignments. If they are going to become remarkable adults, they need to find ways to lift their spirits no matter what the job.* Endless Voyage *will give them an opportunity to practice that.*

All that being said, I fairly bounded into the room today. Why shouldn't I? I really love this project. It involves creating a business plan for a company that helps its clients achieve personal growth. We began our project by writing a journal entry that compared our lives to Hemingway's Santiago, and we watched a clip of Derek Redmond, the UK sprinter who suffered a heartbreaking injury while competing in the 1992 Olympics. Both activities helped set the premise of Endless Voyage, *and we followed up by examining project guidelines and selecting topics to present to a panel of teachers in three weeks.*

Here is where the tricky part of any project always comes in. If I am going to design a task that will allow my students to explore and to grow, then I can't be too prescriptive with my expectations. What good would it do to tell them exactly what I wanted them to create? All I would get in return was compliance, not creativity. I would be producing students adept at following directions but not necessarily skilled in problem solving, not to mention risk-taking. With that in mind, the day of a project launch is a bit unsettling for students, especially those who have high expectations for their performance, and so I give them enough of a preview of where they can go, but I avoid showing them a finished product.

You know what happens? They flounder for a while. They fret and they worry and they sometimes even whine. As I have said before, I have an advantage over them because I know what happens next. I know that I will guide them on Wednesday, will answer any questions they have after they work with the project a bit. I know that they will eventually feel empowered because they will not simply replicate something that I have modeled for them but will instead devise their own plans. When that happens, I will revel in their success.

That is why I was buoyant today. That is why I bounced around the room checking with my teams, smiling right past their doubtful looks. I know that in three weeks, they will accomplish more than they ever dreamed today, and then they just might appreciate the beauty of ambiguity. It's all right to not know exactly where we're going or how we're getting there, just like it's better not to read the last page of the novel before beginning Chapter One. Uncertainty adds excitement to the journey, helps us stay alert. It may not be in vogue in this era of direct instruction and learning targets, but it will always be a hallmark of my classroom. It's all pretty simple: our class is about the students, not the teacher. It's about what they accomplish, not what I do. Why should I limit them to merely following me?

W e've talked about love, now let us discuss joy. It was certainly something I brought into the classroom nearly every day, as did a lot of my students. It was something we could see in each other's faces, hear in our voices. More than anything, it was something that we felt because we were happy to be together, eager to learn with each other. As Eckhart Tolle tells us in *A New Earth*, joy does not result from what we do. Instead, it is something that we bring to our actions, to our participation. It comes from being aware of who we are at a deep level, and with that awareness comes a delight in even the simplest things. When my kids and I were joyful, when we enjoyed being in class, we had fun with learning the *Word of the Day* or noticing subtleties in our reading. We had a ball listening to each other's stories in discussion, embraced activities that gave us a chance to learn in novel ways. Again, it wasn't that we found pleasure in those activities but rather that we brought that feeling to them.

I was, of course, a leader in the joyful movement. It wasn't hard. No matter how tired I felt as I drove to school in the morning, no matter what I had on my mind about committee concerns or grading responsibilities and deadlines, when that bell rang, and I popped into our room, I brought with me an exuberance for the opportunity to be with my students for the next eighty-five minutes. Part of that feeling was based on my experience, of knowing that my kids were about to learn something at a high level because my students had been doing that for years and years and years. Part of it had to do with that wonderful uncertainty that left me wondering just how each year's group was going to come together. It felt like my anticipation when opening a Christmas present from Teresa or one of our children, not really knowing what lay inside that wrapping but believing that because it came from them, it would be thoughtful and based in love. Isn't that what teaching gives us? Every day you will walk into your classroom knowing what you're going to do but not really knowing what your students will do in kind. If you enter into that situation with the awareness that you have much to contribute to the knowledge of your class, and that each of your kids does, too, then how can you not enjoy teaching? How can your kids not have fun learning if they come to believe that they have talents to share with their classmates?

I know that there will be days when you'll feel anything but cheerful. There will be stressful times, and there might be even days when you'll despair. That's only natural. Just appreciate those mornings or afternoons when your kids walk in and you feel a swell in your heart because you realize that there is no other place you'd rather be for the next hour or so. And remember this. Happiness isn't something you receive. It's something that you create. As Joseph Campbell said, "We cannot cure the world of sorrows, but we can choose to live in joy." How true that is. Keep that in mind, and maybe you won't hear yourself saying, "These kids are driving me crazy" or "If I have to go to one more faculty meeting. . ." It's all a matter of choice, isn't it?

What Steinbeck Said: Post #14
Wednesday, October 5, 2016
When I Am an Old Man I Shall Write Purple

I was so happy to start each class today. After five weeks of school, my students were at last ready to submit their first essays, and there was a hum in the classroom as the kids arrived, newly-printed papers in hand, trying to hide grins that would suggest that maybe, just maybe, they had created something worth reading. After glancing at their drafts and conferring with a good number of writers, I had a smile on my face as well.

We celebrate writing in Room 218. We adore the authors that we explore, we delight in our own well-turned phrases and our little victories in the everlasting punctuation battles. We love those just-right words that color our prose, those clever titles that somehow find their explanations in our ultimate clinchers. Did we experience all of that today? Not exactly. So far, we have only been introduced to Frost and Hemingway, and while there are little gems here and there in our writing, we are far from being jewelers just yet. Punctuation? See me in February.

Still, we celebrated today. Cookies! The kids had no idea that they would be served when they came to class, but they are treating me to their writing, and the

55

least I can do is return a sweet favor. I quoted the Chinese proverb at the outset of class: "A journey of a thousand miles begins with a single step." In our nine-month trek toward eloquence, today was the most important stride.

Tonight I will take my customary purple pen, and I will rain ink all over a few essays. I will acknowledge strengths, I will mark errors, I will comment on my students' logic and the clarity of their expression. In essence, I will teach writing each night for the next two weeks. Oh, I will surely devote some time in class to modeling and to sharing lessons on technique, but my true teaching will come in that intimate conversation that I have with each of my writers. It is in those purple words that I will exhort and encourage, that I will question and challenge. More than anything, I will whisper secrets that only the writer will hear. Shhh—time to read another!

Her name was Wendy Neininger. She was not much older than I was, maybe six or seven years. Certainly, she was much younger than any of my other professors in the Department of English at Michigan State University. I met Wendy early in my immersion into Language Arts Education courses, and she immediately became my mentor for the world of teaching. I'm not sure she ever realized what an impact she made on a boy on the brink of manhood.

Wendy was forever patient. No matter how many questions I posed to her—and I asked a lot—she took the time to listen to me with full attention. She took the time to write copious comments in the margins of my papers and my journal entries. I had never known a teacher who took that much care with my writing. Wendy's notes were often questions to spur more of my thinking. At other times, they were personal connections to something I had said, just a few words to let me know that we shared similar ideas or experiences. Most important to me at the time was her encouragement. As a preservice teacher, I was still trying to find my way in so many aspects of the classroom, and I felt grateful for a message as simple as, "You can do it!" I could not wait to get my notebook back to see what she had marked in it.

It was Wendy who taught me just how intimate the relationship between writer and reader can be. And it was Wendy whose spirit sat beside me all those years as I read student essays and journals. As much as I connected with my students during class and before and after school, it was in the writing of those comments crammed into every nook I could find on a page that friendships were forged. I knew that my students often let their friends read my remarks, and that became my challenge, to be fresh and personal with everyone's paper, but there was just something incredibly confidential about my interactions with student writing. It was more than grading, more than reactions. More than anything, it was me telling my kids that we were co-creators of their writing. Did it take time? Countless late nights. Did it take patience? Lord, yes. Did I get tired? To the bone.

So why did I do it? I'll tell you why. Because Wendy was always there in my mind, cheering me on, just as she had done all those years before. Because by spring each year, my students had found their authentic voices and their sense of structure, and I knew that my cheering and encouraging and celebrating had played some part in their success. Because when I asked my kids to write me a letter of reflection at the end of the year, nearly every student told me how much my comments had meant to them.

I don't know what became of Wendy after I graduated from Michigan State. I know that she left the school shortly thereafter, but that's about all I do know. Well, I know something else. My students became better writers, better thinkers, because I had the good fortune to walk into her classroom over forty years ago. Someday, I hope that some of my students can say the same about me.

My wish for you is that if you haven't already found your Wendy, that you do sometime early in your career. When you're lucky enough to have that experience, do everything you can to carry it forward into your own teaching. Extend your mentor's influence to your students, lean on it when times get tough, when you feel that you're not making a difference or when you doubt that anyone appreciates your efforts. Do something more. After you've been teaching a while, keep an eye out for a younger colleague who might be in need of a Wendy. You don't have to wait till you've been in the profession for forty years. All you need to do is open your wing a little bit and offer encouragement, maybe a little expertise.

Finally, if you have had the good fortune to know someone who has helped you shape yourself into a teacher, by all means, find a way to thank that person. As it was for me, you might think of a professor who helped you directly. Or maybe it will be someone who has no idea of the effect that he or she has had on you. Sometimes we aren't aware of our impact on others, especially on our fellow teachers, and when a simple note of gratitude brings that to light, it can not only brighten a day but also inspire us to be on the lookout for others who need a little boost from time to time. Of course, in the end, you know that it is always the students who benefit the most from our kindnesses to each other. Their interest is written on every bottom line.

What Steinbeck Said: Post #15
Friday, October 7, 2016
What Suddenly Emerges

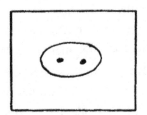

*P*erhaps *you've seen this picture. What does it show? Cell division? An eye with a double pupil? A European electrical outlet? You might not be able to identify what you're seeing, but one thing that we do know is that the drawing is an example of a* droodle, *a riddle expressed in visual form. That's fine, Eric, but what am I looking at? Take another good look. See it?*

A pig coming out of heavy fog.

As I walked about our classroom on Friday, I saw that snout emerging time and time again. Teams that had struggled to grasp the demands of our Endless

Voyage *project were not only finding their grip on the task, but they were now functioning as visionary units. They were researching and brainstorming, creating team names and logos, topping each other with ideas that were so far out there that the kids could no longer even see the box. You know what they were doing really, really well? They were laughing. My favorite sound in a classroom.*

I wrote the other day about embracing ambiguity. That's easy for me to do because I have done this so many times before. It was much harder for my students, who, try as they might, could not see more than a foot before their faces, enveloped as they were by the fog of uncertainty. They saw no landmarks, and they either stepped gingerly along the path to the project's completion or stood frozen at the start, afraid to lose their way. I called to them from down the road, I walked back and guided them to begin their journey. Some came willingly, some fretted and stressed and waited for the fog to lift.

Funny thing about a foggy night. Shine a flashlight or your high-beam headlights into it, and you just get a cloudier view. Creep along in relative darkness, and you eventually find your way. Though my kids wanted me to enlighten them, to show them just want I wanted them to create, I knew that doing so would not promote their learning. I might as well have carried them in my arms down that murky road. Instead, I assured them that the path was safe, that conditions would eventually change in their favor. Yesterday, those conditions did indeed change. As the mist cleared for my teams, and they were suddenly able to see a starry sky of possibilities, the synergy from their collaboration was palpable in our classroom. They can now see the way, and some are fairly running toward the finish. Not a pig among them.

Days such as that one didn't come along all that often in my career. I would like to tell you that every time I met with students, we had an amazing experience, but the truth is, day-to-day life in our classroom was a matter of putting in hard work in a supportive environment. We smiled and we laughed every day, we struggled and we learned, but a class period like the above entry describes was rare and special. It's not that my kids spent most of their time in a fog, but more that, on those exceptional days, a veil was lifted. For

59

just a moment, they saw what was possible, became aware of new dimensions of thought, of creativity. Most significantly, they realized that they were in charge of their own learning. They didn't need to wait for me to explain something step-by-step. In fact, they seemed oblivious to my presence in the room. I felt like a scientist who had set up conditions for a chemical reaction and then watched in fascination at the changes happening before him. Most of the time, I knew how the process would turn out, but there were those days, those special days, when something gloriously unexpected happened.

As I said, that was a rare occurrence. It didn't even happen for all of my classes on a given day. My first period might muddle along, working diligently but not spectacularly, and then my next group would come in, and we had nuclear fusion. Would I have liked to have had fireworks every class period? Sure, though I don't know that the kids and I could have survived that pace over the course of a year. I wish I could have planned for it—okay, next week my classes are going to have an epiphany—but maybe I really didn't. There is a certain serendipity that you will find in your classroom, a turn that you decide to make that takes you out of the fog. A happy accident that is not really much of an accident at all but the result of a carefully cultivated environment that is ripe for growth and for enlightenment. That preparation will be crucial if those special days are going to come along more than once in a long while for you and for your students. Trust me, each one will be something to cherish.

What Steinbeck Said: Post #16
Tuesday, October 11, 2016
Living Poets Society

*I*n the summer of 1989, I attended a workshop at Indiana University entitled Empowering Leadership, *taught by a marvelous woman named Mary Martin. It was a week filled with insights and revelations, a few days of sudden friendships and incredible good cheer. I shared a ride from the airport to campus with a high school science teacher from Minnesota* *named Doug. Even though he was enrolled in a different class, we quickly hit it off, and we ended up eating breakfast and dinner together each day in the dorm's dining hall, sharing what we were learning in our respective sessions.*

On Wednesday at breakfast, Doug suggested we take in a movie that evening. I had heard of a new release that sounded promising, and so after supper we walked a few blocks downtown to see Dead Poets Society. *I wasn't aware of what my new friend was thinking or feeling during those next two hours, but I sat completely mesmerized for the entirety of the film. That was my classroom up on the screen, though my school looked nothing like Welton Academy. That was me in the front of the room, though I was not nearly as dramatic as Mr. Keating, nor did I begin to approach the genius of Robin Williams. Still, that was my dream of an English class. Passion. Wit. Inspiration. Laughter. Tears.*

Magic.

As we left the theater, I explained my interpretation of the movie, in particular Tom Schulman's use of symbolism. This was foreign territory for Doug, but he seemed to get a kick out of my delight in the film's tone. As a screenwriter, Schulman had an ear for school. As a director, Peter Weir had an eye. Williams? He had a heart.

There are days in my classroom when I almost channel John Keating. It might be when I feel a need to raise my intensity, when I am compelled to draw from students what they know and what they feel. No matter how much they love language, kids tend to reserve their emotions, to hide their enthusiasm for wordplay. It's not exactly being "too cool for school," but there's danger associated with being academically playful. When I sense that, I turn to theatrics.

Today I shared a brief lesson on adverbs. Adverbs! How dry is that? Ah, but in teaching my kids the need for strong adjectives (e.g., morose *rather than* very sad*), I asked them to write synonyms for* very happy *and* very tired. *When they were reticent to share what they'd written, I went into Keating mode. I teased, I cajoled, I exulted in words such as* zonked *and* jovial. *I pulled up a thesaurus on the SMART board and showed my kids a long list of synonyms, all with their own nuance and all simply gorgeous to behold. Later, I cavorted around the room, eyes wide, voice modulating as I shared presentation techniques with my kids in* *preparation for next week when as teams they will pitch a project proposal to a panel of teachers. What I saw was a glimmer of hope in their eyes, as if they were daring to believe that this time around, public speaking might not be the scariest thing in the world.*

The Latin word is educare*: "to draw out." The English word is* educate. *Education is not about putting information into students' minds. Rather, it is about helping them draw it out. That's what I did today, what I seek to do every time we meet. These are living poets I'm working with, even if they don't dare to admit or to aspire to that honor. In time, they will.*

By the way, two days later, on our last night together in Bloomington, Doug and I went to another new movie. Field of Dreams. *You know the rest.*

When I was a small boy living in Akron, Ohio, the most haunting place I knew was our local parish, St. Sebastian Catholic Church. Each time I entered that gothic building, its shadows illuminated by candles and daylight streaming through stained glass windows, I felt surrounded by mystery. It was present in the marble statuary, the oil paintings, the incense that burned my nostrils, the Latin intoned by the priest and answered by those kneeling in their pews. If ever I spoke in my native tongue before or after the service, it was in the softest and most reverent whisper. To say anything above a murmur was to profane the sacred surroundings.

On the other hand, the most exciting places I knew, from childhood on, revolved around sports. From the time I first stepped onto a baseball field, I was immersed in sound. In little league, our coaches demanded that we chatter when we were in the field, crying "Hey batter, hey batter, hey batter, swing!" on every pitch, encouraged us to exhort our teammates at the plate when we were on the bench. I ran the bases with abandon and slid into them hard enough to tear the young flesh on my legs and my rear end. I didn't care. I was playing ball, and I loved the energy all around me. A ballpark was raucous, as were the gyms I played basketball in. From the first time I took the floor in uniform for a fifth-grade game, I was moved by the speed and the passion of my teammates and of my opponents. I sprinted end to end on fast breaks (well, perhaps plodded is a better term), I dived on the floor for loose balls. I shouted and I celebrated. Loudly.

Throughout my career, our classroom lay somewhere between a church sanctuary and a sports arena. When my students and I were reading our novels for ten or fifteen minutes at the beginning of class, the silence was reverential. I taught my kids how to gently close our heavy door so as not disturb the peace of our quiet moments, and when an office aide visited and let the door slam, I watched my students flinch as if someone had belched during the Consecration at Mass. Other times, our room was far too noisy for the good of those classrooms on either side of us. When we played a game like Balloon Bounce or we worked together in cooperative teams, creating and celebrating and in general raising a din, I felt bad for the sake of those learners adjacent to us, but you know what? Sometimes school has to be more like a stadium than a chapel.

That was all up to me because I was in control of our venue. It was my hand on the volume knob, on the energy regulator. There were days when I had to tone things down, when my kids were so excitable that I thought it best to calm their levels a bit. Then there were those days like the post before when I injected a little of my own enthusiasm into the mix. If I felt that my students were dragging, or if I knew that the material I was presenting was necessary but less than thrilling, I would hold their attention by being dramatic or funny, and in doing so, I would help them generate their own enthusiasm for the task. After all, I was the stem. My function was to support them and to nourish them, especially on those days when their petals appeared to droop.

No matter what subject you teach, no matter what content you are sharing, there is no reason to bore your students. I know that boredom is something in the mind of the listener not in the delivery of the speaker, but these are young people we're talking about. If they tell you with their body language that they're just not into it that day, it will be up to you to look out for their interests. Maybe someone will tell you that it's not your job to entertain your students, but lord help you if you don't. Bored minds don't stay that way for long. If your kids tune you out, then they will find other ways to amuse themselves, and it won't be by parsing sentences or solving quadratic equations. Besides, it will just feel good to have some fun with your kids, no matter how dry the subject matter. How will you know that you're getting through to them? Count the smiles and multiply by the laughter. That should give you a good idea.

What Steinbeck Said: Post #17
Friday, October 14, 2016
A New Slant on Expression

*I*n preparation for our upcoming project presentations, I have been sharing verbal and nonverbal techniques with my students. We've reviewed some key principles involved in pace, projection, eye contact, expression, and gestures. We've analyzed a number of TED talks and Billy Mays commercials. On Thursday, I opened the jewelry case and took out a clip from Mad Men. Any time we interpret literature in our classroom, we first experience it on a visceral level. We begin by asking ourselves, what's happening, here? What is our emotional connection to the characters? The plot events? Finally we examine issues and motivations, all the while relating the piece to our own lives, to our own perspectives. In a sense, we dive into a pool of interpretation.*

On closer examination, we look at the piece as art. What are the metaphors, the symbols, the images that inform our understanding of the literature to a much deeper and profound degree? In other words, what raises this poem or story or novel or film to another level? What separates it from just another good story?

This is how we worked with a four-minute segment of the Season One finale from Matthew Weiner's exquisite series. Before I showed the video, I reviewed our presentation rubric with my classes, reminding them of the ten different standards upon which I will evaluate each of their presentations throughout the year. I asked them to keep those items in mind as we watched Don Draper lead his team of advertisers in a creative pitch to representatives from Eastman Kodak. If you watch the clip for yourself, look to see how Jon Hamm's character organizes his message, how he uses his voice, his face, and his hands to convince his potential clients that what they are going to be selling isn't a slide projector.

No, what people are going to want to experience is nostalgia, *and the Carousel is going to be their ride to those memories.*

Following our viewing, I asked my students to share their thoughts on Mr. Draper's performance. They noted that he never seemed to rush his pace, that he changed his inflection to emphasize key ideas. They noticed that he used his hands purposefully to indicate movement in his points. I listened and nodded, and when they had finished their analyses, I asked them how the character had employed his eyebrows. His eyebrows? No one had a clue.

Back to the tape! I showed the clip once more, but this time with the sound muted. This move helped us focus on the visual content of the scene, and when we reached the point where Draper calls nostalgia "delicate," the kids gasped and giggled to see how high Jon Hamm raised his dark brows, how he lowered them when he said, "potent."

"How did you miss that?" I asked my classes playfully. I knew the answer. There was so much to which they had to attend when they first watched the video, and at this point in the class, they have yet to learn to focus on nuance.

"When you present to your panel next week," I continued, "you have many tools at your disposal to create an emotional connection with those three teachers. That's what Don Draper does at the beginning of his pitch. He has all the important details ready to go later in the discussion, but in those first few minutes, he has to grab their attention, appeal to their emotions.

"In the next few days, we'll practice using our voices to emphasize, using our hands to illustrate. And, yes, we are going to practice using our eyebrows to highlight our key points. Remember," I said leaning closer to my kids and lowering my voice. "Your eyebrows are the italics of your face."

In a few weeks, we will be addressing style in our next essay, and I will encourage my students to find many ways to emphasize their points in their writing. We'll talk about word choice and punctuation and text features such as bold face and, of course, italics. In that last case, I will encourage my writers to raise their eyebrows in their papers. Will they overdo it? Sure, some will, but playing with those possibilities for expression will in time help my kids become aware of the control they have over their message. When they realize that power, *their words will whisper and shout and sing from the page. That's something even a mad man can appreciate.*

E ighty percent of success is showing up."
—Woody Allen.

I swear, I could have started every class with a different quote from Woody. Or Twain. That one was a favorite, not just because it states what seems to be a basic truth, but because of what it doesn't say. Sure, as I told my kids at the outset of the period, if we merely showed up for class, and that meant being actually present in the moment and not preoccupied otherwise while we were physically in the room, then we would do just fine. Was "just fine" enough, though? "Eighty percent is a B-," I continued. "Is that what you want for a grade in this class?" Of course, not. Those were high-striving kids I was teaching, and just "good enough" simply wasn't. What, then, was the other twenty percent? "That's where the excellence lives," I told them in a conspiratorial tone. "What makes this class special is that we take for granted that we'll all show up. What can we do to go beyond that eighty percent, though?"

The lesson for that day was a great example of what I was talking about. We're used to seeing and hearing things once. We make an interpretation of what we observe, and then we move on to other things. There's little time for contemplation in our day-to-day lives, but school will provide you with a chance to reflect, to replay and reflect again. At least, it can give you those openings. It will be up to you to take the time to do that. To design lessons just for that purpose. In our class, those few minutes with *Mad Men* did more than help us prepare for presentations that came the following week. In addition, they set a tone for our studies for the rest of the year in terms of considering nuance. Subtlety was not something we explored the first few days or weeks of school. Those early classes were like taking a walk in the park. Sure, we might have seen the mountains in the distance, the trees across the way, but it was only after a while that we began seeing more than the branches. In the Draper lesson, I pointed out the leaves. Later, we would look even more closely.

One more thing about opportunities. I know that in your classroom, you'll do everything that you can to inspire your students, and you'll seek all sort of ways for them to expand their learning. That's what great teachers do every day, but opportunity is more than something that is given to us. It's also something we can make for ourselves. It's one thing for teachers to open doors and windows so that their students can see the world in new ways. It's quite another for students to throw wide their own. The *Mad Men* lesson was the beginning of my message to my kids that they must make their own chances. If they could ask their teachers for the time to do so, then great, but that can be a daunting task for a teenager. If nothing else, I encouraged my students to take their own time outside of class to find nuance, to discern subtlety all around them. I loved it when they did that and dropped in to tell me or, better yet, told the whole class the next day. When that happened, we found ourselves in that elusive twenty percent area. And that, well, that was an occasion was worthy of a roomful of raised eyebrows.

What Steinbeck Said: Post #18
Tuesday, October 18, 2016
Hands Up!

*T*his morning and this afternoon, with our projects looming just two days away, I took my students beyond the nuts and bolts of creating visual aids and organizing their presentations. In the past two weeks we have examined a number of videos to better understand verbal and nonverbal techniques, but today I wanted to touch them a little closer to their hearts, to where they hide their fears and, at an even deeper level, where many hide their hopes. To that end, I showed them the last eight minutes of Amy Cuddy's TED talk on power posing. Cuddy, a Harvard psychologist, teaches her students that "our bodies change our minds. . .and our minds change our behavior. . .and our behavior changes our outcomes." It's a simple premise: if confident people act in a certain way, then it follows that if we act that way, we, too, can become confident. She exhorts students who doubt their abilities to "fake it till you make *it!" Cuddy's point is that we become paralyzed by our fears, and rather than succumb to them and quit, we should pretend that we're strong, that we know we can do it. Eventually, she says, it's a matter of "faking it till you become it."*

How do we fake it? How do we jump start our feelings of confidence? Cuddy suggests that just prior to performance, be it a speech or a job interview or even participation in a class discussion, we practice power poses. One has us stand like Wonder Woman, hands on hips, head held high, feet firmly planted. Another has us raise our arms above our head in a sign of exultation or victory. Cuddy's experiments have shown that performers who practice power posing are rated by interviewers or judges to have a greater presence before an audience than do people who practice low power poses such as closed body language. High power posers tend to come across as enthusiastic, caring, and authentic, and those qualities seem to resonate more with audiences than do considerations such as organization, content, and verbal techniques. I can sense that my students want to believe Cuddy. They are looking for ways to feel more comfortable in their presenting, more powerful in their connection with their audience. They may not have told me so today, but I know from experience that some if not many of my presenters will strike a positive pose before they enter the room to greet their panel on Thursday.

We may be faking a lot this time around, but just you wait a few months. It is amazing what we are going to become!

I was a devotee of Amy Cuddy's ideas long before I ever watched her TED talk. I am told that as a young child I was precocious, scoring highly on intelligence tests and seeming to know the answer to every question that the nuns asked me in school. As a result, I was quite secure in my abilities when I compared myself to my young peers. That changed as I grew older and began encountering classmates with similar or greater gifts than mine. Suddenly, a boy who had a reputation for being smart not only discovered competition but also found himself in classes that challenged his thinking and his skills.

Rather quickly, I learned to maintain a brave facade in the face of those challenges to my intelligence. I refrained from asking questions because I feared that each time I did, I would reveal my ignorance. If someone said to me, "You know this, right?" I would nod, and my questioner would often reply, "Of course, you do." If I found myself in a conversation where I was over my head, I would insert key words or facts every so often so that my friends would think that I knew everything about the subject. I graduated from high school with a much lower grade point average than a lot of my friends, and I doubt they had any idea that I was a "B" student. I was definitely a poser.

All of that came to an end in my first year of high school teaching when I met Dan, a rookie teacher like myself and one of the wisest people I have ever known. Our talks basically consisted of him asking me questions. They were often simple in nature, clearly designed to get a better picture understanding of a subject, and I never tired of answering them because Dan seemed so interested in what I had to say. I looked forward to our daily chats because I felt that he respected my knowledge and opinions. He rarely reciprocated with his own ideas unless I pushed him to, but he was always willing to explain his side of things if I asked. As bright as he was, he was totally at ease with listening and asking for information, remarkably humble in our discussions. I never set foot in his math classroom while students were present, and he left the profession just a year later to pursue other interests, but Dan turned out to be one of my most important teachers.

With Dan as my model, I started to ask my own questions when I didn't know something. To my great surprise, no one looked at me as if I was stupid. What a relief! It took a while to get the hang of it, but eventually I became proficient at listening and probing, at rephrasing and asking for clarification. In time it dawned on me that while my friend Dan had shown me respect through his questions, he had also grown in his own knowledge. I had always known that he asked me things that he must have known the answer to, but it was all part of his strategy to build a conceptual framework.

It felt so good to be liberated from posing. Freed from the worry that others would criticize my lack of knowledge, I now felt smarter. At the same time, I didn't worry about how others viewed me because I was finally taking charge of my own learning, finding out what I could about what I didn't understand. Plus, I knew how my family, my friends, and my colleagues felt on the other end of my questions. Dan had given me the chance to feel that.

Years later, looking around the circle in my classroom, I sought out telltale signs of kids faking it. The averted eyes when I asked an open question. The confident head nods when they heard someone else express a great idea. I had played that game, and I knew that I could help my students move beyond those pretenses to open up their learning. The key was to accomplish that in an artistic way, to allow my kids to preserve their dignity while they dissolved their own facades. That meant never telling them directly to stop acting as if they knew it all.

What did I do? I modeled in discussion and in conferences, asking simple questions and also asking if my interpretation of what I heard matched what they meant. I let my kids know that every question was valuable, and I treated each of those queries with great respect. Just as it took a while for kids to start noticing fine distinctions in literature and in film, it took them a while to learn to stop worrying and ask questions. Sure, we had fun standing like Superman before we made a presentation, but that was different because so many of us profess a fear of public speaking, and telling others that we're nervous makes us part of the majority, usually earns us empathy and support. Conversely, asking for clarity can make us seem ignorant, and that's a heavier burden for us to bear. Still, Dr. Cuddy has a point. It's helpful to fake it until we feel truly confident of our abilities, or at least secure enough to acknowledge our vulnerability. As a teacher you can create a nurturing environment that will foster both, and if that means that you'll have to fake it until you figure out how to do that, then put on your best smile, strike your most powerful pose, and convince your class that you've got this. Who knows, maybe you'll all make it at the same time.

What Steinbeck Said: Post #19
Thursday, October 20, 2016
Remembering Old Lodge Skins

I t is an iconic cinematic moment. Dustin Hoffman as Jack Crabb, tending to his grandfather, played with wit and grace by Chief Dan George, as the old man prepares to die on a rainy hillside in Arthur Penn's Little Big Man. Despite his effort to will himself to the other world, Old Lodge Skins opens his eyes and utters the immortal line, "Well, sometimes the magic works, sometimes it doesn't."

Those words came to my mind a number of times today, our first day of presentations for our project entitled Endless Voyage. Three teams from each class pitched a sales plan to a panel of teachers who gave up their planning periods to help the kids practice their speaking techniques. Despite our preparations and our best intentions, it wasn't easy for us to cross over. Each panel missed a member today for circumstances that we just couldn't foresee. An assembly for seniors ran ten minutes longer than scheduled, putting my first class in a time crunch. The software that I prescribed for my students to use decided it didn't want to play nice with PowerPoint, and so most of the teams were left to share some things orally that they had envisioned presenting with impressive graphics. A lot more rain than I had seen in the forecast.

To their credit, my kids pulled through, displaying poise and good humor despite their challenges. To my gratitude, my panelists were supportive and affectionate while pushing the presenters to think critically. It's nerve-wracking enough to stand before the discriminating eyes and ears of professionals who are charged with judging the efficacy of your plan, and it's quite another to do so while the technology isn't cooperating.

As much as I want to sit to the side and enjoy these presentations, I don't often find myself at my best while they are happening because I'm busy taking notes and scoring rubrics, keeping an eye on the clock so that each team gets a fair shake on time, helping out with the computer glitches that often show up at inopportune times. While I struggle to keep all those juggling balls aloft, I often *feel less patient than I normally am, more abrupt in my interactions. My deepest regret today was that I put my students in a difficult spot because of my website requirement for them. Had they chosen their own platforms and encountered problems, I would have felt empathy for them, but I have a responsibility to not only guide my students and place them in situations where they can succeed, but more importantly to avoid throwing them into a disadvantage. I failed in that regard today.*

Despite the occasional downpour, the sun did shine brightly for most of the presentations. We had a chance to process the experience in two of my classes, and I am confident that my presenters on Monday will come prepared for computer contingencies. I told each class that while we may not hope for problems to arise, we can embrace them as opportunities to shine when they do show up. As it turned out, we did glow fairly brightly as individuals and as classes today, and I learned much about the character of my students. That's a rainbow, if you will.

Each afternoon after school, Teresa and I sit with cups of tea and maybe a cookie, and we share our teaching days with each other. Today she had her good moments and a few bumps. When I told her that I'd had better days as a teacher, she gave me that wonderful look of hers and said, "What, you mean it wasn't perfect?" So much of my success in the classroom is grounded in the magic I have in her.

I t really did feel like magic from time to time. Some days things did more than just fall into place, and something extraordinary happened. I can't really say that I ever planned for a miracle, they just appeared. And I can't say that those truly special moments can be attributed to anything that I ever did. Magic in the classroom was always the result of what my students did, and when it happened, I think they were more surprised than I was.

One moment occurred in one of my *Senior Humanities* classes when I taught in Green River, Wyoming. Along with our daily studies, we began each class period with a student's presentation on a composer, an author, or an artist. These were fifteen-minute shots that not only gave the presenter a chance to practice research in a time years before Wikipedia, but also gave the rest of us a deeper understanding of the arts, often by learning about creators whom we had never known before.

Nicole came to me after school the day before her presentation and asked if it would be all right for her to come in early to set up. That wasn't a really unusual request, so I told her that I would arrive a little earlier the next morning to give her whatever time she needed for preparation. She thanked me, and as she turned to leave, I asked her what she planned on doing. "You'll see," she said with a smile. Boy, did I see. And hear.

What Nicole's classmates saw when they came to class the next day was a transformation of our classroom. Housed on an underground floor of the school, our room had no windows, and while I lamented the lack of sunlight throughout the year, on that occasion, it worked perfectly. Nicole had taken our circle of desks and turned them into two sets of rows divided by a center aisle. In the corners of the room she had lit candles (a fire code violation for sure, something that I myself was wont to do from time to time), and as each student came through the door, in a whisper, Nicole instructed them to silently enter and find a seat. As they did, they could hear symphonic music playing softly.

When the bell at last rang, Nicole, attired in a black dress, walked to the front of the room, stood next to the projector screen, and said in a quiet voice, "Welcome to the funeral of Ludwig van Beethoven." For the next twenty minutes, she delivered an inspired eulogy, aided by images she shared with the help of an opaque projector she had borrowed from the library and by musical excerpts that she played on our room's cassette player. Her classmates sat enthralled. I sat proud and incredibly moved by the girl's creativity, her passion. An accomplished pianist, Nicole wanted her classmates to experience just a fraction of what she felt for music. What she did beyond that was to set a standard for the rest of the year. No longer would it be satisfactory to hold up a print of a painting or play a song and then recite facts about the artist. Because of the spell that Nicole conjured that morning, her classmates would have a memory of what it meant to touch not just the eyes and ears of their peers but their hearts as well.

It was moments like that that put my frustrations with technology into perspective. A student who had researched her subject in encyclopedias and books, who had played his music on a device my final-year students had never seen, who projected images with a technology that seems painfully primitive today, delivered one of the greatest lessons I ever witnessed in my classroom. It had nothing to do with what I had done save giving her the assignment. Nearly twenty-five years later I had worried about Blendspace not working perfectly, about the impact that a slightly shorter class period was having upon my presenters. I had forgotten that great moments happen because of the people involved, not the technology that they employ. Sometimes the magic happens and sometimes it doesn't. I could live with the latter because, while the former was a temporary irritant, the magic seemed to change things for the rest of the year. As I've told you before, you can't plan for days like that. All you can do is stay alert to possibility, be ready to realize the benefits of what at first seems to be a problem. In a Zen sense, it's a matter of being aware, of having your eyes, ears, and especially your heart open to a moment that just might be a catalyst to dramatic change in your classroom. It's one thing to not see something coming. It's quite another to not see its significance when it arrives. My advice to you? Be awake every day!

What Steinbeck Said: Post #20
Monday, October 24, 2016
The Second Free Throw

I was a great foul shooter in practice. I was near-perfect from the line in my driveway, too. For some reason, when it came to basketball games, I often struggled to make the first shot when I was fouled. Call it nerves, maybe adrenaline, but I tended to clang my first effort. Ah, but the second. It seemed that the second always went in.

Today was the second free throw for presentations in my classes, and the teams were a little more prepared than were their classmates who launched their proposals last week. Why wouldn't they be? They saw what worked for the other teams, and they heard what the panel was looking for. That's why we always honor those first day groups—they blaze the presentation trail. It was a second try for me as well. Over the weekend, I made some technical moves that ensured that our slide shows would function properly. That relieved my worries about repeating that missed shot on Thursday where I felt that I had in some way hindered my kids from being able to fully demonstrate their skills. It helped today that my panel members arrived early for their tasks, giving us a few precious extra minutes, and that meant that time was much less of a factor than it had been on day one. The result? I entered each class in a lighthearted mood, and that energy transferred to my teams.

On Thursday, whether or not they realized it, I'm sure that my students were a little bit affected by the fact that I felt rushed. Try as I might to be upbeat, when I'm uncharacteristically anxious, there's an undercurrent that permeates the feel of the classroom. Today, I was relaxed, more myself. As I conferred with each team before and after they presented, I felt such a good connection with them. It is something a teacher sees in students' eyes that conveys trust, gratitude for the help they have been given to see them through a challenge. In an educational world now driven by assessment and data, how can we measure that impact? How do we calibrate the heart?

At the end of the period, we processed the project after our panels left, and the kids reported that while they had dreaded the unknown of presenting, in many ways, they surprised themselves with their performances. Considering that this was our first shot of the year, I felt deep satisfaction when I heard that wonderful sound.

Swish!

T he most glorious moments in your life are not the so-called days of success, but rather those days when out of dejection and despair you feel rise in you a challenge to life, and the promise of future accomplishments." I wouldn't say that I had despaired after the difficulties my kids and I had suffered the previous class period, but that day was perhaps a little of what French novelist Gustave Flaubert had in mind when he talked about glorious moments. From the earliest days of my career, I made it a point to never have two bad days in a row. I couldn't help if things went wrong on any given day. Conditions were often out of my control, and I wasn't all that good at control as a young teacher. Still, I did my best to ensure that I wouldn't let a bad day carry over to the next one. I did that for my sake but even more for the sake of my students. I can trace that practice back to one day in the beginning of my career when I was, among other things, a remedial reading teacher at Pennfield High School in Battle Creek, Michigan. I swear that what follows actually happened. I've changed the names, but not to protect the innocent. I just honestly can't remember any of them except one, and you might be able to figure out who that was. This is a long story, so you might want to grab something to sip on and make yourself comfortable.

My first year at Pennfield was a real struggle. I had three class preparations, and while *Honors Freshman English* gave me a chance to teach writing and discussion, the reading classes quite often bordered on unbearable. I eventually developed a decent routine for *Speed Reading*, and some of my kids in time increased their rate and comprehension. I experimented with activity rotations, and by the end of the year, I felt at least semi-competent at my instruction. That never was the case for my other class, *Remedial Reading*, which was full of special needs students before the advent of special education. I worked with kids with poor literacy skills and in some cases, even poorer attitudes. To my relief, I had but one section of the course. Two would have killed me.

I quickly learned that our school's student body was infected with more than a few sassy vocal mannerisms, and it wasn't long before I grew weary of hearing the kids' overuse of those expressions. One of them was "Sorry about _____." I am guessing that started with someone making a sarcastic comment about a classmate along the lines of, "Sorry about Jesse getting his head beat last night." That eventually morphed into all sorts of mutations. "Sorry about your face," or "Sorry about your breath." Another slang term used to exhaustion was *bogue*. In my four years at Pennfield, I never quite figured out the origin of the term. I thought it might have something to with *bogus* or *Bogart*, but no one seemed to know or really care. It meant something along the lines of "nasty" or "horrible." Kids used it as the supreme insult. Homework was bogue. One's parents could be particularly bogue. In at least one instance, I was informed that I was bogue.

It was one of those class periods where I was doing everything I could to hold onto my sanity. I had long before given up on maintaining order. No matter what methods I tried to get my students to read quietly for at least two minutes, I failed. Some whispered, some just talked as loudly as they wanted. The class was making no attempt at following my directions, and I finally reached my limit.

"That's it!" I shouted. Standing up from behind my desk, I took a ruler and smashed it so hard on my lectern that I broke the stick in half. That effectively silenced the room, and while I could have probably quietly reminded the class that it was time to read silently, my temper's control valve was perilously spinning open, and I had no desire to arrest it. At that point in my career, I had not learned how to achieve an advantage and leave it at that. Once I got rolling, I let all of the steam out, violently at times. To my student's misfortune, this was one of those occasions.

"I am sick to death of all the talking!" My voice was growing louder with each word, and I could feel a vein throbbing in my forehead. I'm sure my face was red, and I could feel my body trembling.

My outburst was a first for that class. I had tried to discipline them for weeks, but I had done so in relatively peaceful terms. Oh, I had threatened kids, and I had even raised my voice, but that day crossed a whole new threshold. My students looked stricken at first, but they quickly adopted the downcast demeanor of a chastened group. All they could do was sit and take it, but I wasn't done giving it to them. Not even close to being done.

"If you think I'm going to keep coming in here every day and put up with your immature attitudes, you are CRAZY! I have been way too nice to you guys, and that's going to stop right now! Do you hear what I'm saying?"

Now I was being a bully. Of course, they could hear me. I was baiting them, and I knew I was baiting them, but I really didn't want to stop.

"You are going to sit here for the rest of the period, and you're not going to say one word. You don't want to read? Fine! Close your books and sit. Not one word!"

For one last effect, I reached across my desk and slung three books to the tile floor. They skidded toward the door, but not one of my students looked up to see where they wound up. I was close to hyperventilation now, and I hoped that the Spanish teacher next door couldn't hear my diatribe. As long as her class wasn't disturbed, I wouldn't feel too bad. At the moment, however, I was just praying that none of my kids made a peep until the bell rang.

Much to my relief, no one did. The class ended, and all twenty-two students filed out the door without glancing my way. The only saving grace about the whole incident was its timing. It was the last class of the day, and so no other students would be coming through the door any time soon. That was the nature of my practice that year. None of my kids seemed to have any reason to seek after-school help from me, and on this afternoon, that was good for all of us.

I was miserable at home that night. What sort of teacher goes off on fourteen and fifteen-year-olds like that? What had happened to my easy-going demeanor? My sense of humor? As we ate dinner, I told Teresa about the incident, and she bit her lip to stifle a smile.

"It's not funny," I said.

"I didn't say it was," she replied, but now the smile escaped. "I'm sorry," she said, covering her mouth.

"So, what would you have done?" I said.

"I don't know that I would have done anything different. Well, I probably wouldn't have broken my ruler, but I've yelled at my kids, too."

"Then why are you laughing at me?"

"I'm not laughing at you, dear." She laughed. "I'm sorry."

"Yeah, I can see that."

She got up from her chair and put her arms around me. I sat frozen.

"It's what I've been telling you," she said, still hugging me. "You were too easy on those kids for too long. I get upset, too, but I never let things build up so much that I can't handle it."

I leaned my head against hers. Damn it, she was right, but there wasn't anything I could do with that seventh period group that would rewind us to the beginning of the year so I could be firm with them. Somehow, though, I had to fix the mess.

As I washed the dishes, alone in my head, I resolved to atone the next day for my lack of control. I would go back to that class with positive energy. I would be upbeat and funny and patient. I wouldn't even mention the afternoon's fiasco.

Though I rarely dressed formally for school, the next day, I wore a tie, a pink one at that. I wanted to feel powerful. I was anxious the whole day waiting for the last period to arrive, and when it did, I was ready. My kids straggled in, none of them making eye contact with me as they entered. I smiled at them and welcomed each into the room as they came through the door.

The bell rang, and I sprang into action. "Hey everybody," I said with enthusiasm. "Ready to do some reading?"

"Why do you care?" mumbled a voice from the rear. I looked back and saw Kyle Brunson, lower lip extended in about as pouty a position as I thought possible. Kyle had yet to warm to me, and even as I tried to put a good face on a bad situation, he wasn't about to let me do that.

"I care a lot, Kyle," I said, and the boy smirked. This was going to be a little tougher to pull off than I had thought.

"No, you don't," he said. "You were bogue yesterday."

There it was. God. Not bogue. Call me anything but that. I started to apologize for my behavior, but I remembered that I had promised myself to move forward. I also remembered my sense of humor. I looked at Kirk with a confused expression.

"Yesterday?" I said. "I wasn't here, yesterday."

The boy looked up at me. "What do you mean?" Several kids echoed his question. I had expected them to laugh, and then we'd go on with class, but I suddenly sensed an opportunity.

"I mean, I wasn't here yesterday. I had a doctor's appointment."

I had cast my line into the water hoping for a nibble, but I was about to get a good tug.

"Get out of here," said Randy. "You were, too, here. What, do you think we're stupid or something?"

"Of course, not," I said. "I just wasn't here." If anyone had called my bluff at that point, I would have confessed, but every one of my students looked at me with that look of doubt that only teenagers can show.

"OK," said Kyle. "If you weren't here, who was? Huh?"

Ah. I had been called out. That's when inspiration hit. I feigned disgust.

"Oh, my God," I said, putting my hand to my mouth. "Oh, my God, don't tell me she did that. Oh, no, no, no." I looked wild-eyed at my kids, shaking my head as if in shock.

"Who?" Cecilia said.

"Mrs. Haverford," I replied, invoking the name of our school secretary, the one who scheduled substitute teachers.

"She didn't call my brother. There's no way. I've told her over and over and over to never call my brother to sub for me. My *twin* brother." I looked around the room as if to be reassured, but the kids looked totally baffled. I couldn't say that I was the best actor in the world, but I could definitely say that my kids weren't the brightest in the school. That was an academic fact. They were starting to buy into my story, and I was starting to have some fun with that class for the first time in months.

"Oh, man, I am so sorry, you all. That wasn't right. My brother is nothing like me. I mean, I'm pretty nice to you guys most of the time, right?"

"You weren't nice yesterday," said Kyle.

"That's just what I've been trying to tell you, Kyle. *I wasn't here yesterday.*"

The boy gave me a close look, squinting and frowning. "But he looked just like you," he said.

Randy turned around in his seat to yell at Kyle. "He said he's his twin, you idiot!"

"Shut up!" Kyle shouted.

I raised my hands. "Easy, easy," I said. "Relax."

I paced back and forth between my desk and the first row. "My brother is the biggest jerk in the world." Kids nodded. "I bet he yelled at you."

"Yeah!"

"Did he turn red?"

"Yeah!"

"He always does that when he's mad. Such a jerk. He didn't break anything, did he?"

"He broke your ruler!" shouted Randy.

"What?" I went to my desk and opened the middle drawer. "Where's my ruler?" I asked.

"He broke it!" said a number of kids.

"Great," I said. "You know, one time he was mad at my mom, and he threw one of her flower vases against the wall. Then he tried to blame it on me."

"That's bogue," said Kyle, warming to the occasion.

"The boguest," I said. This was fun. My kids were totally with me now, they were on my side against an evil twin who had usurped my authority. Destroyed my property. The next step was crucial. Did I fess up, have a laugh, and go on? Maybe, but what if my kids got mad at me for lying to them? I was sure that they would eventually figure out the truth, but in the meantime, I had to find a way to transit from my story to the work for the day.

"Man, I am so sorry," I said again. "I know you all can be a little noisy sometimes, and I know sometimes you don't feel like working, but I would never treat you like my brother did yesterday. You know that, right?"

My kids nodded.

"OK, I'll talk to Mrs. Haverford, and I'll tell her that under absolutely no circumstances is she to ever call my brother to sub for me again." More nods and a few smiles. "But I'm going to warn you, sometimes she has no choice, and she just might call him."

"Tell her she can't do that!" said Riccardo.

"Oh, I will, I will. But just in case she does, you guys have to be super cool when my brother is here, OK?"

"Sure," they said.

"How will we know it's your brother?" Kyle asked. Hmmm. Good question. I had to come up with an answer to it and quickly. I looked down, hoping to find one, when inspiration struck for a second time.

I looked up. "There's only one way," I said solemnly. I pointed to my shoes.

"See these?" The kids nodded. "They're brown. That's the only color I ever wear. And the only color my brother ever wears is black. That's the only way you can tell us apart."

I held up my right foot, brown for all to see.

"Wow," said Cecelia. "Thanks."

"You're welcome," I said. "I'm just sorry you all had to go through that. You don't deserve to be treated that way."

"No problem," Tim said. "We know you're cool, Mr. Stem."

The rest of the period was a dream. The kids opened their books and read quietly until the bell rang. Even Kyle. I read at my desk, looking up from time to time to catch a student's eye, smile, and wink. It was a beautiful twenty-five minutes.

At the bell, my class rose to leave, each one thanking me for being their teacher, for being so nice to them. Kyle still looked me over one more time before he left. I nodded at him as he went out the door.

What color shoes did I wear the next day? Why, black, of course. I stayed out in the hall until the bell rang, and I slammed the door as I came in.

"All right, get in your seats and don't say a word till the bell rings," I growled. My students' eyes grew wide. "I said, sit down!"

Randy leaned over his desk, looked at my shoes, and turned to face his classmates. "Shut up, you guys," he said in a stage whisper. "It's his brother!"

I thought I was going to die. I waited for a few seconds, but I couldn't keep the smile off my face. Cecelia was the first to catch on. She gave me a look that said, "I saw what you just did," and Tim followed by pointing at me. "Good one, Mr. Stem," he said. The truth began to filter through the room, at least the idea that I had played a good joke on them by wearing my brother's shoes.

"Wait a minute," Randy said. "Do you really have a brother?"

"Of course, he does," John said. "That's why it's so funny."

"No," said Randy. "I don't even think you have a twin. You just made that all up."

I raised my eyebrows and dropped my jaw. "Are you calling me a liar?"

"Yeah," he said laughing.

82

"That's the sort of thing my brother would do," I said with a smile.

"You don't have a brother!" Cecelia said, shaking her head.

"Why, Cecelia, I am hurt," I said, winking at her.

"Whatever, Mr. Stemle." She looked around the room at her classmates. "There's no brother!"

The kids looked back at me. I held my hands out in front of me. "All I can do is tell you the truth," I said. The kids looked at each other and back at me. I grinned. "In the meantime, you all ready to read?"

For the remainder of the year, we had a good time with the twin story. If the class got a little antsy or hard for me to manage, I would just mention my brother and things quickly settled down. Sometimes the kids themselves would invoke the threat. "Shut up, man. He might bring his brother in if you guys don't stop screwing around." It was fun, and by the end of our time together, nearly everyone had finally caught onto the joke. All but one, that is.

As we were wrapping things up the last week of school, I asked the kids what they had learned about reading. I asked them what they would remember from being in our class. They shared a number of good ideas and agreed that they had come a long way in their abilities.

Then Kyle raised his hand. "The best part of this class was that your brother never came back."

"There is no brother!" most of the class seemed to shout together.

"He said there was," Kyle said, looking a bit more confused than usual.

"He was joking!" said Randy. "God, Kyle."

"Shut up, Randy. You're so bogue."

My days of yelling at classes are long in the past. In fact, in my final year, one of my students asked if I had ever raised my voice in the classroom. When I assured that I had, many times, and even more as a coach, she and her classmates seemed incredulous. My emotional maturation may have spared them and a lot of other students a good tongue-lashing over the years, but then again, they also missed a lot of the creativity that I employed in my early days to cope with my frustrations. I believe they were happy to keep the familiar version of Mr. Stemle. I certainly was.

I don't care how laid back or chill you are, you are going to have days in your classroom when your emotions are going to come to a boil. You might even have a situation like I had with that seventh period class when you feel out of control and say things that you instantly regret. What's important to remember when that happens is that kids are remarkably resilient. They might be hurt or embarrassed by your blowup, but they will also forgive you pretty quickly if you treat them with good humor soon after. That timing is the key, however. Kids won't hold a grudge if you make amends the next day, but if you hold onto your anger, if you wait for your class to change in order for you to treat them nicely, then you just might find yourself in for a long emotional siege. After all, you are going to be the adult in the room. It will be up to you to make the first move toward reconciliation. If that hurts your pride a bit, I'm sorry. If you cling to the belief that your demonstration was justified and demand that your students show you that they're sorry, then you might get that apology, but you'll also lose a bit of trust in the bargain. However you choose to deal with the aftermath of a bad day with your kids, remember that you're the one who has to make the first move. Your class will appreciate the gesture, and you'll buy a little bit of good will that you can spend later on in the year.

What Steinbeck Said: Post #21
Wednesday, October 26, 2016
Here Today

I am at my desk today, preparing for a curriculum committee meeting next
week. The classroom is empty because my students are off visiting college
campuses with the rest of the class of 2017, and I find myself deeply
immersed in a research study about elementary reading programs when a
familiar voice calls my name.

I look to the door to see a girl smiling and heading to a desk near the
window. A now successful woman as she appeared in my Green River classroom
some thirty years ago. Before I can comprehend this situation, another of my

former students greets me.

"Hey, Mr. Stemle," she says. "How's it going today?" She waves at the first girl and sits across the way.

"I'm fine, I guess." I have a dawning sense that a Bradbury story is coming to life before my eyes. Two of my favorite students, miles from their original schools and decades removed from their participation in my class.

"What are you all doing here?"

The girls look at each other and giggle. "We're here to discuss Chapter Five," the first student says.

"Chapter Five?"

"Yes, Mr. Stemle," says the second, her palms upraised. "You know, Great Expectations?"

In walk three adolescent boys, chatting easily and nodding my way as they find their places in the circle. They were not contemporaries many years ago, but they seem like the best of friends as they lean back in their desks. Within two minutes, the circle is filled, and by the time the bell rings to start class, there are as many as fifteen more students sitting on the floor within the circle. They are my kids from classes gone by. Navajo Community College in Arizona. Pennfield High School in Michigan. A junior high, a middle school, and a high school in Green River. Even some bright faces from the past few years in Evanston, another Wyoming town that became our home.

I accept the fact that I have somehow fallen asleep at my desk—curriculum study can do that to a body—and I embrace the fantasy with a hopeful heart.

"So," I say, shaking my head as I look at my room bursting with alumni. "Chapter Five?"

The class period is a blur. I sit silent while my kids question and answer each other, while they compete to see who can find the most incredible interpretations. It is a teacher's dream come true, and I am sure that's exactly what it is. A dream.

The bell sounds, and I hug each of my guests on their way out, thanking them all for a most extraordinary experience. They all look at me with puzzled expressions as if the day has been just like any other in Room 218.

"See you tomorrow," the first girl calls as she passes through the door.

I return to my desk, sure that I am about to awaken, when more visitors arrive. Four girls shining with excitement, followed by Ellen and Paul. Wait—those are my children, there. They're teaching in their own classrooms in Utah right at this moment, but no, here they are chatting with two kids they have never met, let alone heard me mention.

"Did you bring the cymbals?" a girl asks.

"I'm sorry," I say. "Symbols?"

"For Cool Hand Luke. *We have to have the cymbals today."*

Oh my God. Standing at the back of the room while my class watches Paul Newman's classic, clashing cymbals right over kids' heads when a visual symbol appears on the screen. One of my favorite teacher moves ever. I get to relive that today?

Each class period brings even more memories somehow transported to the present. We read Romeo *and* Juliet *aloud with smiles and discuss "Flowers for Algernon" through tears. We break down Langston Hughes' "Dream Deferred," comparing it to our own aspirations. We feel of the courtroom scenes in* To Kill a Mockingbird *and* Inherit the Wind. *We laugh, and we act as if all of this is not only possible but already real.*

The last bell comes at 3:10. By 3:15, I am out of hugs, alone again in my classroom. A dream? Not really. A figment of my imagination? I know it seems that way. It's not. The veil has merely lifted for a day. Truth is, all of you are with me every day, even after all of those years. Though many of you have grown and married and have raised your own children, your love and your support have carried me every step of my career. Everything that I do to help and inspire today's students comes from sharing the wonder of learning with you. Thank you, dearest friends. Can't wait to feel your presence when my kids come back on Friday!

I used to believe in coincidence. I'd be thinking of a friend to whom I had not spoken in years, and within a day or so, who do you suppose would give me a call? I'd suddenly remember a scene from movie I had seen long before, and which film do you think I came across while surfing my television that evening? Happenstance, right? I changed my mind about all that on February 27, 2003, the day my younger brother Drew died.

Many years before that fateful date, as we listened to the second movement of Beethoven's Seventh Symphony, Teresa turned to me and said, "This is so beautiful. Promise me that you'll play it at my funeral." "Only if you play it at my funeral first," I replied. Our children know of this arrangement, and someday, hopefully in the very distant future, we hope that loved ones who attend our services will be as moved by the music as we are each time we hear it.

I learned of my brother's passing when I came home from school and found a message from our mother on our answering machine. After calling her back and talking with her briefly, I got back in my car to pick up Ellen from middle school. My mind was filled with questions, my heart with numbing sadness. I turned the ignition, listened to the engine as it engaged and then to the radio as it played Beethoven's Seventh, second movement.

At that moment, alone in my car, still parked in our driveway, I felt an incredible sense of peace. There was no doubt that this was a message from Drew, and when I mentioned it to Teresa that evening, she told me much the same. From that day on, I have given much less credence to coincidence. I'm sure it happens from time, but I am also certain that there are forces at work in my life that lie beyond my consciousness. Reality must be more than what I perceive through my five senses, and while I am by no means psychic, I do believe that we are all somehow bound together by thoughts, by feelings, by some kind of energy beyond our perception.

While the reverie that I described in the previous post was at first nothing more than my fancy left to roam a bit on a day when there wasn't much to write about, the more I thought about it, the more I believed that my students have stayed with me. I invoked their memories whenever I read one of their comments on my blog, but it went further than that. I have a feeling that every time I read aloud the final pages of *Of Mice and Men*, my students from classes past somehow felt, if only for an instant, the pangs of sorrow they experienced in the circle with me. Every time my classes read in unison the opening of paragraph from *A Tale of Two Cities*, they were joined in a silent chorus by hundreds of others students. I'm not sure I conjured any spirits when I taught non-restrictive clauses, but I suppose there is only so much psychic energy to go around.

Whether you believe that such connections and occurrences are mere coincidence or, like me, you have a sense that there is something going on at different levels of our awareness, remember that what will happen between you and your students will most certainly have an impact on their lives. It may be in the form of memories that remind them of the power of emotion, or it may be something subliminal that affects them without them realizing it, but the vibrations created in your classroom will go on forever. That may be a burden if those vibes are negative, a blessing if they're loving. Surely it's the latter that keeps us in touch over the years. Facebook brought me back into conscious contact with folks who graced my classroom in the eighties and nineties, and it was fun to watch their comments pop up under my posts. But as that entry suggests, it all goes beyond that. On a day when no corporal students filled the seats in our circle, the spirits of countless others did. Thus, a veil was indeed lifted, a boundary crossed, and there will be no going back until the strains of a certain symphony are softly played.

Germinating

Watered and warmed by our first two months together, feeling more anchored as they came to know each other and me as fellow learners, my senior seeds began to sprout. I, the stem, extended roots to draw upon my knowledge and experience to nourish each student as an individual and each group as a class. At the same time, I began to rise in my responsibility to lead them to the light. As they felt more and more comfortable with our environment, they were more willing to try things, emboldened to take academic chances. They were developing leaves that soaked up the sunlight of new ideas, and as they welcomed those opportunities, the process of educational photosynthesis kicked in. Their growth was now happening at a faster rate because they were discovering energy in their exploration of concepts, and they were also becoming stronger in their ability to take on challenges. They were enjoying the sunshine, and while they were about to encounter harsher conditions, the rains and winds that come with mounting expectations on assignments, it was becoming clear to us all that this was a vital and exciting time to be in our class.

Eric Stemle

*T*here's a small rectangular sign at the top of the outside of our classroom door that reads "Now Playing." Below it we have a movie poster so that anyone passing by can see what book we're currently studying. As my students arrived on Friday, they saw that The Old Man and the Sea had been replaced with a collage featuring Armand Assante in his role as Odysseus. The poster wasn't the only thing changing in the room yesterday.

"Patience is power," began our opening quote. "With time and patience, the mulberry leaf becomes silk." I choose our quotes to focus on what the day will entail, and I wanted to start by honoring my kids' efforts. This was a day when we were handing in our second essays, trading Hemingway's novel for Homer's epic. Looming next class period is the initiation of another paper, and in less than three weeks, we'll be discussing the poem. It's a time of transition.

"Today, we move from a brief story of personal transcendence to a long tale that transcends western literature," I told my students while I held up the book. I looked around the circle, knowing that they were tired, having just come through a fall season of extracurricular activities while maintaining an increasing number of responsibilities in our class. I knew that the last thing they wanted to hear was that we have more reading ahead, more writing to do. Still, as we began our guided reading of The Odyssey, my kids were right there with me. As I looked into their eyes, I saw something that every teacher loves: trust. Though they have only known me for nine weeks, they know that I have their best interests at heart. I will push them, but if I have one hand on their backs, I will have the other around their shoulders. That's why I showed them all sorts of love as they handed me their essays and shook my hand. That's why last night as I put purple on papers, I celebrated them for their progress and encouraged them going forward.

Silk is in our future!

P atience and trust go together, don't they? It's easier for me to wait for something if I trust that the outcome I want will eventually come about. I can be patient awaiting an online order to be delivered, even as I wish it would get to me faster. I can bide my time till dinner is served, even if I'm hungry. On the other hand, waiting for the rain to stop so I can play golf does at times strain my patience, even if the radar map suggests it will just be another hour or so. What enables me to be patient in some circumstances and not in others? My experience with certain companies tells me that they will deliver when they promise, and Teresa is remarkably prompt with meals. Unless she tells me otherwise, I can expect to sit with her at the table at 6:00 each evening. If only the weather forecasters could guarantee results as well.

Trust is not really a matter of faith. Sure, if we have faith in something, we count on it, but what creates trust is more about consistency than our simple belief in it. Barnes and Noble's books arrive when they're due on a regular basis. If they didn't, then I wouldn't trust their estimates. Our dinner is served at the same time each night, and I plan my time around that consistency. It's easy for me to be patient if I know I can depend on others to do what they almost always do.

Your students will yearn to trust you as their teacher. They will want to feel secure in knowing not only that you will act in their best interests, but that you will also provide them with an environment that they can rely on. To that end, I made sure that our classroom was a haven of consistency. I began each period exactly the same way, and I established a few routines that my kids could anticipate for the outset of each period. For instance, in the last few years of my career, we had a poster on the inside of our door that read, *Omnis, partis, referent.* That's a phrase I borrowed from director David Simon, who continually reminded his actors and crew on *The Wire* that "all the pieces matter." Our daily routines started with the bell ringing and me walking into the classroom from my post in the hallway between classes. My students already seated, I turned off the overhead light, a signal for us all to chant the Latin phrase. When we finished, I flipped the switch again to in a sense suggest that we were going to be enlightened from that point on.

No matter how I was feeling physically or emotionally on a given day, I always entered the room with a smile and a cheerful greeting. My kids needed that opening as a reassurance that no matter how things were going for them, they could count on Mr. Stemle to be upbeat. Not that it was a chore for me to say hello in a happy way, for even if I was feeling a little overwhelmed by things, I was always glad to see my students, to have yet another eighty-five minutes to spend learning with them. Still, there were days when I may have done a little acting in those first moments of class. I doubt that my kids noticed—all that mattered to them was that their class was starting the way it always did.

From there, we would examine our quote for the day, learn our *Word of the Day*, and spend fifteen minutes in silent reading of books of our choice. Every day. Did kids ever find such a routine a drag? I'm sure that some did, but I did my best to add humor and enthusiasm to even the most mundane of tasks. For example, I could have presented a new vocabulary word each period by projecting its definition on the board and asking my students to add that information to their notebooks along with a sentence that used the word in a meaningful context. That is in essence what I did each time, but deep down I knew that just doing those steps in a perfunctory manner would soon become drudgery. Instead, I began that activity each day by using my best television announcer's voice to intone, "It's time to play. . ." That was the cue for my kids to respond with gusto, *"Word of the Day!"* If for some reason their response was less than exuberant, I would start over. We had to do it right, right? Even on our sleepy or grumpy days, we could always wake up the classrooms on either side of us with a loud announcement that vocabulary was about to be explored. As I said before, corny? Absolutely. Fake it till you make it? Yep. You know what? It worked.

Students can put up with a lot of stuff if they trust their teachers. As long as they know that someone has their backs, then they are willing to push through frustration and weariness. That's why I worked hard to create a stable environment for my kids. It's why I did everything I could to encourage them, to inspire them. As you work hard to build trust with your students, and you will have to work hard for it, remember the importance of time and patience in creating anything worth having.

What Steinbeck Said: Post #23
Tuesday, November 1, 2016
Bit of a Giggle

O *f all the mnemonic devices I have used (test me to see if I can name the Great Lakes, homes), it seems that nothing better cements learning than laughter. I'm not sure of the neurological connection between a chuckle and long term memory, but I sense that it does help my students retain information. Tuesday, I used humor twice in delivering material to my classes. The first came during my first class of the day as my kids were practicing the punctuation of compound sentences. Now, you wouldn't think that I would have to insert some comic relief into that activity, right? I mean, where I come from, comma placement is a guaranteed guffaw, but as I watched partners giving each other independent clauses and putting them together into complete thoughts, I decided we needed to lighten the mood.*

"Hang on a second," I said, interrupting the conversations. "Let's make this a little more memorable." I changed my instructions so that Partner A would announce an independent clause (e.g., "The dog is barking"). Then, in unison, the pair would say "Comma!" and then Partner B would vigorously nod her or his head and say "and" and follow it with another independent clause (e.g., "it's too cold to open the back door").

More energy. Kids were now smiling, especially when they said "comma" together. When they finished that practice, I asked them to change and to but.

"This time, when you say but, I want you to stick out your conjunction." I saw quite a few puzzled expressions, but then a couple of kids demonstrated by extending their derrières, and we were off. Much more energy. Laughter. Compound sentences flying everywhere!

We finished our exercise by pantomiming the rowing of a boat when we said or as our connection between clauses. Now refreshed, my kids returned to their seats.

"*I can see you now,*" *I said.* "*You'll be writing your essay next week doing this,*" *and I went through each conjunctive action. Great laughter. You know what? When they do sit down to write, they will hear the word comma loud and clear in their minds, and they'll feel each* and, but, *and* or.

Next came my introduction of our next assignment, an argument paper. I prefaced it with an iconic sketch from Monty Python. The kids loved it, and again, they laughed, even when Michael Palin rapidly explained to John Cleese that an argument is not a series of contradictions but rather "a collective series of statements to establish a definite proposition." If I had said that to them, if I had written it on the board, they may have remembered it for tomorrow. If I ask them on Thursday what the guy from Python said, they will more likely have a good idea. We might not laugh our conjunctions off, but we'll smile and get on with more learning.

I s there any better sound in a classroom than laughter? Not the derisive kind where kids are celebrating the misfortune of others, but that genuine outpouring that brings everyone together for a moment or two of shared emotion. As you walk down the hall of your school, listen for the peals of laughter coming from various rooms, and you can instantly tell if it's joyful or insulting. Maybe it's the spontaneity or the explosiveness. It could be that ripple effect of individuals finding out just exactly what is funny to everybody else. In any case, more than the best medicine, laughter is a bonding agent for a class.

When I first started teaching, I used my sense of humor much in the way I did at the dinner table with my family or at a party with good friends. I had a deadpan delivery that involved puns and references that could be a tad obscure. The payoff was delightful for those who caught my drift, but a lot of times, I'd nod at one or two students who got the joke and then move on, not wanting to play the game of, "That's a joke. Get it?" After a while, my kids came around to my style and started listening for wit, but even then, there still seemed to be a divide in the class between those who understood an allusion and those who didn't.

Years later, I made peace with the fact that my students didn't necessarily have to comprehend my sense of humor at its most arcane. I began tailoring my comments so that most if not all of my kids would catch what I was saying. The result was a closer-knit class where pretty much everyone was in on the joke. That didn't necessarily mean that I had to dumb down my humor for the sake of unity, though. I just learned to aim a little over their heads, and I tried not to pause as a cue that they were supposed to figure something out. Instead, I would make a comment in response to something someone said in discussion and then move on. If no one laughed, then I knew that I had gone too high. It wasn't their fault, and I wasn't about to show any disappointment in the situation. If that happened a few times in succession, I usually quit going for a laugh for a while, leaving that to others in the circle.

I once had a colleague who asked me whether I could tutor him on being funny. He said he admired my sense of humor, and he thought that if he could somehow develop a more comedic approach with his classes, he would connect better with his students. Think of the money I could have made were it actually possible to teach someone how to be amusing. I might have just as easily taught my friend how to fly or read other people's minds.

On the other hand, I do believe that it's possible to learn occasion and timing. I often used humor when chairing a committee or sitting in a staff meeting, and the key always seemed to be knowing when a little levity would help to wake people up or relieve tension. I once delivered a committee report to my building faculty who were none too pleased with our lack of progress. As I stared out at faces that looked either bored or unhappy, I felt the moment slipping away from my grasp. Then one of my colleagues grumbled quite loudly, "That's the problem with this district. Nobody wants to make a decision." My friend glared at me when he finished, and I knew that what happened next would largely determine whether our committee's work would ever be respected by that group.

"I think I know what you mean," I said to my accuser in as earnest a tone as I could muster. Then I paused. "But I'm not sure." The laughter that followed, including his, was most certainly one of bonding. I went on to assure folks that I shared their concerns, that I was just as frustrated by the glacial pace of our committee's work as the rest of them were. I could have said the same words without the joke, but I'm not sure that they would have found as many open ears.

The key to humor in your classroom will lie in its intention. If you deliver it in order to make yourself look good, then it will have limited value to the learning environment. If you use your wit in order to bring everyone together for a moment of mirth, then all sorts of learning can ensue because of the power of that shared emotion. Funny how that works.

What Steinbeck Said: Post #24
Thursday, November 3, 2016
Buoyed

F or the past few days, I have found myself drifting farther and farther out to sea. Normally a good swimmer who stays at least in sight of the shore, I have been carried out beyond my depth, and I've felt myself fatigued as I've struggled against the tide. For years I have been comfortable in this water. I know the currents, I anticipate the breaking of the waves. The swimming has always been vigorous, but I have been sure to float on my back from time to time or alternate my strokes in order to conserve my energy for the next rise coming.

This fall has seen a sea change. By coincidence, I've taken on a number of unexpected responsibilities, from facilitating a curriculum committee to participating in two book studies. Any one of those activities adds a commitment beyond my customary preparation for my teaching and my grading of essays. Together with an unusual number of evenings away from home in the past week, those new duties combined to form a perfect storm, and I gradually came to realize that the swells that storm was creating were taking me far away from my routine. As I awoke this morning, I felt the ominous tug of the undertow. How was I going to make it through the day?

Thank God a life preserver showed up. During my first period planning time, I graded two essays, and while I gave each the care that I extend to all papers, I felt my strength ebbing. I was exhausted. Then my second period students began coming into the room, happy and ready to learn as always. With no idea that I was struggling to keep my head above water, they quickly hoisted me up atop the surface. I was suddenly focused not on what lay ahead but rather on the beauty of the moment. After all, isn't this why I teach? Isn't all that I do outside of class time done merely in service of these few minutes I share with my young ones every other day? Refreshed, I taught with fervor, engaged my kids with banter and affection. I felt renewed, but still I wondered whether I could somehow ride that wave to shore. Was it a temporary boost, or had I caught my second wind?

There is a certain synergy within a great classroom. On any given day, some of us are on a high, and others are feeling a bit low. Still, a community that is dedicated to learning can be remarkably buoyant. Today, I not only swam with my students, but I splashed and kicked and reveled with them in the water. I also kept an eye out for those who may have entered the day much as I had, looking to see who was hesitant to get into the water and who might be there but flailing. I did what I could to keep them from sinking, to lift them as that first class had lifted me. By the time the bell sounded to end each period, everyone seemed at least at ease with the sea's conditions, and I felt a sense of gratitude to my students for their willingness to dive back in from day to day to day. In the meantime, I have many more papers to mark and many more chapters to read. I'm sure that I'll go to bed tired tonight, and I know that my weekend will be busy, but come next Tuesday, I'll be ready to swim, again.

Anybody say, "Surf's up"?

A s you age as a teacher, you will be caught in a Catch-22 when it comes to stamina. Near the end of your career, as your reservoir of energy naturally dwindles, you will tend to have more and more responsibilities. As a young teacher, when you have all sorts of bounce and vigor, when you are ready to try new things, you will be free to solve the mysteries of the classroom without being called to do much outside of it. My early principals took care of me by letting me focus on learning the ins and outs of the profession without asking me to do too much else. Oh, I was busy enough, with papers to grade and sports to coach, but because I was a novice, my administrators did not expect me to contribute much to the direction of the school. I'd like to think that my absence on committees was more of a consideration of my need to find my way in the classroom than it was a dismissal of my youthful naiveté, but my experience was fairly typical in the profession. To this day, it is usually the more veteran teachers who are asked to serve in leadership positions on their faculties, to serve on district and state committees and commissions.

That dynamic might wear you down years and years from now as you enter the December of your career. Talk to teachers who have recently retired, and they will tell you that the primary factor in their decision to stop teaching was not that they had tired of working with young people, but, rather, they had become exhausted by all of the bureaucratic demands on their time and especially on their energy. My case was complicated by the fact that until the very end, I was excited by trying new approaches, by finding even better ways to inspire my students. I was not so much a cyclist coasting to the bottom of the hill as I was a distance runner sprinting slightly uphill to the finish line. Now imagine me carrying a backpack with someone running beside me, adding more and more weight to its pockets. That's the feeling I had on that early November morning in my final year. I was running as hard as ever, but my legs were growing wearier.

As always, it was my students who picked me up, even though they had no idea that I needed their help. As I reflected, I thought back to a junior high basketball practice some forty years before. I ended that practice by asking (well, sort of) my players to run a series of sprints, among them a set that called for them to run to the other end of the floor and back thirteen times in three minutes. It was in part a conditioning task, but even more importantly, it was designed to make my team tougher mentally and emotionally. Two of my kids finished ahead of the rest of the team, and as they stood catching their breath, they noticed that one of their teammates was laboring. There was no way that he was going to beat the time limit, but it meant a lot to all of us that everyone at least finished the thirteen up and backs. Tired as they must have been, my early finishers returned to the floor to run beside their teammate, and as they did, they talked to him, encouraged him. The trio reached the end of their run quite a bit over the three-minute limit, but they did so to the cheers of their teammates and their coaches.

Sometimes I was the coach with the whistle. Other times, I was the kid in the middle, trying to catch my breath as I put one foot in front of the other. As the latter, I was fortunate to have students and colleagues who carried me through the tired times. Even as a young member of a faculty, you might have to run beside your fellow teachers if your school is going to work effectively. In the long run, helping your fellow teachers can only make the culture healthier for everyone.

What Steinbeck Said: Post #25
Tuesday, November 8, 2016
Three Options

*W*ith my students working on their first drafts of an argument paper due on Thursday, I took two opportunities to today to help them better understand the task. First, I invited them once more to join me in the Flatland as we call the area inside our circle of desks.

"You have been writing essays for years," I told them as we gathered round the cardboard ring that we had used to preview the year from a multidimensional perspective in August. "I'm guessing that as you work through a paper, you are focused on moving from point to point, but today I want to show you how things look from above."

With the help of color coding, I showed them how topic sentences relate to the main idea of the thesis, how paragraph clinchers tie back to the impact of that main idea. I talked about how the final sentence of the essay can hearken back to the title to bring the piece full circle. I shared those factors so that my kids can have more control over decisions regarding the organization of their writing. We'll see if it makes a difference in a couple of weeks when they submit their essays.

After our discussion of structure, we turned to style by examining the art of argument. Today's concentration was on decisions we can make when faced with a strong point from our opponent. In that case, we basically have three options. We can ignore the point, we can attack the point, or we can use humor to deflect or change the mood. I showed them a three-minute clip from Inherit the Wind *where Spencer Tracy has two opportunities to exercise those options in his cross examination of Frederick March. I paused the clip just before Tracy's moves to give my kids a chance to predict, and some were spot on both times. It was fun to hear them chuckle at the histrionics of both attorneys.*

That exercise is particularly helpful in an oral argument, but I challenged my students to think of ways they could use those three approaches in their written arguments as well. Perhaps the best way would be to present an opposing point in the form of accommodation and then move on or refute or make a little joke. I'll encourage them to try all three in their final drafts. In the meantime, if you find the clip, enjoy it!

In *The Wizard of Oz*, L. Frank Baum's travelers are given green-tinted spectacles upon their arrival in the Emerald City. This little detail is, of course, a divergence between the book and the movie, for in the latter, everything is green by nature. In the former, everything appears to be that color when viewed through a different lens, but that raises a question. Do the glasses change the outward appearance of the city, or do they allow wearers to see its true nature?

From time to time, I reminded my students that one of the purposes of our class was to help them develop different perspectives. It didn't matter to me that they tried on green or rose-colored lenses, whether they looked through a microscope or a telescope. As long as they weren't trying to see the world through dark sunglasses, I was all right with their choices. It could be tricky at times when kids or their parents thought that I was asking them to change their values, but that wasn't my intention at all. All I wanted for my students was for them to look around when they found themselves on a learning path, to look at the sky and the trees and the flora, not just the ground before their feet.

That lesson on argument was all about perspective. The first part, where we examined an essay from a point above the Flatland, allowed us to see the structural nature of a paper. It is so easy to find ourselves trapped in a two-dimensional world where we travel from word to word, sentence to sentence, introduction to body to conclusion. In a proverbial sense, we can't see the forest for the trees, and the result is often writing that lacks coherence and flow. We move from trunk to trunk, seeking a way out of our logical proposal, but sometimes we don't quite end up where we said we were going at the beginning. By employing a visual aide in the form of our ring, I handed my kids a new pair of glasses to try on. By inviting them to join me on the carpet, I was giving them a chance to physically move from one circle in order to observe another inside. I'm pretty sure that not all of my students made that connection in those few minutes hovering above the Flatland, but that's why we have a school year and not a school day.

Speaking of time, it is certainly as relative as a visual perspective is. The more experienced we become in an art or a sport or a skill, the more control of the performance we seem to have. Athletes talk about the game slowing down for them as they become more seasoned, musicians don't feel as rushed playing a piece when they become more practiced with it. What happens when time seems to expand? We begin to see things more clearly, more completely. That was a point embedded in our viewing of the clip from *Inherit the Wind*. At that stage in our study of argument, things were going pretty fast for my kids. When I shared the three choices we have when our position is attacked in an argument, I, in essence, made time stop as I paused the video and asked my kids to predict which option Tracy's character would choose. Over the course of the year, my kids were able to slow things down, to look for openings in discussions and in their writing. As for that particular lesson, there were layers to explore. Did any of my students realize that as an experienced lawyer, Tracy's Henry Drummond was experiencing his heated discussion with Matthew Harrison Brady in a slower time? I don't know, and at that point, I guess it wasn't important whether they saw that possibility. What did matter was that they had another pair of glasses in the drawer if they chose to put them on.

As you gain experience as a teacher, you will also become a master of time rather than its servant. Not only will you learn to manage minutes when planning each lesson, but, on occasion, you will also find yourself in a flow while making decisions on the fly. Part of your ability to take things slowly will come as you learn to anticipate the consequences of the choices you make, and you will understand those results better when you experience years of such decision-making. Another part will stem from the confidence you'll develop so that no matter what happens following a move in your teaching, you will be able to adjust, to correct and move forward. That's not something you can necessarily pick up from attending a lecture or reading a text, but it is something that you can look forward to acquiring with practice. All in good time, of course.

What Steinbeck Said: Post #26
Thursday, November 10, 2016
We Walk the Line

T he Art of Argument *continued today. We watched clip from* To Kill a Mockingbird *in which Gregory Peck delivers a speech that surely helped him win an Oscar, his summation to the Tom Robinson trial jury. The film is a masterpiece in many ways, a superb adaptation of Harper Lee's novel by screenwriter Horton Foote, and a tour-de-force performance by a legendary actor. If for no other reason than its singular brilliance, it was worth showing my students.*

Of course, we went beyond that. We watched the seven-minute segment to study Peck's use of gestures and facial expressions. We noted his nodding and his pointing as forms of emphasis, and we marveled at his use of his eyebrows to signal the jury that he has just made a salient point. We listened as well, attending to Peck's rhythms, his dynamics, his deft use of pauses and long silences.

"The challenge is not to see how you'll use those rhetorical devices in speech because you already incorporate them quite well, whether or not you are aware that you do," I told my kids at the end of the video. "Rather, the question is how you will use them in your essays. How will you pause dramatically in your

writing? How will you change the volume? Raise your eyebrows?"

We brainstormed those possibilities, discussing italics and exclamation points and boldface that will change the inflection and the amplification of our words as well as the ellipses, diction and simple sentences that will expand the space of our writing. One student asked if he could uses emojis, and in response, I smiled, winked, and gave him a thumbs up. I cautioned my classes to go lightly with any of those features, but you know what? If they go a little over the top in the next paper, we'll be fine.

Fine.

It's a fine line that I walk with my writers. On one side of that line, our rubric requires them to strive toward mechanical correctness and a coherent structure. It demands that they present textual evidence and interpret it deeply in light of their thesis statements. It holds them to a rigorous collegiate standard of written expression. On the other side of the line lie creativity and inspiration and fun. Especially fun. As I guide my students in developing each essay, I remind myself to keep an eye on that center line and a foot on each side of its path.

On Monday, I will read my students' second drafts of their argument essays. I will revel in their early steps in the process, and as I walk that line, I will carry thoughts of Atticus Finch and his eloquence, of Gregory Peck and his command. I might even raise an eyebrow or two.

I stood a bit hesitantly on the platform, eyes on another that seemed to rest too far away. Stretching between the two was a taut wire, lying deep beneath was a net that didn't look all that sturdy. In each hand I held a ball for a feeling of security and to keep myself steady. I took a deep breath and stepped forward, not at all certain that I could make it all the way across.

Teaching often felt just like that. As a beginner, I knew that balance was going to be essential, I just wasn't very good at achieving it. You may find that your early lessons are indeed a tightrope act as you try to remain aloft, planning in your right hand, spontaneity in your left. At other times it might be discipline in one hand, play in the other. Each time the bell rings, and you climb up to that platform, do your best to keep your composure for the sake of your students. In those early days you might worry that no one will learn a thing if the teacher falls off that wire, but eventually, you'll realize that your kids are the net itself, ready to catch you if you topple.

As for me, by and by I became more certain of my footing and developed a sense of proportion. Like any acrobat, my success relied on not just on balance but on the confidence to take that next step, on the intuition that told me just where to place my foot, how to lean to avoid going too far to one side. I found that I couldn't think my way along the rope. Instead, I had to feel. Eye on the goal, I learned to trust my instincts and put one foot in front of the next, to pause when I felt out of balance and to regain my sense of calm.

In my later years, I learned to truly enjoy that trip from one end of the rope to the other. It was exhilarating to not just walk but to juggle those balls, to stand on one foot, to celebrate the challenge of finding new ways to traverse that wire each day. I also came to realize that I wasn't the only circus performer in the room. Every time my students began an essay, they climbed to their own platform, and as they moved step by step, draft by draft toward the goal, they worked hard to build a solid organization while holding their reader's interest with an engaging style. I followed their progress from below, encouraging them to keep moving, prepared to catch them if they fell. Every presentation found them on the high wire, balancing fear and excitement, the need to inform and the pleasure of entertaining. On those occasions, there was more than me there to cheer them on, to support their efforts, trembling though they may be. We may have been clumsy at first, careless at others, but there were those days that it truly felt that we were the greatest show on earth.

What Steinbeck Said: Post #27
Monday, November 14, 2016
Anybody Feel a Draft?

*W*hen I was a lad, the word draft *meant more about the window I left open overnight than it did about writing. I had no sense of what a first draft was or how it differed from a final one. In my days at Saint Thomas Aquinas Grade School and at East Lansing High, my approach to completing papers was simple and consistent. I would glance at the prompt, devote a little time to think about what to say, or if I was inspired, gather some evidence, and then, the night before it was due, write the essay.*

Once.

Why would I do anything else? I got A's on nearly every piece I wrote, and I was told by every one of my teachers that I was a good writer. Writing was like turning on the faucet and filling a glass of water. How complicated could it be?

Enter my college days. That little word draft *now conjured local pubs downtown, and soon thereafter the specter of Vietnam, but when my first essay for* Freshman English *at Michigan State was returned with a C- scrawled next to my name, I decided that my writing habits had to change. I began to produce several versions of each paper, to prune and nurture my ideas and phrasings. I got to the point where I was writing up to five drafts, though only one was ever required by my professors. They didn't care how I got to the product. That was my business, and it was something that I began to take seriously. It was partly about getting back to that "A" level with my grades, but it was more about wanting to know that I was considered a good writer again.*

Check that. I wanted to know that my teachers thought I was a great *writer.*

Enter my teaching days. In my undergraduate methods classes I was taught ways to instruct my students in the writing process. Prewriting. Drafting. Revising. Editing. Publishing. This was a no-brainer. Having taught myself how to develop a polished paper, I was now a true believer in drafting, yet as I began teaching, I found myself on the other side of the essay. I was the one holding the red pen, and as I read through stacks of papers in those early years of teaching, I

105

discovered an unfortunate truth.

Not everyone in my classroom knew how to turn on a faucet.

After over forty years of teaching writing, I have come to realize just how much work is required of a good writer. Sure, some students are facile with language, some are like that boy back in the sixties who could fashion a good enough essay without too much effort, but for the great majority of my kids, that five-step process is essential to success in writing. It's also critical for those writers who seem to excel with little effort, for I realized a long time ago that in my first few years of teaching, I cheated my good writers by not pushing them to become great, shortchanged my great writers by not challenging them to become outstanding.

Enter tonight. After doing the dinner dishes, I began commenting on my students' second drafts of their argument paper. I wield no pen at this stage in the process, instead typing my comments in little boxes on the right side of their Google documents. It's a remarkable change in the process since I began grading in 1976. Rather than waiting for me to return their drafts on Wednesday with comments scribbled in the margins, some kids are reading my suggestions in real time as I type them. Some will respond to me on the document or e-mail me later on in the evening with a question about my notes.

Unreal.

Here's the deal. While our technology has dramatically changed our communication opportunities, and while I have become much more skilled at guiding my students in their writing, human tendencies remain the same as they were when I was a sixth-grader in Sister Thomasella's language arts class, dashing off an interpretation of Edgar Allen Poe without breaking a sweat. As I settled in tonight to read assignments online, I discovered that exactly half of my kids had submitted any sort of a draft at all. Many of those documents consisted of an introduction and nothing beyond that. A great majority of those submissions were first and not second drafts. It's hard to help someone improve on a piece that really hasn't taken form yet.

On Wednesday, I'll have a short talk with my classes. I'll let them know that I really do relate to their struggles to go beyond a single draft, but I will also help them understand that they can do so much more if they will commit themselves to the writing process. In me, they have a resource I don't recall having as a student all those years ago. Then again, maybe I was just too cool or too lazy to notice that my teachers were waiting for me to take advantage of their expertise.

The draft coming through that window, kids? That's opportunity calling. We'll keep it open, if you don't mind.

T hat class period began with a quotation from James McNeil Whistler, an artist we know more for his portrait of a mother than we do for his use of words. "I maintain that two and two would continue to make four, in spite of the cry of the amateur for three or the cry of the critic for five." My kids and I spent a little extra time discussing Whistler's statement because I knew that his message would soon have an impact on them, and I wanted to give them an opportunity to let the idea percolate in their minds a bit. My purpose for choosing the quote was to help my students see that their efforts to score well on our writing rubric need not lead to frustration. Some had complained that the values for some of the standards were too difficult. An amateur lament if ever I heard one.

"Remember," I told them, "this rubric will help you on every paper this year, but it is also aimed at your future. It's designed to help you produce excellent collegiate writing." I assured them that if they scored fours on those standards, then they could expect to receive good grades on their papers when they were on campus. The standards weren't easy or hard. They were guidelines, simple as that. Want to write a strong thesis? Here's what it contains. Want to present convincing support for your points? Here's how you do that. The rubric was an instrument to help them create great writing. It was a tool, a map, maybe even a formula, but it wasn't paint by number. There was plenty of room for creativity, for expression, for art.

As I told you earlier, even though I was the developer of the rubric, I made it clear that I was not a critic. "Hey, I'm on your side," I told them. "My job is not to judge your writing. The rubric does that. I'm your coach, and I'll do whatever I can to help you satisfy its demands."

107

Now, you and I can argue whether, as the designer, my kids were in effect satisfying me and my notion of what good writing is. In the end, it didn't matter because they adopted that perspective. Bottom line, the rubric wouldn't call a three a four, and I certainly wasn't going to demand a five. The rubric played the role of judge, I played the role of helper. At that moment, what mattered as much as anything was that my kids weren't taking advantage of the opportunities to draft, to craft, to improve. Because I had taken myself out of the grading equation, I was free to push, to cajole, to inspire them to try harder. I had a long way to go.

While it's true that much of your success as a teacher will be the result of acquiring experience, I'm sure you already know that it will take more than simply putting in time. Making it to ten or twenty or thirty years in the classroom, will not guarantee that you will acquire a feel for when to push your students and when to massage their bruised egos because developing that sense will also require you to reflect often and to take emotional risks regarding both your feelings and those of your kids. There is a knack to reflection that takes years and years to hone and to appreciate, and as much as you may think you're in tune with kids when you start teaching, there are no shortcuts to artistry. You may have innate talents that will contribute to your effectiveness as a teacher, but true greatness is only achieved with incredible effort, with a rock-solid faith in yourself as an agent of change. Find that commitment to excellence every day, turn those days into years, decades even, and you will become a teacher who can inspire kids even when they're not looking to be inspired, when the last thing they want to do is write one more draft, read one more chapter. That all starts with your belief in yourself, even on your most discouraging days.

What Steinbeck Said: Post #28
Wednesday, November 16, 2016
The Gift

*W*e opened class today with a quote from American distance runner Steve Prefontaine: "To give anything less than your best is to sacrifice the gift." Standing outside our circle, I told my kids Pre's story, his phenomenal record as a competitor, his unmatched desire to excel. His death in an auto accident at twenty-four. His legacy that lives on over forty years following his passing. Here was a man who squeezed every drop out of his ability.

"Think of the gifts you have been given," I said to my students. "Think of your talents, your opportunities, your second chances." I gave them the present of a few seconds of reflection before we launched into our day, but I returned to Prefontaine's message later in the class period.

As I told you in Monday's post, I planned to have a talk with my classes about their work ethic. Nothing too serious. Nothing approaching an ominous tone. Just a gentle reminder of that generous window of opportunity. It was a quiet talk, lasting but a minute or two. I took a seat in the circle, and as I looked around it, I explained with love and understanding that whether or not they follow all of the steps in the creative process, whether or not they avail themselves of the services offered to them every day inside and out of Room 218, that gift is always available.

Our class is built on choice. Kids choose the topics they write about, they choose the partners with whom they collaborate. They choose whether to share their ideas with their classmates or to keep them hidden in their hearts. That ever-present choice is my gift to them.

Aren't they fascinating, Prefontaine's choices of words? Give. Sacrifice. Gift. *All suggest something surrendered freely. None implies something stolen, something taken away. I love that the passage avoids the idea of waste. We sacrifice the gift, we forego it for another choice. That does not necessarily mean that we have sinned.*

My brief conversation with my students today wasn't a warning, nor was it a threat. It was simply me shining a light on the situation. In implicit terms, I was telling my kids to be sure of their options, to check to see whether they are truly giving their best. It's a long race, this year-long pursuit of ourselves. When we near the finish, we'll each take a look over our shoulder to see how far we've come.

Today?

Today we took the time to see whether our stride is all that it can be, to see whether our feet are taking us on a purposeful path.

Keep your eyes on the prize, kids.

My teaching, well, my life, changed in the 1990's when I was introduced to the ideas of William Glasser. My first mentor in that journey was Kathy Curtiss, who came to our school district to offer introductory courses in Control Theory and Reality Therapy. Teresa was in the first group to work with Kathy near the end of March, and after the first day, she came home and told me, "You are going to love this workshop when you take it this summer. It is you."

So it was that I entered Kathy's *Basic Intensive Week of CT/RT* in early June, anticipating a fresh approach to psychology but totally unaware of the hold it would take on my imagination. In the span of a few days, I came to understand Dr. Glasser's concepts of the Quality World, our basic needs, and the behavioral system. I learned that all of our behavior is grounded in choice, and that we make choices in order to get what we want. When we do get we want, we meet at least one of our needs for love and affection, power, freedom, and fun. It all made sense on a surface level, though I wasn't sure that I wanted to go much further with it than that. When the week came to a close, and Kathy suggested that I might go on to take other classes on the road to certification from the Glasser Institute, I told her that I would think it over. I'm forever glad that I did.

Within a few years I achieved that certification, and after that I became an instructor of classes in what had become known as Choice Theory. Not only did my deepening understanding of Glasser's ideas have an impact on the way I saw the world and my place in it, but it also influenced my teaching. I forsook coercion as a means of getting my students to act appropriately or to hand in their homework. I set up a classroom environment that promoted choice and natural consequences. I found myself less frustrated, and I released my lifelong sense of guilt for just about anything I did. I became a more relaxed teacher, and in turn, I was blessed with students who took more responsibility for their actions.

By the time my final group of seniors arrived in Room 218, I had spent over a quarter of a century building a choice-driven, learning-centered classroom. No rules posted on the wall, no threats hanging over kids' heads. No broken rulers or sudden outbursts of teacher anger to punish or to "motivate" them to work and work hard. So it was on that mid-November day that I sat in the circle and talked with my students about gifts and sacrifice. I never used the word *should*, never uttered the phrase, *you'd better*. Instead, I reminded them of their opportunity, and I offered them my assistance in a loving tone. At that point in the year, that approach seemed to reach most of my students. By spring, it would touch them all.

Of course, there are many schools of philosophy, many psychological approaches that we can apply to education. Glasser's was the one that opened doors for me, but you may begin your time in the profession by walking through an entirely different entrance. Over the course of your career, you might stay with your view of human behavior and continue to learn more and more of its intricacies. Or it's quite possible that you will end up being like me, one who started his teaching grounded firmly in behaviorist tenets, perhaps not totally a devotee of B.F. Skinner but certainly one who believed in cause and effect and in pushing the right buttons and pulling the right levers, and after teaching a while, you may find another perspective. I'm not going to advise you as to the best way to set up your classroom environment, how to create and manage conditions that will affect your students, but I will shine a light on what you might consider in making those important decisions.

First, what will you do to secure your learning environment? You'll have to think about how you will ensure that your kids feel safe both physically and emotionally, how you will minimize distractions so that they can concentrate on their tasks. Does that mean a clear list of rules? Perhaps a system of dealing with issues with student input? Nothing is more important to your kids and their parents than your assurance that they will be allowed to function in your classroom without the fear of harassment or chaos. Nothing else will matter if kids feel that they can't learn under your roof.

Another consideration is student motivation. Will you use rewards and punishments? Will you provide incentives? Will your students feel empowered because you provide them with options that allow them to make choices about their learning? You might find yourself in a school that operates primarily on the promise of extrinsic rewards for achievement and the warning of negative consequences for failure. If that system does not mesh with your own personal philosophy, how will you function within that context? You might not know that answer yet, but in any event, the approach that you take in your classroom will have a real impact on your students' success.

Finally, how will you create a culture in your classes that will promote qualities such as curiosity, perseverance, and cooperation? How will you capture your kids' imaginations, encourage them to stick with their assignments when they feel disheartened? How will you bring them together as a unit instead of a loose collection of learners? How will you help them carry their desire to learn beyond the walls of your classroom?

Whether you set that classroom up on the principles of Abraham Maslow's hierarchy of needs or you take a constructivist approach and lean on the ideas of Jean Piaget, whether you align yourself with Maria Montessori's child-centered methods or Benjamin Bloom's work on the acquisition of higher levels of thinking, having a consistent framework for your decision-making will be essential for the efficacy of your teaching. Just remember to be intentional, thoughtful in the way you set up your classroom, and you will have a foundation upon which you can rely when things get sideways. And they will get sideways from time to time. Think of your psychological framework as your instructional gyroscope, an instrument that will help you find your bearings and orient you toward your goal on those occasions when you feel things spinning out of your control.

For me, Glasser's theory was my gyroscope, in some ways my GPS. Because I understood the underpinnings of his ideas and could apply them to every situation surrounding my teaching, I was confident that I could deal with difficulty and could build on accomplishment. More than anything, I could develop an environment in which my students felt secure enough to take risks, felt supported enough to give their greatest effort, felt welcomed enough to create lasting friendships. Do you know who else received those same benefits from that environment?

Me.

What Steinbeck Said: Post #29
Friday, November 18, 2016
Still Going

A fter more than forty years of teaching, I suppose I should be in a rut, comfortable with lying low and letting the educational world pass me by. In another sense, maybe I should be coasting downhill, no desire to pedal any more. As I reflect here on our living room's love seat on a cold, Friday evening, a bit weary from a long week, I find that I am neither stuck nor taking things easy. A look at the past two days might explain why.

Yesterday morning, I arrived at our central administration building at 6:45, waiting a few minutes in the snow for someone to come down the stairs and open the locked door. Once inside the board room, I distributed agendas around a long rectangle of tables set up for our elementary reading curriculum study meeting. One of our district office assistants was busy laying out breakfast on a table near the windows, and I was awaiting the arrival of some thirty-five teachers who are dedicating their precious time every other week to learn more about reading instruction, something that they already know much more than I ever will.

Earlier this fall, our elementary curriculum director, asked me to chair this group's efforts, and I accepted his request without hesitation. I have a lot of experience with facilitation, and while I was happy to serve in that capacity for this study, I was also excited to learn more about initial reading instruction. After all, I am the ultimate beneficiary of the work of these talented teachers in the early grades, and I couldn't wait to understand the intricacies of their practice. Well, maybe not understand as much as appreciate. To truly understand a teacher's work, one must do the teaching. My time leading this committee this year will at least help me see what is involved in perhaps the most challenging task in education.

It was a wonderful meeting yesterday. The teachers had come prepared to discuss a forty-page chapter from the National Reading Panel's analysis of reading pedagogy. They had highlighted and noted, and as we broke into small groups, they shared their insights and their questions with each other. These were consummate professionals at work long before their young students would arrive in their classrooms for a day of learning, and I marveled at what I was hearing as I went from group to group and eavesdropped. What a wonderful opportunity for me to learn.

After we adjourned and left for our respective schools, I scooted to a book study being held in the high school media center. Our facilitator for that meeting was our secondary level curriculum director who had convened the secondary principals and a fellow instructional coach to discuss Tim Westerberg's book on standards-based grading. Now I assumed a role different from the one I had played an hour earlier across town. I was once again a listener, but I also had the opportunity to share my thoughts and feelings about the reading assignment. While my elementary committee is charged with exploring a possible change in our reading program, this group will be examining the possibility of taking our grading practices in a new direction. I will make no decisions for either committee, but I will have a chance to lend my expertise, more importantly to serve.

Today my classes continued examining The Odyssey, *and I was once again the facilitator. I got the conversation rolling by reviewing the menu of topics that my classes had brainstormed on Wednesday and then asking who wanted to start the discussion. I did very little after that but listen and ask an occasional follow-up question. Oh, and I smiled and laughed. A lot. My kids were so insightful, so dedicated to figuring out the multiple layers of Homer's epic. I was on Olympus.*

After school, two students came by with questions about their essays that they will submit next Tuesday. Each presented me with a second draft that was well-documented and thoughtfully argued. In an otherwise empty classroom, we huddled before their laptops, parsing sentences, searching for nuance, listening for rhythms as we read parts aloud. As much as I love working with my colleagues, as exhilarating as it is to sit in a circle of interpretation and watch ideas fly like a koosh ball around the room, my favorite teaching still happens with a young mind sitting in a desk next to mine.

As this forty-first year unfolds, I find myself not in a rut but a groove, not coasting to the finish but sailing toward the clouds. Have a wonderful weekend, my friends. I have some notebooks to read and comment on. . . .

Another one of my mentors along the way was a kindergarten teacher turned educational consultant named Joel Suzuki. In the 1980's, Joel was one of many experts brought to our school district in Green River to augment our professional development. I had the privilege of attending his first class, and over the course of a few years I found myself working more and more closely with Joel as I, too, started to take on a consulting role in my district.

Joel was a consummate presenter who modeled techniques as he taught them to us. As he showed us about lesson design, he took us inside his planning for the day. When he taught us about active participation, he asked us to practice a variety of ways for students to share. I sat captivated as he unveiled secret after secret about our profession. A few years later, I traveled to his hometown of Minneapolis to participate in an intimate workshop that taught me and four others the ins and outs of workshop presentation, including planning, speaking techniques, and troubleshooting. As I left to fly home to Wyoming, I felt as if I had been inducted into a select society. In many ways, I had been.

One of Joel's messages to us in our very first class in Green River dealt with teacher profiles. He proposed that there were three types. The first were the "DeLoreans," named for the designer of the car popularized by *Back to the Future*. Joel reminded us that the DeLorean was constructed of stainless steel, and as such, was resistant to rust and wear. DeLorean teachers, in Joel's eyes, were impervious to change. Their lesson plans never altered from year to year (in fact, Joel mused that they were most likely laminated), and their basic approach to learning was, "I teach it. If you don't learn it, that's your fault." Principals tended to appreciate DeLoreans because they had few discipline problems. Their students might not have learned a whole lot, but those teachers sure knew how to keep kids in line.

The second type of teacher Joel called "rustouts." Continuing his car analogy, these were folks who had started with all of the best intentions, but somewhere along the way they had become bored with the day-to-day life of the classroom. Mediocrity crept into their teaching as surely as rust forms on metal if there is no vigilance to prevent it. These were the colleagues who you could go to if you needed something because they had ordered materials from year to year but didn't necessarily use them. Posters? Rustouts had a closet full. Colored pencils? Check the bottom drawer. Construction paper? Well, you get the idea. Rustouts weren't particularly favored by their administrators because they tended to get overwhelmed by circumstance. They knew how to manage their classrooms, but they simply lacked the execution that was required.

That left just one profile, Joel said, and it was the type of teacher that we all want for our kids. Departing from the automotive pattern that had seemed to be emerging, he called this desirable type the "burnouts." Wait, I thought, why would a school want to employ a teacher with that label? Burnouts were bums or drug addicts. I tried to imagine the benefit of having either one of those in the classroom. Joel described the burnout profile as someone who had for all intents and purposes given up, a victim of stress and mental and physical exhaustion. These were dangerous to classrooms because those teachers had lost all enthusiasm for the job. They were tired, cynical, and often surly. These were the teachers Joel wanted us to emulate?

"I know this sounds crazy," he told our class, "but remember, in order to burn out, you must have once been on fire."

Oh.

Joel went on to explain that it was our stars on the faculty who were most at risk of burning out. They were the ones who principals called on to serve on every committee, the ones with huge classes because parents wanted their children in that room. They were the ones who were continually seeking a better way, pushing themselves to study and create better and better learning opportunities for their students but at the same time sacrificing other parts of their lives for the sake of their profession.

"So," Joel continued, "if this is the standard that we want a teacher to achieve, how can we help those people avoid turning into burnouts? It's simple. We help them add another log to their fire."

What were those logs? Professional development, for one. Encouragement another. Novel approaches a third. If teachers who were really on fire were to avoid flaming out, more fuel had to be added to their teaching. DeLoreans don't need any more logs, thank you. Rustouts wouldn't know what to do with them. But burnouts are always looking for something new, some little magic.

When people asked me how I maintained my enthusiasm for teaching for over forty years, I told them about the stack of firewood I had available to me. Working with colleagues certainly was a log for me. One-on-one time with on-fire students was as well. Opportunities to learn more about my practice were essential to my ongoing development as a teacher. Was I tired at the end of a day like the one described in the post above? Of course, I was. But it was a good tired. A satisfied weariness. I knew that the next morning I would awaken and stoke the fire a little more. And if I came across a colleague whose flame seemed to be flickering a little, well, I had plenty of logs to share.

You might think at this point that you'll never fit any of Joel's profiles. You'll care too much to be a DeLorean, persevere too much to become a rustout. You'll be on fire throughout your career, and you'll never run out of fuel. I certainly felt that way when I stood before my first class in my student teaching, full of ideals and certain that I would never have a bad day of teaching. I'm sure you won't be as naïve as I was as a pup; nonetheless, it is the true believer who is most at risk of falling if not careful. Things won't always be easy—sometimes they might seem near impossible—but it will be up to you to find those logs in order to keep your fire burning. Don't wait to be asked to take an extra course or to attend a conference. Make that happen for yourself. Don't shut yourself away in your classroom when you start to lose hope or confidence in your ability to lead young people. Seek out your older colleagues and ask their advice. You'll find that they have gone through all of the rough experiences you are suffering through. And you know what? They'll appreciate that you have come to them for help. Who doesn't want to be held in such esteem?

On those days when the non-teaching aspects of the profession are more than you think you can stand, find refuge in your classroom. I can remember leaving early morning faculty meetings feeling that if I was asked to fill out one more form, reminded one more time that our test scores were too low, or informed once again of a last-minute assembly that was going to impact our learning time, I was just going to keep walking out to my car and drive home for the day. Something always saved me on those occasions, however. I would stand outside of my room while students walked past on the way to their first periods, smiling and nodding at those I knew and some I didn't, talking all the while with the teacher I shared a wall with, either commiserating about our meeting woes or taking our minds off them altogether by discussing the game the night before or the most recent episode of *Better Call Saul*. Then the bell rang, and I would saunter into my room, a smile and a cheerful greeting for those young hearts who were just waiting for me to arrive so we could all learn together.

There's your best firewood.

What Steinbeck Said: Post #30
Tuesday, November 22, 2016
Hard to be Great

*T*wo posts ago, I told you the story of my talk with my classes about Steve Prefontaine's immortal line, "To give anything than your best is to sacrifice the gift." Indeed, it appeared that many of my kids were forfeiting opportunities to excel, to test their limits.

Well, well.

Within a day or two, a few of my students stopped by to confer with me on their argument papers. Several of them told me that this was a hard assignment, that it was the toughest of our essays to date. I acknowledged that the prompt requires extensive research as well as accommodation of the opposite side of the issue. Quietly, I was thrilled that although my kids were troubled by the demands of the assignment, they were nonetheless seeking to accomplish it. They were going out of their way to get help to achieve that end.

I thought about my kids' complaint for a few days. "This is hard." So often, teachers seem to pull back when they hear those words, seek to mollify their students' anxieties.

"Don't worry, you'll be fine."

"Oh, it's not that hard."

I've done my own share of assuaging, but today, I decided to embrace my students' feelings. Our opening quote came from Jimmy Dugan, the baseball coach in A League of Their Own. *When his star player tells him she's quitting the team to return to her soldier husband because "it just got too hard," Dugan replies with more immortal words: "It's supposed to be hard. If it wasn't hard, everyone would do it. It's the 'hard' that makes it great."*

It's the hard that makes it great. We're not just talking baseball, are we? I reminded my kids that our class is indeed difficult, that they have to earn their way into the room were it happens. Not everyone qualifies for College English. *As for the hard, well, yes, we do read complex material. Our essay prompts are challenging. Our discussions push us to dig deep, to express our ideas with conviction and a sense of exploration.*

"There is no reason to be afraid of the hard," I told my kids. "No, we must embrace *that challenge. That's what will make us great."*

What I didn't tell my students is something that has long glowed warm in my memory, a passage from The Grapes of Wrath. *In Chapter Twenty-Three, John Steinbeck details ways in which the Okies traveling to California sought pleasure and amusement on the road. They found it through music, and they found it through alcohol. They even found it though religious conversion. One form of pleasure that Steinbeck shares holds a special place in my own heart: "The story*

119

tellers, gathering attention into their tales, spoke in great rhythms, spoke in great words because the tales were great, and the listeners became great through them."

What benefit do we derive from accomplishing easy tasks? Do we really feel good about our efforts when all we achieve is what is expected of us? Sure, great literature can be hard to comprehend, difficult to interpret. Because it's great, however, we will become great by experiencing it. We will become great by taking on the rigorous essay, by engaging each other in vigorous debate. That's something for which we'll all give thanks.

Enjoy the holiday, my friends!

I n my second or third year of teaching, one of my students remarked during class that she was dreading English the following year because she'd be taking a class with a teacher that she'd had before, and he had been "hard." She was quickly supported by most of her classmates, but along with the anxiety they expressed about that upcoming class, there was an undercurrent of excitement as well. Perhaps it was nothing more than misery loving company, but I sensed it was more than that. The kids were quietly relishing the prospect of being challenged.

"Is that the way you feel about this class?" I asked my kids. They looked around at each other and laughed.

"Oh, Mr. Stemle," said Susan, one of my better students. "You're funny."

"It's not hard?"

"Of course not," said Joe. "This class is easy."

Great. The bell rang, and the kids scooted out the door, leaving me to figure out why I had this sudden ache in my stomach. I had worked diligently to make lessons relevant for my students. I had assigned them plenty of homework, and I had demanded good writing for them if they expected good grades. Where had I gone wrong? At home that night I stewed quite a bit, and I resolved that from that point forward, I was going to be tougher. I was going to earn my kids' respect by making class harder.

For several weeks it bothered me, and while I tried not to let it affect my teaching, every time that a student mentioned that another class was difficult, I couldn't help but think that while my kids seemed to enjoy my class, as an instructor I was pretty much a lightweight. I grew jealous of my older colleagues, and I wondered whether I would ever be regarded as a demanding teacher. One day, as the ending bell was about to ring and my class was putting away their books, I casually brought the matter up.

"So, I've been wondering why you think Mr. Sanders' class was so hard and this one isn't."

"What do you mean?" asked Robbie.

"You know. You all are always talking about how difficult it is. The same with Mr. Porter's and Miss Macy's. I was just wondering why this one isn't."

"Oh, Mr. Stemle," said Susan with a laugh and a shake of her head. "Don't you get it? Your class is easy because you explain things so well. Those other teachers just give us assignments and make us figure things out for ourselves."

Well, I must say that I felt stupid. Here, I had taken pains to make sure that my students understood what I expected, and when they were successful, I had somehow convinced myself that I was failing them. In their minds, however, I had facilitated their learning so that it seemed effortless. My relationship with hard and easy continued over the years, and I continued to seek ways to make learning as simple as possible, but I also came to realize that if I could do that, then I could also increase the rigor of our content and push my students to interpret at deeper levels. The result was a different kind of hard. It was not born of confusion or uncertainty but, rather, of complexity. The first two can cause us a certain amount of frustration, but the third can bring exhilaration. Like your students, I'm sure that you will be willing to work hard if you know that you're being supported, if you are confident that it's OK to struggle, even to fail. It will be the depth of your challenges that will define you in a competitive academic sense, that will separate your effort from the more mundane tasks in your life. You'll find that the hard does indeed make it all great.

There is a lesson for you here that goes beyond how your students are going to perceive your teaching, their learning. My question for you is, how will you know what your kids are thinking and feeling? It's easy to make assumptions when you don't know. As I did, you might take a comment or some laughter and interpret it as a criticism. Or you might project your own feelings, ones that you had when you were in school. Maybe you'll figure that if you felt that way when you were a kid, then your students must, too.

What can you do to get a clearer understanding of how your students view your class? One obvious way is to ask them, though I wouldn't recommend that you continually say things such as, "Did you like what we just did?" A more open-ended approach can come in a number of forms. I used to hold brief meetings every so often to check the temperature of our class. I'd pose some general questions to allow my kids to reflect on their feelings about how we were doing. "What parts of our class are working well for you?" "Is there anything about our class that is especially difficult for you?" "If you could change one thing about our class, what would it be?" I learned a lot during those meetings, and while I was sometimes surprised by what was bugging my kids, and while it was hard not to take negative comments personally, I learned to view all feedback as helpful to improving my teaching. Those sessions also helped us develop trust in each other because we learned that we didn't have to keep our feelings secret.

There are other ways to ascertain how things are going for your kids. You can ask them to describe their experience in journal entries or in letters they deliver to you. You can encourage them to drop by and see you outside of class time if they have concerns. You can also arrange reading or writing conferences that can open avenues for discussing other matters pertaining to class. Some kids may never feel comfortable opening up to you in any sort of format, but if you can develop a general sense of where things are for your kids, you can apply that understanding to making your teaching stronger, your classroom culture more nurturing. It might save you a stomachache, too.

What Steinbeck Said: Post #31
Tuesday, November 29, 2016
Through a Glass Dizzily

*F*rom my childhood till my late twenties, I wore glasses. Thick glasses. I endured broken frames, cracked lenses, constant slippage down the bridge of my nose. When I made the move to contact lenses, a luxury that I had long considered cosmetic, I was stunned at how much better I could see. Sure, there was the inconvenience of caring for my lenses, but the benefits were well worth the hassle of cleansing and storing. Reading was so much easier. I no longer played basketball with the lurking fear of getting hit in the face and being rendered blind. My life in many ways changed.

It changed back again on Sunday. I awoke to reddened, swollen eyes, an infection that told me immediately that I wasn't going to be wearing my contacts anytime soon. I fished around in a dresser drawer and found a pair of wire-rims that I had purchased five or six years ago as emergency eyewear. A visit to my optometrist on Monday confirmed my self-diagnosis, and I immediately began a week-long regimen of drops and an antibiotic.

In the meantime, I did my best to grade essays with my specs, and I waited for my eyes to adjust to a much different acuity. While my contacts had brought things closer to me, my glasses were now shrinking them into the distance. I knocked over teacups reaching beyond their position, not favored with a sign that read, "Objects in your visual field are closer than they appear." I could see straight ahead all right, but anything near the edge of my vision was distorted like a funhouse mirror.

And this will last for a week.

Today I went to school, grateful to be able to see at all and knowing that my kids would be curious about my appearance. Some didn't seem to notice, while others complimented my new look. As I always do when I find myself in a challenging situation, I put great energy into my teaching. Not that there was much to teach on this day, for my kids were engaged in an in-class writing on

The Odyssey. *My class period would be spent checking on them from time to time and grading papers at my desk while they created their own essays. As long as I sat inert and marked my comments, I felt fine. Anytime I took a tour around the circle or went down the hall between classes, I threaded my way through a kaleidoscope. The more quickly I traveled, the more disorienting the effect.*

And this will last for a week.

God bless my students. They gave their best today. As they came to my desk to hand in their essays and their copies of the text, they smiled with the satisfaction that comes from the knowledge that they had prepared and executed. This was our one timed writing of the year, our one glimpse into the college world that they will soon explore, and I believe that they secretly enjoyed the challenge.

There was another reason for their smiles. They knew I was operating at less than one hundred percent today. They knew that I, too, had given my best. It is on days like this that I love to reflect, to slow down and keep my focus in front of me, to ignore the whirling images on the periphery of my life and appreciate the real reason that I love teaching. It is more than my love of literature, my delight in the wonder of language. It's more than guiding students to explore their hearts and minds to find beauty. What it is, more than anything, is that look in their eyes, that smile that tells me that they are beginning to realize that a door has opened for them.

And this will last for a lifetime.

A thletes are often praised for playing hurt. They shake off pulled muscles and broken fingers, sprained ankles and back spasms, in order to keep playing, especially when they are part of a team that depends on their presence in the arena of competition. How often do we give the same credit to other performers? Who gives kudos to the secretary struggling with carpal tunnel syndrome? Who lauds the mechanic who tunes an engine while dealing with a throbbing headache? Who notices when students and teachers give their best even when they're not feeling it?

I never was one to ask for sympathy from my students or my co-workers. I figured that if I felt well enough to show up to school, then it did me little good to complain about my condition. Who wants to hear that someone isn't feeling great? Sometimes it was just too obvious for others to miss, however. I used to cringe when friends would say, "Man, you really look tired today" or "Are you feeling OK?" but I knew deep down that they were merely showing their concern for my well-being. When I showed up wearing glasses at school, it had to be clear that something was different, and when I told my kids about my eye infection, they immediately gave me their sympathy. I could have played on that feeling, milking it for a few days in order to get more out of my students, but the fact that I projected a teaching-as-usual vibe must have had an energizing effect on my classes. When we watch someone handle difficulties with grace, we are drawn even closer to them emotionally.

Here's the important thing, though. How aware are you going to be of those who are acting gracefully at any given moment? Sure, you'll see it in someone who has a visible physical injury, a student crutching down the hallway with a boot on her foot. You'll observe it when you see someone insulted in a discussion and watch to note how he handles the attack. But how good will you be at noticing graceful behavior when someone is holding close a secret? The quiet boy in the room who is abused by his stepfather. The girl who has just lost her grandmother. The friends who have had an argument and haven't spoken for days.

In the 1973 film *Bang the Drum Slowly*, Robert DeNiro's character Bruce feels sorry for himself because his teammates are continually putting him down. Few if any know that he is dying of Hodgkin's disease because he has chosen not to tell them and instead puts on his catcher's gear every day and plays. Never a great hitter, not much of a defensive player, he simply ignores the taunts of his clueless teammates and goes about his duties. In a moment of self-pity and candor, he tells his one confidant, Henry, the team's star pitcher played by Michael Moriarity, "Everybody would be nice to you if they knew you were dying." Henry replies, "Everybody knows everybody is dying; that's why people are as good as they are."

Was I dying on that late November day? Not any more than usual. Was anybody in my classes? Not that I knew of. Yet, somehow we came in every day, despite our troubles and our concerns, and we learned together, discovered together, played together. As I said, that will last a lifetime.

What Steinbeck Said: Post #32
Thursday, December 1, 2016
Beyond the Grade Book

I looked forward to my classes today because I knew they would involve one of our most important activities of the year. It was a day of transition as we said goodbye to our work with The Odyssey *and said hello to our study of short stories. In one way, we enjoyed the anticipation of new learning, of forming new teams and of drawing lots for great pieces that we'll teach each other about next week. In another, we honored each other by sharing a little about our lives. I have told you that I have an advantage over my students because I already know what they'll know later in the year. What I know tonight is that this morning and this afternoon, we grew closer as classmates. I'm sure my kids felt that to some degree, but they really don't understand yet how that will benefit them for the rest of the year.*

Last week, I handed each of my students a large piece of construction paper and encouraged them all to symbolically represent the highs and lows of their lives. The purpose was to give them a chance to reflect on their own personal odysseys, to map out their journeys to this point and perhaps beyond. I shared my own map, a spiral that places my birth on the edge and all of the other events in an ever-tightening curve toward the center. I told my kids that the format represents my belief that as I have grown older, I have looked more and more inside for my answers. As for their maps, I told them to create, to risk. "You can make a timeline, if you wish, or you can draw a tree or a flower or a musical staff. Better yet, you can create something I have never seen. Please!"

At the end of each period today, we gathered once more in a circle on the Flatland inside of our desks. The kids shyly kept their creations hidden, laying them face down on the carpet or curled into a cylinder on their laps. They had the option of sharing their maps with their classmates, of narrating the flow of their trips so far, or of waiting to let me look over their drawings in private. In each class, eight to ten kids shared, and we delighted in the colors and the designs, the outright genius of the eighteen-year-old mind. And we laughed. Not the laughter that follows a witty remark or a slip of the tongue, but the sound of intimate recognition of each other's humanity. Of our vulnerability and our willingness to let each other in.

We learned so much. Some of us have been adopted. Others have suffered through divorces, lost grandparents who have passed and best friends who have moved away. Many have endured injury, both physical and emotional. We heard about travels and championships and hopes for more of each. More than anything, we got to experience the miracle of us.

One of my students asked whether her life map would be graded.

I grinned.

"Not everything receives a grade," I told her. "In fact, the most important things we do in here cannot be measured by a letter or a number." There are essays and presentations that will earn points in the coming months, and my kids will work hard to be worthy of those marks. That's a big part of our experience in this class, but the real treasure will be discovered in the weeks ahead when we learn together. Because of today, my students will be braver about sharing their ideas in the circle, will listen with more empathy for each other and with more love. What possible grade could I ever place on that?

Outside of Tom Joad's farewell to his mother, for me the greatest paragraph in *The Grapes of Wrath* comes in Chapter Fourteen where, in just a few sentences, John Steinbeck describes the transformation of a group of individuals into a community. Folks who have lost close to everything somehow find a way to share, to move from "I to we." For three months, each of my classes and I had moved toward that kind of relationship. I had worked to build a bond with every student, had provided opportunities for those students to team together and depend on each other, had created a safe and nurturing environment in which we all felt secure in our sharing. It wasn't until that day, however, that I felt that each of my classes had reached the beginning of "I to we." As we sat close on the floor, near enough to each other to speak in gentle voices, to look into each others' eyes, we shared in wonderfully creative ways some personally meaningful events from our lives. There were several kids in each class who kept their maps confidential, but each and every one of them listened because that was no ordinary discussion where classmates were espousing opinions about literature. Rather, those were friends opening the doors to their memories, to great celebrations and to great loss. In those tight circles, there was laughter to greet each life revealed, there were tears from time to time as well. It wasn't just a moment in a class period.

It was *the* moment.

In Chapter Fourteen, Steinbeck is warning the great land owners of the change that is about to come, that the growing unrest among the small farmers and itinerant workers, the emerging unity of purpose, is a result, not a cause. Paine, Marx, Jefferson, and Lenin were results, not causes. A revolution had begun, an economic war that the great owners were too late in stopping. For my students, a different kind of change had arrived. No, there would be no one trying to bomb it or crush it. Nonetheless, where we had been a collection of *I*'s, each class had taken the first true step into *we*. Make no mistake, it is emotion that creates a great classroom, that bonds teachers and students together into an organism that feeds on learning.

I had principals who warned me that emotion was a dangerous thing in a school, that I should avoid asking my students to reach into their hearts and share their feelings with their classmates and their teacher. I have to wonder whether those leaders ever sat on the floor of a classroom, ever felt the energy that an emotional release has upon a group that is ready to become one entity. Whenever I could, I left the door open to our classroom, happy to let passers-by see the beauty of the learning therein, shutting it only when the sounds of that learning might disturb other classes, or when noises from the hallway might bother us. The day of the life maps was a time that I closed our door because the power we were creating was too precious to let escape.

We had, indeed, created the room where it happens.

Your classroom can become that, too. No, it won't come on schedule, and it might not happen with every class or even with every year, but when it does, you will realize the sublime feeling that only teaching can give you. You can't force the "I to we," but you can create a culture that fosters it, and you can keep your eyes and ears open for signs of it developing. Just be prepared when it does arrive because it will empower your class to work together in remarkable ways, and it will energize you in ways you cannot imagine.

What Steinbeck Said: Post #33
Monday, December 5, 2016
Highlighting the Hidden Pictures

*A*s a boy, I actually looked forward to sitting in the waiting rooms of our dentist and our family doctor. Even though my mother and I would wait for what seemed an hour past our appointed time, I never minded because I had the chance to read* Highlights. *Here was the classic children's magazine, chock full of stories and jokes and puzzles. By far, my favorite feature was "Hidden Pictures," an elaborate sketch in which was embedded ten or twelve common objects. I might at first be presented with a sketch of young Abe Lincoln splitting wood, but I was tasked with also locating a saw, a book, a turtle, a cat. When I was four, this challenge could be quite daunting, and if I struggled to find that first item, my mom would gently ask me if I wanted help. Most of the time I was stubborn and refused, but every once in a while I just could not find what I was supposed to see. In that case, all she needed to do was give me an area to focus on, and once I spotted a hidden piece, I was on my way.*

To my delight, I got to be my mom today. My students met in their newly-formed teams to discuss the short stories that they will start teaching to their classmates at the end of the week. I asked them to start by discussing the plot so that they could agree on what happens in the story. Once they got that done, they were to figure what their story is about. Those are two wholly different things, by the way. The plot consists of events. What a story is about is its theme, its message. The ultimate goal is for each team to develop a lesson plan with discussion questions and activities designed to help their classmates interpret the deeper meanings of each piece.

That wasn't today, however. Today was about figuring what in heaven's name William Faulkner and Flannery O'Connor and John Updike are talking about. As I went from pod to pod, kneeling beside the teams to be at their eye level, I asked for their initial impressions of their stories. Some had a firm grasp on the plot and were already discussing symbols and imagery. Others looked lost. I knew those kids were going to be all right, even when they admitted they had no idea of what was happening in "A Rose for Emily" or "A Good Man is Hard to Find."

"That's OK," I told them. "I'm not sure I know, either."

Right. What are you selling, Mr. Stemle? How can an English teacher not know everything there is to know about literature? Well, kids, it's really quite simple. If we're going to read the most honored short stories, pieces of great merit, we are going to have to dance with ambiguity. There's not a lot of black and white. Forget the shades of gray. We're talking infrared and ultraviolet. It's not about what I can tell my students. Rather, it is about helping them find it for themselves. With that in mind, I asked each team where they were with their stories, I listened to them converse about possibilities. When I sensed that they had reached a struggling point, I intervened.

Just as my mother always would.

"Do you what the name Della means?" I asked a team preparing a lesson on Amy Bloom's "Hold Tight."

"Have you looked at the different ways that Sammy describes Queenie?" I asked another team working with Updike's "A&P."

We talked about the relative morality in "A Good Man is Hard to Find," the concept of healing in Joyce Carol Oates' "The Night Nurse." I didn't point out the hidden pictures in each story, but I did suggest where my kids could begin looking. It was fun to bounce from team to team and find out what progress they'd made since I'd spoken to them ten minutes earlier.

It has been decades since I wore a whistle around my neck, but I still do a lot of coaching in my classroom, just as I did a lot of teaching on the court. Because all those years ago my mother had the grace to coach me in the right direction but never give me an answer, I have the faith today to trust my students to find their own hidden pictures. All I have to do is ask the right questions.

Thanks, Mom.

I n my final year of teaching, one of my students asked me during class if I had ever coached. When I told her that I had, much to the chagrin of many referees, she and her classmates seemed incredulous that I would ever raise my voice in any arena, athletic or academic. Here it was, almost spring, and they had never heard me speak in anger or show any sign of great negative emotion. All I could do was laugh because early in my career as a teacher and as a coach, I had a pretty quick temper and a biting tongue. As a coach, whether it was in practice or a game, it seemed that I was always talking to and yelling at my players, and while what I said was probably ninety percent positive, once I got in a vocal mode, it was hard not to shout at the officials as well. Were I to return to the bench today, I would be a much mellower coach because I would trust my players to carry out our practice plans without my constant reminding. That's how I taught, letting my students find their own way of implementing what I had shown them. In trusting my kids to learn a lot on their own, I learned to trust myself as well.

Coaching and teaching are certainly related, but there are definitely distinctions between the two. When I was in high school, I saw little connection between the approaches. My teachers were people who shared information with my classes and showed us how to solve problems or organize our ideas. I don't recall receiving much specific feedback on my work. My geometry proofs were marked as either correct or incorrect (mostly the latter), though they might also be labeled as partial credit. I took objective tests in my social studies classes and my answers were judged as either right or wrong. Even my English essays came back with scant comments and occasional errors marked, the grade at the top of the paper being the one important part of my teacher's perception of my paper.

Overall, that's how the system worked.

My coaches took a different tack. While my academic work was done in private, either at home or in the classroom, and it's evaluation was almost always done outside of my presence, on the basketball court and the baseball diamond, the opposite was true. Every effort I made happened in front of my coaches and my teammates, and not only was feedback given directly, but it was also almost always public. If I was sloppy in executing a crossover move in practice, my coach would pull me aside and remind me of the proper technique. He might even show me how to do the step again. If I did the same in a game, he might bring me over to the bench to remind me or ask me to sit to give me time to think over my sins. In batting practice, if I was dropping my hands when trying to hit a high fastball, my coach would show me how to keep them up and then would throw me four or five more in a row to let me practice. It was immediate and specific feedback.

Of course, my coaches did a bit more shouting than my teachers did, and if the team really messed up, we did a lot of wind sprints and pushups, something I don't recall ever doing in my chemistry class. Still, a major difference between being a student and a player was that my coaches worked much more with me as an individual. That included pep talks when I needed them and dressings down when I needed those, too.

Because the United States is one of the few countries with school-sponsored athletics, we also have the unusual situation where most of our coaches are certified teachers. While this setup can be quite grueling for those teachers who also coach, it does provide some helpful crossover opportunities. If that turns out to be your experience, then you just might find that because you are teacher, you can be effective in demonstrating what you want from your athletes, and, because you are a coach, you can be effective in working one-on-one with your students and in encouraging them when it comes time for them to perform publicly. I know that as I became more and more adept as a basketball coach, designing tighter and tighter practices and adjusting to changing conditions during games, I found myself more comfortable with lesson planning and dealing with changing conditions in the classroom.

The longer I was in the classroom, the less I taught and the more I coached. I continued to explain instructions and provide models before I asked my students to begin an assignment or a project, but I devoted much more of my time and energy to sitting close by and watching my kids engage in their learning, ready to point them in a direction to find an answer or to create something new. As a result, I had a much deeper understanding of what each of my students knew and could do, and I found it easier to guide each one in specific terms, to provide encouragement that together, we could do great things.

Oh, and without a single pushup or sprint. Imagine that.

What Steinbeck Said: Post #34
Wednesday, December 7, 2016
Anybody Seen My Broom?

*O*ur lesson designing continued today. Teams moved beyond discussing the plots of their short stories and began exploring themes. Moving from group to group, I listened to their conversations about the author's message, to their early attempts at writing discussion questions, their wondering about activities or demonstrations that could enable their classmates to delve into the subtler aspects of their pieces. I observed that nearly every team was more animated than it had been on Monday, and as my students built upon each other's ideas, they grew more and more excited about possibilities for their teaching.

This effect came as no surprise to me. Whether or not they realized it, my students were creating synergy, the energy released when people collaborate to create a sum greater than their single contributions, and like a sun worshipper, I couldn't wait to bask in the glow of each team's burgeoning ideas. As I did on Monday, I asked them questions and helped them focus their energy on the various tasks demanded by the lesson. As I worked with each team, I waited for the right time, and then I leaned in closer to them, the better to softly deliver some instructional tips, veteran teacher to novices.

133

"Whenever I start a discussion," I told them in a collegial tone, "I ask a question that anyone can answer, a personal response. I might ask you all to tell a partner about a time you were afraid or to discuss a problem you see in our school today. The idea is to let your students loosen up before you ask them to think deeply.

"It would be like taking you down to the end of the hall and asking you to run as fast as you could to the gym. That's about one hundred yards, right? Imagine how your legs would feel when you reached the end. Your lungs. Your heart."

I looked into each student's eyes, watched them nod.

"But what if, instead, I asked you to stretch for a few minutes, to jog up and down the hall a bit before you took off on your sprint? How would you feel then?"

I waited. Nods and smiles.

"We're all cold at the beginning of a discussion. Stiff. If I ask you to talk about a symbol you found or the deep meaning of the story, you're not going to be ready. You're going to hesitate. You might look down or start fiddling with your pencil. That's because you're not ready to run yet.

"As you plan your lessons, think of a way to engage your classmates at the start, to let them loosen up a bit before you ask them to interpret. Once you get their energy flowing, you'll be surprised at how much better they will share."

Is there more fun for a teacher than letting students in on the magic of the profession? The best part for me came when I returned to teams to check their progress. Not only had they developed more of their plans, but some were near giddy in their expectation for the lessons. They had discovered a reservoir that they probably never knew existed. They were getting a glimpse of what it means to be on the other side of the lesson, and in the next week, they'll understand to a small extent why we teach, what keeps us coming back at the end of every summer, what fuels our smiles each morning when we greet our first classes.

Why do we teach? It's simple. We teach because we long to feel that synergy, to see that dawning light of realization in their eyes. As teachers we are the purveyors of hope, the merchants of opportunity. We are the sorcerers who *conjure the conditions necessary for success.*

Starting Friday, I will have a classroom full of apprentices exercising their nascent teaching powers. As teams, they will come together to lead their classmates toward discovery, to tap into that energy that only a classroom of seniors can create. Will my fledgling teachers have complete control of their lessons? Maybe not, but today they all saw the bright light of possibility. Is there any question as to why they're so excited?

I f teaching was talking, think of how smart we all would be."

—William Glasser

Of course, teaching, as Glasser suggested, is a lot more than just talking. We talk about tricks of the trade, but a great teacher is one who inspires students to see beyond illusion, to realize that learning is alchemy. Why? Because it turns ignorance and inability into gold. Yet, how often do we invite kids into the sorcerer's workshop to learn the secrets of the craft? What, do we fear a Mickey Mouse disaster? Teams out of control like multiplying brooms, flooding the classroom when given the power to teach each other? Maybe we just think that teaching should be left to the professional in the room, but I truly believed that everyone was a teacher in our classroom. That's why I was so happy to move about the room that December day, to share inside information about my practice to help my younger teachers prepare to lead their classmates. With four decades of experience in my pocket, I was confident that I could not only guide my kids as they prepared their lessons but could also help them weather any calamities when it was their turn to teach.

At first, you might be a bit wary of unleashing the power of a room full of teenagers who are, to put it politely, exuberant. I know that in my early years, I enjoyed all of that spirit, but I was always a little nervous that what started out as an enjoyable exercise could quickly turn into a riot if I turned off the cruise control. This was especially true of my middle school classes. An activity that brought laughter and movement could escalate into a frenzy with little warning, and once that happened, it was hard to put the genie back into the bottle. Of

135

course, you will be cautioned by your veteran colleagues to beware of having too much fun in the classroom or for allowing your students to express too much of any emotion, but can you imagine teaching from day to day in a sedate, perhaps even a sterile environment? Do you really want to drag your kids along class period by class period? If you bind them with rules and warnings to tamp down their enthusiasm, that's exactly what you'll have to do in order to move them along academically.

In the long run, you'll come to understand that classrooms run on energy. When you become a successful teacher, you'll know how to harness it, how to use it to create even more, to spin excitement into greater learning. There was nothing harder for me than to try to jump-start a dead class battery. On those days when my students were lethargic, maybe even apathetic, it was a major chore to get them to engage in the lesson. On the other hand, if my kids bounded into class full of noise and movement, I welcomed the chance to dance with that energy because it meant that their spirit was high that day. As I glided around the room among my young apprentices and whispered words to help them learn to conjure, I was one happy sorcerer. And you know what? I couldn't find a single scrap of base metal.

What Steinbeck Said: Post #35
Friday, December 9, 2016
The Rookies Step Up

*I*t's a familiar story. An aging ballplayer, the end of his career in sight, taking aside a first-year player and teaching the youngster the finer points of the game. The veteran, sacrificing minutes for the good of the team while passing on wisdom acquired over the years. It's how the culture of a team is preserved, how the game is honored. I love that story.

Now, don't get any ideas. My teeth may need a little trimming, but I'm not exactly grooming my replacement quite yet. Rather, as I told you in my last post, I shared some teaching tips with my students on Wednesday as they prepared lessons for our short story unit. Today we kicked off that unit, and my apprentices tried their hands at teaching. Because our school was hosting the Evanston Invitational wrestling tournament, classes were shortened to forty-five minutes, just enough time for one team per class to execute its plan. As fate would have it, two of my classes delved into our most challenging stories: Flannery O'Connor's "A Good Man is Hard to Find" and William Faulkner's "A Rose for Emily." As I told you the other day, my advice to my teams was to start simple and build some energy before asking their classmates to interpret deeply. Now, here we were, without a chance to stretch, about to begin our short story experience with two doozies.

After introducing each team, I sat at my desk with rubrics labeled and ready for marking, outside of the circle, removed from playing the game. On the inside were young hearts and minds ready to guide their classmates, trusting that they had prepared for the moment. My student-teachers were understandably anxious. I was simply curious. What direction would each lesson travel? What discoveries would each class make? Who might say something in the course of twenty-five minutes that would open my eyes to an interpretation I had never considered?

Of course, each class had a different experience. One started slowly but then found its footing and came up with a thoughtful interpretation of Faulkner's classic. Another was hot from the start, digging deep into O'Connor's dark tale and finding symbolism that supported its examination of moral questions. The third used apples as a metaphor for looking beyond appearances to find true character in Joyce Carol Oates' "The Night Nurse." Oh, and we even got to watch a clip from Monsters, Inc.

For a first day, this was a good set of lessons. The kids collaborated, both teachers and students, to create meaning from text. They pushed each other to find answers and credited each other when they were found. In the end, they warmed the heart of an old ballplayer who saw promise emerging.

Want to know what's really cool? We get to do this two more days!

P art of building a community in our classroom involved developing protocols that helped us treat each other with kindness, compassion, and respect. If my classes were going to bloom into the beauty that I wanted to see, then I, as the flower's stem, had the responsibility of feeding them, of rooting them in a stable environment. To make that happen, I began the year by teaching my kids how to share their learning with each other, and by the time we reached the team presentations in December, the ritual was well-grounded. They knew that whenever it was their turn to stand and deliver to their friends, they could expect that I would first rise and formally welcome them all to a day of lessons, that I would lead them in gentle clapping that followed the announcement of those presenters, and that I would join with that audience in a healthy round of applause at the conclusion of their teaching. It was our way of showing our sincere appreciation for the time that our classmates had invested in creating their presentations, for the courage they had displayed by standing before their fellows and accepting the risk that came whenever any of us stepped into the spotlight, whenever any of us submitted the fruits of our preparation for the consideration of a room full of critical eyes and ears.

As you know, during the previous class period, I had shared some secrets with my apprentice teachers, and now the time had come for them to move beyond the knowledge of what I had told them so that they could experience the excitement that teachers feel when they are guiding the learning of others. So it was that I delighted in watching my seniors teaching their friends, going far beyond the simple presentations they had made to a panel in October. I loved the energy that each team brought to the circle in that first round of lessons, the creativity that informed their questions, the fun that infused the activities that they led to help their classmates better understand the meaning of a particular short story. By the end of the period, I wasn't sure who had learned more, those who had participated in the lessons or those who had facilitated them. Maybe the one who had learned the most on that day was the old ballplayer sitting on the bench outside of the arena defined by our circle, the one who felt an affectionate kinship with all of those teachers in his past who had passed on their wisdom and had provided him opportunity after opportunity to stretch his mind, even if he had not always taken advantage of those gifts.

Maybe the ultimate lesson for you is this: in the end, the players come and the players go, but the game remains the same. Teaching and learning is essentially a series of moments, strung together from class period to class period, from day to day, year to year in the lifetime of a school, of a community. That evening at home, while I was writing comments at the bottom of each presenter's rubric, I paused to reflect on some of the moments I had shared with my students and colleagues over the course of my career, and I suddenly realized that while I was looking back, the kids to whom I was writing had their hearts focused in the other direction, on the moments still to come in their lives. Our first lessons taught and class ended, we had gone our diverse ways, I captivated by my memories, they liberated by their imaginations. Our hearts would intersect again when we met once more in our classroom, our concentration not trained on what had happened two days before or what would take place two days after, not two years earlier or two years hence. On that occasion, those next presenters would hear a heartfelt introduction from me and a soft sign of appreciation from their colleagues. Then they would feel the exhilaration of a precious moment of teaching. Is there anything in the world more worthy of an ovation?

That is something to keep in mind not only when you enter your classroom on any particular day but also when you give your students a chance to step into their own teaching shoes. It doesn't matter what subject you teach, you can share instructional responsibilities with your kids. It doesn't have to be every day, even every week, but there is something about successfully putting plans into place that is incredibly satisfying, and why should you be the only one in your classroom to feel that satisfaction? It will be more than just executing what you want to happen, however. Every lesson will bring surprises as well, responses that you won't be expecting, openings for deeper investigation that you will never anticipate. When your students get to feel the thrill of helping their classmates learn and grow, they will in turn be more motivated to learn more from their peers and from you. Why wouldn't you want to make that happen?

What Steinbeck Said: Post #36
Tuesday, December 13, 2016
Inner Circle

I love this week every year. Not because it's almost time for Christmas vacation, though it is. Not because I am having a ball watching my kids teaching each other, though I am. More than anything, these December days are special because I often hear from my students who have moved on. I used to call them "former" students, but that isn't really true. None of you who have ever graced my classroom will ever stop being my student. The koosh ball is just a longer throw now.

I received one of those wonderful e-mails this week. The type that always seems to come when I am weary from staying up late with essays or am slightly overwhelmed by responsibilities that loom, the type that always seems to know that I could use a chance to smile. This message came from a student who sat in our circle a few years ago. She wanted to let me know that she had recently been accepted into her university's honors program, and she credited our class with helping her develop the writing skills that enabled her to prepare a project proposal that led to her acceptance into the program. I assure you that this young woman came into our class as a fine writer. I did guide her as she refined her skills, but while I might show my students the clouds, it's up to them to find the wings to fly. Still, I loved her thank you note, just as I love it when my students return from campuses to see me in our classroom, regaling me with tales of their college adventures.

This week, as I reflected on my relationships with students both now and then, I saw the layers of our connections as concentric circles. The outermost circle consists of people who know me outside the classroom. These are family, friends, colleagues, parents who have one thing in common: they might be familiar with what others say about my teaching, but they have never been students in my classes. Oh, they may have even visited our room, may have observed me on a formal or an informal basis, but unless they have sat in the circle every other day, unless they have shared their minds in discussion and their hearts in their writing, they aren't part of the middle circle. Those of you who have been students in my classroom know me on a much deeper level than those who haven't. It's hard to explain the experience, isn't it? There is an intimacy born of our co-creativity, of those magical moments such as the ones that occurred today as my teams inspired remarkable interpretations of stories by Updike and Faulkner and Oates. There was a feeling that coursed through our class' bloodstream, a rush that we might try to explain to those family members, friends, and colleagues, but nonetheless a feeling that words cannot totally describe.

That brings us to the innermost circle. I'm sure that those of you who populate the other two have always realized that there was a deeper level, the one that has been locked inside of me all of these years. When I opened this blog at the beginning of the school year, I invited you all into that long hidden region, and for the past three months, I have explained what informs my teaching. It has been wonderful to hold this conversation with you, to connect with you in ways that we never have over the years. Thank you for reading, thank you for your likes and loves and comments. As for my part, I'll continue to share, and who knows? We might just find another circle!

L ate in her teaching career, my wife Teresa discovered *Music Learning Theory*, an approach developed by Edwin Gordon that describes musical acquisition as analogous to the way we learn language. One of the key elements of the theory is *audiation*, the phenomenon that occurs when we hear sounds in our minds and associate meaning with those sounds. A toddler might hear her parents talking and, wanting to join in on the fun, babble right along with the conversation. Audiation doesn't occur, however, until the child realizes that the sounds she is making are not the same as those that her parents are speaking. One aspect of Teresa's use of *MLT* was to determine whether her elementary students had developed the ability to audiate because, once they did, she could instruct them in a more sophisticated way. She liked to look for a cue that Gordon called "the audiation stare," a moment when a student suddenly realizes that what he or she is singing isn't what everyone else is. Kids basically shut down for a short while as if they are trying to figure out the discrepancy. In Teresa's mind, that was always a cause for celebration.

I had a celebration much like that once, and it involved the circles I spoke of in the previous post. For a couple of years, I participated in a group of teachers who took turns inviting each other into their classrooms to observe and study their teaching. We took one day a month, arranged for substitutes to cover our classes, and then spent the beginning of the morning going over the lesson plan. Sometimes we offered to take part in the teaching, while other times we watched and listened with specific intentions such as taking notes on transitions or checking for the level of engagement among targeted students. It was a fun way to learn more about teaching and about our colleagues, and perhaps my favorite part of each of those days came at the end when we met in a conference room to process what had transpired during the classes we had observed. The group also included our principals and our curriculum director, and their input added a great deal to our analysis.

On a day that I hosted the group, I sat with my colleagues at the end, answering questions about decisions that I had made and about my impressions of the lesson. One of my colleagues asked me why I began every period with a quotation, and I explained that the quote was the first of many layers each day. I chose a passage because it had some significance, whether it helped us focus on the content of a literary work we were reading or to serve as inspiration for a challenge my kids were facing. I went on to say that I sought to layer each part of the class period, to intertwine elements from the quote, the *Word of the Day*, maybe a writing piece we were working on or a chapter that we were discussing. It didn't necessarily all come together every day, but when it did, I felt like a weaver creating a tapestry. And when my students caught on, they gained entrance into the most fundamental layer, the innermost circle of my teaching.

After I explained my layered approach, the group went around in a circle giving their own feedback on the lesson and on my explanation. When my head principal's turn came, he stared at the table, apparently in thought. "Come back to me," he finally said. When everyone else had spoken, he looked up at me with tears in his eyes.

"I'm sorry I couldn't say anything before, but I was just trying to wrap my mind around what you said. Your lesson seemed so straightforward and simple. I had no idea of how complex it really was."

And right there, I understood exactly what Teresa was always looking for. The audiation stare. It was a moment when my principal, a man with whom I had shared many a good and long conversation about teaching, had an epiphany about what I had been doing all along when he visited my classroom.

Want to know where professional development needs to go? Right there. Workshops are fine, and I hope you find something valuable for each one you attend. Regional and national conferences can be useful, especially if you find a way to take your learning from them and apply it directly to your teaching. What will be tremendously valuable for you, however, will be the dialogue that you have with other teachers on the nature of your practices. It will go beyond planning together or sharing materials. It will delve into the meaning beneath your teaching, the layers that not everyone can see. If you will take the time to share your purposes with your colleagues, to ask them questions and to help them reflect, then you will help in some small way to create a tighter and more coherent educational system. As a teacher, you will in time know the depth of what you do. Sharing with others could add level upon level, circle within circle to everyone's understanding. That will be more precious than anything you'll take away from a workshop, a conference, or a class.

What Steinbeck Said: Post #37
Thursday, December 15, 2016
A Christmas Kiss

A tradition I began some thirty years ago happens at the end of the last class before Christmas vacation. No matter what is on the menu for the first hour of that period, we pause to gather in a circle on the floor and spend the last twenty minutes or so reflecting together. It's one of my favorite moments of the year.

Today, we began, of course, with a symbol. With the lights off and the shades down, I placed in the center of our circle a red candlestick in a pewter holder. After lighting it, I asked my students to tell me about the nature of a candle. We discussed its composition and how that contributes to the burning, how the wick conducts the melted wax to serve as fuel. We observed the flame and talked about its physics and its behavior, about the way it dances and the varying levels of heat we associate with its blue and black and yellow.

Once we established the attributes of the candle, I asked my kids to compare it to our class. Ideas buzzed around the circle.

"It's bright, like we are."

"As it burns down, the flame gets brighter, just like our learning is getting easier and easier to see."

"Near the top, the wax is almost transparent, but it's dark near the bottom. That's like the learning that we haven't had yet. Eventually it's going to come to light."

In the flickering glow, I saw smiling eyes.

"Even though each of us is an individual, as a class we have one flame. All of our learning shines together."

As I said, I love this moment.

Next, I asked my kids to think of something they're thankful for. I gave them no other directions other than to call for the koosh when the spirit moved them to share. It didn't take long. They expressed their gratitude for family, for friends. They spoke of their freedoms and their opportunities, of the benefits they enjoy living in a small Wyoming town. Sometimes a voice broke, and a few other times, tears were shed. When that happened, I took the time to remind my students of the gift that their classmates had just bestowed upon them. What greater way is there to demonstrate trust than to cry in the presence of friends?

After each student shared, I tossed her or him a Hershey's kiss. It was a small token, but on this cold and snowy day, as we sat around a tiny flame, it was a way for us to commune together. This was a quiet symbol, and while we didn't discuss its significance, I hoped that my kids saw those drops of chocolate as a sign of the sweet affection I have for each of them. As the clock ticked toward the ending bell, I shared my thanks, my appreciation for the opportunity to teach them and to learn with them. I leaned near the candle and told them just how excited I was for the weeks and months to come.

"You think you've gone deep so far?" I asked them. "Just wait till you see what we do second semester."

What lies ahead includes Of Mice and Men, Our Town, A Tale of Two Cities. *In* The Tempest, *Shakespeare tells us, "What is past is prologue." This will be true for my kids as we travel on together, for the best is yet to come.*

"Now, you might be thinking that if we're going away for a couple of weeks, what will happen to the light that has burned from the first day we came together? If that flame dies out while we're apart, how will we light it again?"

I looked around the circle. "You all know that there's magic in this room, don't you? So, even if that flame does go out, even if our candle grows cold, when we come back—" I lit another match, blew out the flame, and reignited it by lighting the smoke swirling above the wick. When the candle's light seem to magically return, the circle gasped as one.

"—we'll glow even brighter than we have before."

Merry Christmas!

That class period began with a thought-provoking quote from Frank Gaines: "Only he that can see the invisible can do the impossible." Perhaps, at the end, when I added my career all up, what we essentially did in our classroom was to strive to see the invisible. I know that as a teacher, that was my elusive quest, to help my students discover truths that lay within themselves, to see beyond the ordinary, beneath the surface. It wasn't my interpretation that I wanted them to see. Rather, it was their insight that mattered. My role was simply to get them to look.

How do you see the invisible? Not with ordinary eyes. That would be like trying to see through an iron door. So it was that year after year I sought metaphors and symbols to help them unlock that door. What they saw when it was opened was up to their imagination. The candle ceremony was one of many keys that I handed to my students, and as we sat shoulder to shoulder on the floor, it wasn't anything that I said that played a part in their understanding. It was more the opportunity that I gave them to observe the candle and its flame, to watch wax and wick come alive and to interpret the fire that burned before them. But that wasn't all.

After they offered their impressions of the candle and what it might mean, I encouraged them to share their gratitude. What they said in those intimate few minutes was important because it gave us a better sense of what each speaker felt, but what was more valuable was the feeling that we got of who we were becoming as a group. Each sharing was the lighting of another match, an addition to the flame that now burned more brightly in our collective heart. Maybe we learned that before we can see, before we can hear, we must first feel. In the quiet of that close circle on the last day before vacation, we felt something more powerful than we ever had before. And as I told my kids in a near whisper, we had so much more before us. At that point, one of my students pointed out that we weren't just looking at the candle. The candle was us, and it would light our way to that most important door. Once it opened, we knew that nothing would be impossible.

As with many of the methods and approaches that I am sharing with you, it's not the specific activities that matter, it is spirit with which you employ them. You don't have to light a candle at Christmas to get to know your students better, you don't have to share M&M's with them or read *The Old Man and the Sea*. You don't even have to teach language arts, though your life would most certainly more blessed if you did. What you do need to do is find ways to not only get more emotionally close to your kids but also to help them develop those kind of bonds with each other. That emotion is the fuel that they will burn together as a learning group, and the more it burns, the brighter they all will become.

What Steinbeck Said: Post #38
Monday, January 2, 2017
The Other Gold

ake new friends, but keep the old;
One is silver and the other, gold."

Today, I welcomed back my silver friends. After a two-week break, it was wonderful to see my students again. As I always do with my planning, this first week back is a gradual return to activity. We caught up with news from our vacations, and we learned that some people went as far away as Florida, while others nestled at home with family. Some went to concerts and bowl games, others read and read and read. Though we weren't far removed from the celebrations of New Year's Eve, the groups looked relaxed and glad to be with each other. I'm quite sure that the happiest was me.

My first gift to my students in the new year was practice with commas. A traditional present, right? It's definitely a useful one, but I also used it as a chance for us to concentrate a little and to have fun with each other. As the kids worked in pairs on an exercise of some twenty sentences, I walked about, answering questions and discussing nuances of punctuation. Commas are a challenge because there are so many rules, but I stressed the need for clarity that proper punctuation addresses. We talked about why leaving a comma out can be dangerous. Take the comma out of the sentence, "Let's eat, Grandma" and what do you have? Exactly. I also advised them that a confused professor is not likely to assign a high grade on a paper that muddles his thoughts. As we ended the session, I assured them that other seniors have been just where they are at this point in the year, and that by the time the last snow melts (I know, that might be June), they'll use commas pretty well. I'm not sure they believe that quite yet.

We also rehearsed for the first draft of our essay on short stories, and once again, I had the chance to talk with each student about her or his plans. This is the closeness that they might not experience in their college classes. I recall feeling a certain distance from my instructors unless I visited during office hours, but whenever I have a chance to co-create with my students, I honor the occasion. That's what felt so good about having them back in the circle today. As I had promised them when I blew out the candle before Christmas and relit it without touching the wick, we were going to step right back into the magic after New Year's. It sure felt that way today.

Today, I also welcomed back a few gold friends. Our guidance department had invited two dozen of our recent alumni to speak to seniors about their college experiences, and some stopped by to see me on their way in or their way out. I adore those reunions. I love seeing the confidence that my kids bring back to me, the strength that they have developed by making it through that first semester on campus. It's hugs and smiles and the look in their eyes that says, "I'm a little farther down the road than when I saw you last." Here's a secret for you all: I am, too!

I also love the fact that my current students often witness my excitement when an alumnus returns. I want them to see that they'll not only be welcome if they come back to the old classroom, but they will be cherished as well. After all, they're not that far from being those college kids home on break, not too far from being gold.

At that point in my final year of teaching, I really wasn't sure that it was going to be my last. Teresa and I had discussed the possibility of retirement, but we were still mulling over some things the day I wrote that post. Still, it was enough in my mind that I thought a bit wistfully about special occasions such as our return from vacation, wondering whether this would be the last time I would greet my students back from Christmas. Whether that group of seniors would ever be able to drop by Room 218 to say hello and tell me all about their college experiences. I didn't let on that either of those situations was possible, but the prospect of this being my last go-around certainly did touch my heart from time to time.

The longer I taught, the more I thought of my classroom as my home at school. In my early years, I decorated the walls of my room with posters and art work to inspire my students, but I mostly cared about creating a functional environment. It was a while before I started adding more personal touches such as family photographs, my diplomas, and such creature comforts such as an electric tea kettle and a microwave. I bought paper plates and plastic utensils to store in my cupboards, boxes of Lipton and Truvía and chocolates to store in my desk drawers. While I reserved the walls of my classroom for student-made work, I did find a way to make my own little corner of the room quiet homey. After all, I spent as many waking hours there as I did in our house.

In time, I sensed that my students saw 218 as their home as well. Sure, they had a lot of sisters and brothers to share it with, but they were quite protective of the space. When the counselors asked to use my room for ACT testing and my students stopped by for a second before school, they seemed truly shocked by the sight of rows in place of their familiar circle. When visitors came into the room to observe my teaching, my kids seemed to take pride in their home, but they also showed a certain wariness toward those strangers. And my poor substitute teachers! The kids often told me that, nice as the sub had been, they wished I wouldn't upset their routine like that ever again. I tried not to.

That's why I loved seeing those joyful expressions on the faces of my alumni when they appeared at my door in December and early January. While I rarely hugged my students while they were enrolled, those returning from college were gleefully embraced. That was a perk granted upon graduation, and on that first day back, having excused myself for a few minutes to catch up with two visitors, I returned to the circle, knowing that the kids sitting there might never experience a moment like the one they had just witnessed. I let them remain in their blissful ignorance and picked up where we had been. Perhaps, I thought, there would be other ways for them to capture that feeling someday.

I encourage you to try something when you go about getting yourself settled into your first school. As you work to transform a sterile space into a welcoming environment, take some time to visit other classrooms in the building. Check to see which of them are inviting, grounded in emotion and affection, places that open imaginations and celebrate young hearts. Check, too, to see which rooms look more institutional. Nothing more than desks and hardware, walls adorned only with rules and reminders. As you make your tour, use your ears as well as

149

your eyes. Note who is speaking as you visit. Is it primarily the teacher, or do you hear younger voices? What is the energy level in the room? Is there an excited buzz or a low hum? In other words, does the classroom belong just to the teacher, or does it belong to the students as well? Teresa and I may have owned our house when our children were growing up, but by all accounts, it was as much their place as it was ours. The question is, what message are you going to send your students when they first walk into the classroom that you all will share for the year? Will they see themselves as visitors or as family members coming home to learn each day?

What Steinbeck Said: Post #39
Wednesday, January 4, 2017
Scaling Down our Practice

A s musicians, we love to play pieces, to sing songs. We enjoy the beauty of a polished performance, and yet, if we are to reach a high level, we have to practice in a variety of ways. There are scales and exercises to do, techniques to refine. We learn difficult sections at a slow tempo and then increase the speed as we become more adept with our playing.

We are applying those same elements to our classroom this week. While as individuals we have begun drafting our short story essay, we have spent our time together as a class working on the fundamentals of college writing. That practice has included exercises with comma punctuation and with writing clinchers at the end of paragraphs. We have also examined a sample literary analysis to examine subtleties in structure. As author James Collins wrote, it's a matter of finding ways of taking our writing from "good to great."

I have kept our class menu simple this week, allowing time for kids to collaborate on our exercises and time for me to meet with them all to discuss the effectiveness of their practice. This was especially important today as I looked over their clinchers, those final sentences that not only summarize the evidence in the paragraph but also show how that information relates to the thesis. At this point in their writing careers, seniors know how to clinch by rephrasing the topic sentence, but they don't always understand how to return to the paper's main idea and its impact. It's hard to concentrate on any one particular aspect when writing an essay because there are so many features to which we must attend, and that's why it was critical that we took the time today to narrow our focus to just one piece of the puzzle. In a sense, we worked on the musical scales of our writing, and we'll see how that practice transfers to our essays at week's end. I anticipate some pretty sweet tunes coming my way.

In each class, we had ten or fifteen minutes left at the end of the period, and I decided that my kids needed a little levity, so we played Spell Down. *It's a game that gets them on their feet, gets them thinking, and most importantly, gets them laughing with each other. After working hard in pairs, it gave us a chance to play as a class, to appreciate everyone's good humor. As the first semester nears its end, we are growing closer and closer as classes, depending more on each other for help and for support. We're right where I want us to be, and now comes the great work of the year in the next five months. Stay tuned, my friends. The best is truly yet to come.*

I have always believed that analogy was the soul of great teaching. In school, when I labored to learn a concept, I found little comfort in my teacher repeating what she had already told me during her instruction. I did much better when I was presented with another way to think about the problem. An example of that came when I was learning to play the piano. One day as I was working through some easy exercises and feeling pretty good about my progress, Teresa sat down next to me and suggested that I was holding my hands too low over the keyboard, essentially my wrists below my fingers.

"If you're going to play better, you'll have to keep your hands arched," she told me. I tried to do that, but she shook her head.

"Like this," she said, holding her hands in a classic posture. I tried to imitate her, but I was still not doing it quite right. A less-skilled teacher would have told me to watch again and try harder, but Teresa is truly gifted.

"All right," she said with a smile. "Let's use something you understand. Put your hands out as if each one was holding a softball."

That was easy. I did as she asked, and she smiled more broadly. "That's it!" she said. She stood and started to walk away. "Just remember to do that every time."

I'd like to say that I did just that, but after a few more weeks of exploring the instrument, I decided that I was better suited to playing guitar. Maybe it was just a matter of being able to take my case wherever I wanted when it was time practice, to not be confined to the living room, but what ended up being important was not so much what I learned about hand placement that day but my wife's reminder of the power of examples in teaching.

It would have been nice if all of my students had been musicians or athletes who were used to drilling and practicing elements of their playing. Those kids who did knew the importance of breaking down their performances in order to focus on particular skills, knew that perseverance was necessary to improve beyond a basic level. In reality, I had lots of students who knew very little about how to practice anything. Oh, I'm sure they had interests such as video games that required them to develop skills, but rebooting a game and starting over is not the same as picking out a three-measure run and playing it ten times in a row on your clarinet or practicing three-foot putts again and again and again. When I wanted to reach those kids and help them understand the importance of intense, focused practice, I had to seek other ways, especially if they were not used to having much success in school. Sometimes all I could ever really do was set aside a few minutes during class so that I could work directly with those students individually or in small groups. When I was young in the profession, I was impatient with those moments because I felt that we were wasting precious time doing things that my kids should have come into the class able to do. It wasn't till much later in my career that I learned how much fun it could be to help struggling students master basic skills. There were days when I felt that I was having much more fun teaching than they were having learning, but I somehow got past that notion.

What was the secret? It all went back to relationships. When I sat next to a ninth grader who could not grasp the concept of topic sentences—and frankly, couldn't have cared less to learn it—I spent a good part of our time together working on *us*. I used humor, I used my knowledge of his experience outside of class, I let him know that I believed that he could eventually figure things out. Some days I spent far more time building trust than I did instructing on language principles, but in the long run, it was the fact that we worked together on a problem that enabled my challenged students to learn some secrets of studying as well as a variety of approaches to learning. In that case, it didn't matter that I taught English. My more important task was to help my kids develop their thinking skills, their questioning skills, their persistence. If they learned to write well and had a chance to read good literature, all the better, but if my kids left my class at the end of May knowing more about how to learn, then I had accomplished my mission.

It will be easy for you to tap into the interests of some of your students because you'll know them outside of your classroom. They might live in your neighborhood, or they might be the daughter or son of a friend. They might be the brother or sister of a student you taught two years earlier or the friend of one of those kids. You can also learn something about your kids by going to their games or their concerts, but I'm not going to suggest that setting aside that time after a long day will be easy for you. There will be nights when you're too tired to leave the house or too busy preparing for the next day, and while I know that you might not want to sit through two hours of *The King and I*, whenever you make the effort to attend an activity, you will give yourself an opportunity to learn more about your school's students, even the ones who aren't enrolled in your classes. And you know what? Even if you don't personally know a sprinter you watch compete in a dual meet after school, you cannot overestimate the power of catching that kid's eye in the hall the next day and saying, "Good race last night." It might not seem like much to you at the time, but that student might just end up sitting in your classroom the next year or the year after that, and you'll have at least one connection point with that kid from day one.

It's pretty simple, really. The more that you know about your students, the easier it will be for you to conjure parallels and metaphors to help them understand what they don't comprehend. And the more often you and your students find a way to work through a challenge together, the better the chance that they will try to overcome the next problem on their own. Success breeds success, and when that happens, word will get around. Kids tend to tell their friends which teachers are willing to devote extra time to help, which teachers have a knack for making material easier to grasp. Even if it might not always seem that way, kids do want to learn. They want to find people who can help them, too, and when they sign up for your classes, they will do so with the expectation that they will do whatever it takes to achieve because they've heard that when kids walk into your room, they're important to you. They will believe that their hard work will have rewards. Believe it or not, all of that success may just come back to the fact that you went to hear the band and noticed who played alto sax.

What Steinbeck Said: Post #40
Friday, January 6, 2017
Out of Love

F*riday my kids had a responsibility due in Google Classroom. The plan was for them to submit their first drafts of our short story essay so that they could share with a partner in class. As we've done all year, I had a set of directions ready to go, but as I checked each student's assignment on my computer at the beginning of the period, I saw that only one kid had completed a draft. That's one out of seventy for my three sections. What should I do in that case? I had a few minutes to decide.*

One thing I could do was lecture my classes. I certainly did that years ago. I made it clear that I wasn't happy with their effort, questioned their work ethic, reminded them that this was a college class. All of that. For the most part, that worked because kids know what they're expected to do. In this case, however, it was, with that one exception, every student who had failed to meet the due date. Something was different.

I contemplated possible reasons for the situation. Had the kids enough time

154

to complete the draft? I had assigned it on Monday, giving them four nights to put something together. As I have told them many times, first drafts do not have to be polished, simply completed. I could understand a number of kids not being ready, but all of them? The time allotted didn't seem to be the answer. Were the kids preoccupied with other classes or activities? I supposed that could be true, but they've been busy all year. That didn't really explain the lack of readiness. I at last decided that the kids just didn't see the value of sharing their paper with a partner. They knew that I would be checking their second drafts, and so perhaps they just didn't push themselves. After all, they don't receive effort grades, and so there was no real penalty for not having the assignment done. Yeah, that was probably it.

As I prepared to speak to my classes and adjust the lesson, I ultimately decided that the cause didn't matter. We were either going to make good use of the time remaining in the period, or we weren't. As gently as I could, I told my kids that we were going to work to complete the draft in the next thirty minutes. I received no resistance. As the clock ticked, I went around the circle, conferring with each student to not only check status but to also give advice on how to proceed. Some kids wanted me to check their thesis, others weren't sure how to begin. A few had yet to choose a story to write about. By the time the bell rang, I had helped each of my students in some way.

I could have chosen my actions from two places on Friday. One could have been from fear. If I was afraid of setting a precedent by not punishing my students, I could have given them a piece of my mind. I could have let them know that this dereliction was never going to be acceptable, that they darned well better have their next drafts ready ON TIME. At what cost, however? Instead, I chose to act out of compassion. I forgave them for not fulfilling their responsibilities, even though I never used those words. Instead, I simply moved on and did what I do best. I listened. I encouraged.

I loved.

I've been doing this a long time, and I know that teaching from love eventually brings the best out of my students. It may not make a great difference on this essay, but in time, my kids will work harder than they've ever worked *before. That's worth waiting for.*

I f William Glasser taught me more about choice, then Neale Donald Walsch taught me more about love. More than twenty years into my teaching, I read *Conversations with God*, and suddenly what I had thought I had known about love and fear and joy were suddenly illuminated in a whole new way. Glasser had written in *The Quality School* that one of the basic tenets of a choice-driven school is the driving out of fear. In his book, Walsch explains that every human action is grounded in either fear or love. Quoting his dialogue with God, Walsch says that "fear is the energy which contracts, closes down, draws in, runs, hides, hoards, harms. Love is the energy which expands, opens up, sends out, stays, reveals, shares, heals."

Those words spoke to me in a way that no other writing had. A child of the fifties and sixties, I had been immersed in a culture of fear, of warnings and threats and consequences for my sins and mistakes. That is how it was at home, at church, at school. I never knew any more powerful motivator than fear, and it was understandable that I used it as a tool in my early years of teaching. It's what I knew. It's what my students knew. Suddenly, a voice Walsch attributes to God was telling me that in order to achieve my highest self, I would naturally choose love.

Choose love.

It seems incredibly simple, but that's what I started doing in my life. When I disagreed with someone and considered how to express my side, I thought about what I could say based on fear and then what I could say based on love. As Glasser taught me, everything I said to someone would either bring us closer or drive us farther apart. I found that, with some practice, I could counter someone's idea in a loving way. When I wanted to discipline our children, I thought about how I could do it in an affectionate manner. It all came down to being who I wanted to be in any situation, not acting out of fear that my choice might cause me problems later but instead choosing to be kind and loving.

I took that same approach with me to my classroom. By no means had I been an ogre for twenty years as a teacher, but now I devoted myself to behaving as if

I truly loved my students. Of course, all teachers say that they love their kids, but I began to wonder whether the manner in which I treated my students in difficult situations reflected that I actually did love them. Did I treat them the same as I did Ellen and Paul?

As I reflected more and more, I realized that there was always a little bit of a distance between me and my students that didn't exist between Teresa and me, between our children and me. There were many reasons to explain that gap, and they all related to fear. I was afraid that if I always came from love, some of my students might take advantage of the situation and manipulate me the way I knew that they played their parents. I was afraid that my colleagues and my principals would see me as a weak disciplinarian, a bleeding heart. I was afraid that if I used the word *love* in the classroom, someone might think I had inappropriate intentions. None of these were by any means irrational reasons, but perhaps that was the problem. I was approaching the situation with my head and not my heart. I thought of Joseph Campbell's suggestion that the mind "is a secondary organ; it's a secondary organ of a total human being, and it must not put itself in control." I knew that I needed to, in more of Campbell's words, follow my bliss, and that meant to lead with love.

The choice to love wasn't something that I taught to my students, just as my spirituality wasn't something that I passed directly along to them. As a teacher, you can be spiritual without making it a part of your curriculum, and you can be joyful without instructing students on how to achieve that feeling. Yet, all of those elements were present in my room indirectly. It was just who I was when I was around my kids. I couldn't help it. When they walked into my room each day, I felt love, I felt joy, and I felt the spirit that somehow connected us all. As the year went on, I'm sure they felt all of those as well. That's why there was a such a special energy that had a home in Room 218. That's why I loved going there every day. You can do the same. If you find yourself happy each time that the bell rings to start a class period, if you feel just the slightest bit disappointed when it rings to end the class, then you will surely have a long and rewarding career. I don't know, just a feeling.

Budding

E ach flower now taller and stronger, our garden was green and growing. Buds were appearing as our skills were surfacing. I continued to tend and nourish by moistening my students' minds with ideas and their hearts with hope, but I was also giving them opportunities to grow on their own. That meant more options for exploration, more chances to work together as teams in order to create their own learning. I kept an eye out for weeds or frost, but my kids were getting heartier every day, excited to keep reaching toward the sky. As a veteran gardener, I knew that some of those buds were liable to pop at any time, but I also knew that each flower was unique. Some were slow to develop and needed a little extra care, others needed a little extra space to grow more quickly. As a stem that was growing myself, I delighted in finding new ways to nurture my students. The first semester was coming to a close, and we were ready for a dramatic change, the conditions right for taking our learning to an entirely new level. My kids were definitely starting to appreciate the beauty of our communal flourishing, but they had no idea of just how spectacular the garden was about to become.

What Steinbeck Said: Post #41
Tuesday, January 10, 2017
Fade In

*M*y students' lives changed today. Oh, not in any way that anyone would notice. No one got any smarter. No one got any prettier or more handsome. No one won the lottery. All we did was begin our reading of Of Mice and Men. Some of my kids had read Steinbeck's little gem in middle school, most did not. All are about to experience literature in a way they have never imagined, about to see layer upon layer of meaning.

"Though this book appears to be a novel," I said before I began my guided reading of Chapter One, "it is, in effect, a six-act play. As each chapter opens, Steinbeck pulls back the curtains to reveal the set. Once that we as readers have observed the scenery, he brings characters in. That will be true of every chapter, and if you'll please join me on page one, we'll see just what there is to see."

I then read aloud the first two paragraphs of the novel without pause. When I finished, I asked my students to take two minutes on their Chromebooks to look up whatever they wanted to learn more about from the passage. Some looked up the location of Soledad and the Salinas River and learned that both are found in north-central California. Others searched for images of sycamore trees and the definition of recumbent. My purpose with this brief interlude was to give power to my kids to learn what they desired, to send once again a message that we will build interpretations together, that they will not have to wait for me to teach it to them.

When that brief discussion ended, I asked the class to help me construct the novel's initial setting in our classroom. "I'll start," I said, pointing to the wall to the right of our windows. "Let's stipulate that the Gabilan Mountains are over there." I pointed to the carpet. "The Salinas River runs through here, and there's a pool that we can place over there." I then asked the kids to fill in the rest of the scenery, and we established where the sycamore limb was, where the ash pile lay. We looked to the wall opposite the mountains to imagine the highway and ranches beyond. This is a critical step in our understanding of the novel on *different levels. On Thursday, we'll see the dichotomy that Steinbeck has created in this setting, the river of life that separates the wild from the domestic.*

I read on. George and Lennie appeared, and the kids grinned to hear my take on the latter's voice. I know I overplay it, but at this point in the proceedings, it's important to paint the contrast between the two friends. I read Lennie as childlike in Chapter One because his underlying menace isn't available to us yet. Instead, we focused today on his animal-like qualities. He's described as a bear, a horse, a dog. We start building sympathy for him from page two, and if we can giggle at his mannerisms early, his later behaviors will be all the more powerful.

The bell rang as George discovered that Lennie was carrying a dead mouse in his pocket. As good a place as any to stop because when we continue our reading, we'll see not only George's frustration with Lennie but also their shared dream. Steinbeck lays this foundation flawlessly, and next week when we discuss Chapters Two and Three, we'll learn how he builds on that base. In the meantime, we have rabbits to meet!

Over the course of my career, I developed a deeply personal relationship with a great number of literary works. I loved that each fall I got to return to Maycomb, Alabama and introduce my students to Scout and Jem and Atticus. I was honored to travel with the Joads to California, and I forever held that masterpiece in awed respect. Each time I read the opening to *A Tale of Two Cities*, I marveled at Dickens' command of language. Yet, were I to fill a bookcase with all the novels, stories, poems, and plays that I shared with my students, *Of Mice and Men* would occupy a most special spot. Oh, it wouldn't be the first cover your eye would light upon, and you wouldn't even find it on the top shelf. No, I'm thinking you'd discover the book in a corner near the bottom of the case, tucked away as it always has been in my heart. I'm not sure if it was Steinbeck's incredible character development or the connection I made between Lennie and my two special needs brothers, but there was something singular about that compact story that transported me every time I opened to its first page and, with Steinbeck's words, began painting the setting for my students.

It's hard to describe the feeling a teacher has when channeling the genius of a great artist. I sat in the circle with my students and read aloud, "A few miles south of Soledad, the Salinas River drops in close to the hillside bank and runs deep and green," imagining that this was how as a conductor felt signaling the downbeat for a symphony, how a minister felt standing before a couple about to exchange wedding vows. This was sacred territory, and I was privileged to step into that space time and time again. As I continued reading the remainder of the novel's first page up to its first break, I held one fervent wish, to read that initial portion without error, with just the right inflections and tempo. I didn't always meet that expectation, but when I did, I felt that I had not only served the work, but I had also done my students a service by not distracting them from the solemnity of the story's dawning.

Why was that important? Would a slip or a rushed phrase ruin the experience for my kids? Would they even notice that I stuttered on a word or truncated a suffix? I never asked them, and while I was sometimes anguished to disturb the flow with a narrative mistake, there were times when I exulted as my performance approached art. When that happened, it was a quiet joy, something between the author and me, but in that final year, on that last run through *Of Mice and Men*, I sensed that my seniors knew that something special might be happening. They would know for sure in a few short weeks.

What can you take away from my experience? Well, it is by no means a call for you to seek perfection in your interactions with your students. That's not what drove me to create a pristine performance of Steinbeck's words. I didn't concentrate just so my kids would marvel at my reading ability or sit in awe at my artistic sensibility. I simply didn't want to get in the way. I saw myself as a conduit from the author's mind to their ears, and I did what I could to keep that channel clear. The same will apply to you whenever you present material to your classes, whether it comes in the form of a dramatic reading or an explanation of a process. It won't be about you. Instead, it will be about how your kids find ways to get in touch with things that will enrich their lives. Will they appreciate your contribution? Some will. There will always be those kids who pay close attention not only to what you say but how you say it. Others may seem oblivious to your effort, but I wouldn't worry too much about whether everyone in your class understands your role in the dynamic as long as they comprehend the communication. In any event, you can find satisfaction in knowing that your students had a special moment without distraction. The more often that happens, the better for all of you.

What Steinbeck Said: Post #42
Thursday, January 12, 2017
Adding a Dimension

*W*e continued our reading of Chapter One of Of Mice and Men *today, and while we got to know the characters of Lennie and George more fully, we perhaps got to know John Steinbeck even better. This was a day to discover the foundation of the novel, and it was also a moment to observe the writer's craft. I asked my students to develop the former, and I took the lead on the latter. This is just another example of the power of co-creativity, and we all worked to our strengths.*

For years, these kids have been interpreting characterization and symbolism. When I asked them to brainstorm traits for the two men, they readily rattled off lists that were insightful and accurate. When we reviewed the setting, I suggested that the river might represent life, and they quickly shared ways that the metaphor would be true. They decided that the mountains on one side of the Salinas represent wilderness, while the valley on the other side, with its ranches and its highway, stands for civilization. As I read the conversation between George and Lennie, we continually picked up on imagery that gave us a finer understanding of the nature of their relationship. Lennie at this point seems innocent and even pitiable. George, the kids pointed out, is more than frustrated.

As for the author's craft, I did a lot of pointing today.

"Look at this."

"Think about that."

"What's going on, here?"

I explained that Steinbeck often interrupts the dialogue to give us a look at the scenery. In one paragraph he mentions a carp rising from the depths of the pool, forming rings on the surface and then returning to the "mysterious deep." I asked kids what they knew about that species, and they told me that carp are bottom feeders.

"Here," I said, "we have a creature that comes up from the dark, stirs things up, and returns. Do you think this might be a bit of foreshadowing?" I also asked the kids to think back to where they'd seen rings on the surface earlier in the chapter. When they answered, "Lennie," I waited until someone made the connection between him and the carp. What deep dark secret does Lennie hold for us?

My favorite part of the day was more subtle. We have a large, framed poster of John Steinbeck hanging on our classroom wall, and whenever I read a particularly brilliant piece of writing in the novel, I point to the author's image and say, "This guy's good." There were two such examples today. One came as George asks Lennie to go get some wood to build a fire. Steinbeck writes that "Lennie lumbered to his feet." Isn't that wonderful? I imagine the author writing, "Lennie rose to his feet," and then shaking his head and retyping with a hint of a smile. Another instance came when we read that Lennie considered crossing the river to escape to the "nature side" of the valley. "Lennie looked wildly across the river." Of course, he did.

Noticing the writer's craft is like viewing a 3-D poster. It might seem at first to be nothing more than a colorful pattern, but once someone teaches us to look at the print differently, we suddenly see the hidden image in depth. I spent today teaching my kids how to focus their eyes in a new way, how to patiently let the picture change to reveal its treasure. With practice, they'll be able to find that meaning without me pointing at all. When that happens, literature will never be the same for them.

any years ago, I had a student who I affectionately nicknamed "Mr. Literal." It seemed that whenever we discussed metaphor or symbolism as a class, he would raise his hand and say with a tinge of disgust, "Do you really think he meant to do that?" Did I really think that Norman Maclean meant to compare the Big Blackfoot River to life? Why, yes, I did. Did I really think that director Stuart Rosenberg meant to portray the title character in *Cool Hand Luke* as a Christ figure? Well, yeah. Whenever I answered his questions in the affirmative, Mr. Literal would roll his eyes, shake his head, and mutter, "Whatever." He couldn't believe that authors would represent ideas in a figurative fashion, saw no utility in it. He was an excellent math and science student, and though I had no idea whether he was colorblind, it was clear that Mr. Literal saw the world in black and white. At first, I was a bit exasperated when he would challenge my interpretations as if they were nothing more than fantastic nonsense, but after a while, we had fun with the game, even to the point of him seeming to relish the moniker I had bestowed upon him. As the year progressed, he even started to concede that perhaps, just maybe, there was something going on under the surface of a story, but I don't think he ever truly bought into the idea.

I thought about Mr. Literal from time to time I asked my kids to consider different layers of meaning in a piece of literature, and I even had a few other students who took a similar tack, though never to the extent that the master had. I kept those skeptics in mind whenever we delved into the writer's craft, for while I wanted to provide lots of windows through which my students could peer into into a story, I wanted to avoid imposing my own takes on what the author intended. I remembered my college literature classes, when my professors were lecturing on the deeper meanings of Dreiser and Howells and O'Neill, and I felt incredibly inadequate, almost stupid for missing those symbols in my reading of the texts. What was worse, there always seemed to be classmates who could engage in discussions with our profs, who could hang with them in those interpretations. Maybe that's why I felt some empathy for Mr. Literal, perhaps even some admiration. I had been in his place, struggling to see the hidden image in the 3-D poster, but I had not possessed his courage to speak up, to question and to ask for clarity.

Pointing out Steinbeck's wordplay in Chapter One was fun, but the key lay in how I did it. I invited my classes to become co-conspirators with the author, to in a sense, place a finger to our noses like characters in *The Sting* and indicate that we were in on the job. Of course, there were times when my kids suggested symbols that were a bit more than farfetched, but it was critical that we maintained a sense of possibility, again, that embrace of ambiguity. That's how my students and I built a culture of wonder and discovery in our classroom, and that's how you will do the same. You will find incredible power in allowing your kids opportunity after opportunity to create their own analyses, their own explanations. That might seem time-consuming at first because it will simply take longer for you to let them learn by doing rather than by just reading or listening, and they will surely flounder a bit when you invite them into the pool of interpretation to swim beside you, but once that dynamic is finally established, you won't believe the power that you'll all have together. In the end, it won't be about how smart you look to your students, it will be about how much they learn with each other and teach to each other. Yes, you can open the door, and invite your kids to enter a new way of thinking, but please be patient if it takes them a while to make their way through that entrance.

What Steinbeck Said: Post #43
Tuesday, January 17, 2017
Walk the Character

*W*e do a lot of talking in our circle. That's the nature of a language arts class—the development of interpretative and communicative skills— and my students are well-versed in analysis and support for their ideas. As I said last week, however, our unit for Of Mice and Men takes them down a whole new path in interacting with a text. Today was no different.

Because of a snow day last Wednesday, our school shuffled the class schedule for today, finishing semester exams in the morning and then kicking off the second semester of our classes in the afternoon. To accommodate that arrangement, two of my classes were forty-five minutes and the other was thirty (please don't ask). That didn't give us much time for our plan to discuss Chapters Two and Three, but it did allow for a different approach. We began with a familiar task as I asked my kids to visualize how our classroom could represent Steinbeck's description of the bunkhouse. We determined where the windows were set and how large they were, where the bunks lay, where the stove sat, where to place the table and chairs. They did this all pretty well because we visualize often in school.

That accomplished, I explained that we were going to understand character by going beyond visualization to actualization. The traditional means of characterizing involve what one says, what one does, and how one is described by the author and by other characters. Again, this practice is achieved primarily by talking about it or perhaps writing about it, but years ago I decided to find another mode. Today we walked before we talked.

"Tell you what," I said to my kids. "In order to get a better feel for each character, you have to consider Atticus Finch's advice to his daughter, Scout. You have to walk in that person's shoes." I asked them to go out to the hall, and I gave them a minute to decide with each other how they would walk back into our classroom/bunkhouse as the boss of the ranch. I made a path by moving two desks away from the circle and then waited across the room from the door.

It took the kids a while to decide which characteristics to reveal through their gaits, but eventually, one or two brave souls entered the room in the manner of the portly man. Some walked with their thumbs hooked in belt loops, and some affected a bowlegged stride. Many strode into the room with a steely gaze, and there were some who just came in as they do every day. When all were in, we processed their decisions. We talked about what informed their choices and determined that their moves reflected the boss' power, his sense of authority.

In the next few minutes the kids walked back out to the hall as themselves and returned as Slim, George, Lennie, Curley, and finally, Curley's wife. With each turn we learned more about their traits as we first felt what it was to be that character and then explained that feeling based on the character's words, actions, and description. With each turn we laughed with each other as we strutted and loped and preened and swayed. Most importantly, we felt.

On Thursday, we will build on that feeling by interpreting character motivations based on what we know about each one. As we discuss interactions between Curley and Lennie and between George and Slim, I will ask my students to remember their walks with those characters. In doing so, we will draw on a skill that we rarely develop in school.

Do you feel me?

M ind the rules."
"Keep this in mind."
"Do I have to remind you again?"

It seems that teachers spend a lot of time talking about their students' heads. That would be all right if all learning took place between our ears, but you know as well as I do that we learn with our entire bodies. Look at a dancer swaying to the beat of the music before beginning her steps. Watch a tennis player hitting shots against a wall, adjusting his body each time the ball comes back to him at a slightly different angle. Every day in gymnasiums, music rooms, and industrial technology shops, students go out of their minds with learning. They get in touch with their physical senses and their emotions, and they push themselves to go beyond what they thought were their performance limits. Why can't they do the same thing in an academic classroom?

Turning our classroom into a virtual representation of the novel's settings allowed my students in a sense to sit inside the book as they interpreted it. I asked my kids to walk like Steinbeck's characters to give them a chance to experience the novel in a novel way. For some of them, the exercise was heaven because their primary preference for learning was tactile/kinesthetic. They loved not only being free to get up and move during class but also to learn in that mode. At the same time, those kids who were more visual or auditory by nature needed a chance to stretch their style preferences a bit. If you had sat next to me and watched my seniors enter the room in the ways they perceived those characters' traits, you would have seen that the first few walkers for each round came in with enthusiasm, followed by a stream of kids who looked a bit sheepish as they performed the gait as best as they could. There was always a kid or two who waited till the line was almost through so that there would be a bigger audience for a dramatic interpretation. Those performers were always rewarded with heartfelt laughter. And almost always, the last student to walk into the room clearly wasn't going to play the game, exerting absolutely no effort whatsoever to climb inside of anyone's shoes.

I had choices with those deadpan students. I could have encouraged them to have a little fun, or I could have just ignored their lack of engagement and moved on. I had a pretty good idea that kids who seemed reluctant to step outside of themselves were afraid of drawing attention to themselves, but I often took a chance and reached out to them with humor. "I've got to hand it to you, Carla," I might say when we had completed the exercise, "you are one subtle actress. I had to look really hard to see the difference each time you walked in." This would invariably invoke some gentle chuckles from the rest of the group and almost always a hint of a smile on the shy student I had addressed. I may have been risking embarrassment on the part of the Carlas I had in every class, but I thought it was worth it if there was a possibility that I had strengthened my relationship with those kids by giving them some public attention. You never know, it could be that they were like middle school students at a dance, standing against the wall but secretly hoping for someone to walk over and ask them out onto the floor. It takes courage for young people to step out in front of their classmates and perform, but it also takes some daring to draw them out of their comfort zones and into a powerful learning situation.

Leonard Bernstein once declared that music completely bypasses the mind and goes "straight to the gut." I often held the maestro's words in my mind as I planned my lessons, asking myself not only what my students would be thinking during a class period but also what they might be feeling. In the long run, the latter was what really inspired a deeper form of the former. It's just another example of educating the whole child, and if that is truly what you want to accomplish, then you can't be afraid of your students' feelings, even if they aren't readily expressed.

What Steinbeck Said: Post #44
Thursday, January 19, 2017
Doggone

*M*y classes had so much to talk about today as we discussed Chapters *Two* and *Three of* Of Mice and Men. *There were characters to define, plot elements to explore. As we usually do, my students opened the circle by asking questions and selecting topics to look at. This process fascinates me because over the course of three class periods, those openings are remarkably different. They require me to listen carefully so that I might better facilitate the flow. In a discussion like today's, that flow was crucial because Steinbeck uses his second chapter to set up his third. I spent the better part of an hour in each class listening to comments, asking follow-up questions and directing the conversation so that we could somehow understand the context created for the action that occurs later.*

My lesson plan called for us to look at a number of symbols sometime during our discussion, and where that examination fell depended on the twists and turns of each conversation. In one class, I addressed all of those ideas at the end of the period. In another, one of the kids brought up a symbol as our first topic. In the third we sprinkled them here and there. It was my call as to when we would move from plot and character to symbol. It's all part of the artistry of teaching.

My favorite moment in each discussion came about as we listed dog references that Steinbeck has made in the book to this point. As the kids ticked them off, I wrote on the SMART board: Lennie as a dog, Candy's dog, Slim's dog and her puppies, a coyote calling on one side of the river and a dog answering from the other. Eventually, we arrived at the word bitch. *Having already covered the use of taboo words, I took my classes through the evolution of the word in our society. They knew that a bitch is a female dog, and I told them about my mother scolding me for "bitching" when I whined to her. She just seemed to grow tired of hearing that doglike sound coming from me. We talked about the use of the term to demean women.*

"Did you know," I asked my kids, "that there is a dog term that applies to

men?" When no one answered, I walked back over to the board and wrote cur, *explaining that the word is derived from a German word that means "to growl." There are cur dogs that are mixed breeds, and while they can be male or female, to call a man a* cur *is to hold him in contempt. After my explanation, I waited for the information to sink in. Once I saw a few eyes widen, I turned back to the board.*

"So, Steinbeck has created a character named 'Curley.'" Once more to the board, where I wrote Cur-ly.

"We take a word that refers to a man as a dog, and we add a suffix that means 'having the qualities of.'" Mouths dropped open.

"How is Curley like a dog?" I continued. The kids quickly pointed out that he is aggressive, that he likes to bark and to attack. One student suggested that he marks his territory, while another reminded us that other characters refers to his wife as a "bitch."

We weren't finished with our canine inspection. If Steinbeck presents these allusions throughout the first three chapters, then surely he is inviting us to make other connections that involve dogs, isn't he? We turned our focus to the relationship between Candy and his ancient Airedale. Because the author draws a clear comparison between the old man and his old dog, the euthanasia performed by Carlson casts a troubling shadow over Candy's prospects on the ranch. If an animal is killed because it no longer serves a useful purpose, can an elderly and crippled worker hope to keep his job for long?

Right now, I'm throwing a lot at my students. There are so many layers to this novel, and as we hop from level to level in our discussions, I know that they are a bit overwhelmed with how it all comes together. That's OK. I want my kids to learn to embrace ambiguity, not despair of it. They might be chasing their own tails at the moment, but eventually, they'll find the scent to track. At that point, I can unleash them to explore without my direction.

One of the gifts that comes with teaching English is the depth of interpretation that we develop by reading and discussing the same work for years and years. You might think that after a few tries I grew tired of bringing out *Julius Caesar* or "My Papa's Waltz," but that never seemed to be the case. After a while, I developed an intimate relationship with a piece, and I benefited from ideas generated by my students or research that I did in order to delve more deeply into a book's character. Sometimes I just made my own discoveries. That's a present I loved sharing with my classes.

Of Mice and Men was probably the novel I danced with more than any other. Some years I read just an excerpt in service of a teaching point, other years I set aside several weeks so that we could make a detailed study. Sometimes in digging farther down in my analysis I would come across one of those glittering nuggets hidden beneath the surface of the book, an insight into the author's deeper art. The Cur-ly idea came to me one year late in my career when I was writing on the board. I stepped back, wonderfully amused at suddenly realizing another gem of word play that Steinbeck had buried in his book. This was beyond the "lumbered off" and "glanced wildly" examples that I had pointed out a few days before. No, this was a window into the character's nature, a key to unlock an extended metaphor that ran throughout the story.

Of course, whenever I told my kids that I had just noticed something about our reading, they would let me know that they weren't having any of that nonsense.

"Sure, Mr. Stemle. You just saw that. Right."

"No, seriously, I did," I would say in earnest. "I swear."

That seemed to bother my kids. I think they wanted to know that what I shared with them about literature was a result of what some professor had taught me in college or what some study aid had said when I consulted it. If I could mine cryptic references in a text and, even worse, understand them without any assistance, how would they ever be able to keep pace with me? Like video gamers who resort to cheat codes, they were looking for shortcuts, a little extra help as they sought to contribute meaningfully to our circle.

I had no problem with my kids using outside sources to prepare for discussions, and while I never called any of them out for presenting someone else's interpretation as their own, I did encourage them to give proper attributions just as they would cite those sources in an essay. At the same time, I wanted my students to develop the ability to make their own discoveries. I shared my little epiphanies with my kids because I wanted them to remember that I was a learner just as much as they were. I did not come into class each day to dazzle them with my knowledge. Instead, I dedicated myself to showing them that there is more to literature than simple storytelling, to leading them to the curtain so that they could make their own breakthroughs. Those moments were not something I could write into my lesson plans, and that is why I became so excited when a jaw dropped for one student or for a whole class. Or for me, for that matter.

Of course, you won't be able to plan those moments in your teaching. All you'll be able to do is be open to their possibility when they arrive. It's easy to get hyper-focused on a lesson and concentrate on directing your class to a certain understanding. Even if you do notice something new while executing your instruction, you might feel that sharing it at that time will be a distraction. How you deal with your aha moments is up to you, but I encourage you to let your students in on your sudden insights from time to time. They will need to see you not only as a teacher but as a learner and an excitable one at that. The classroom is certainly no place to hide your light under a basket.

What Steinbeck Said: Post #45
Monday, January 23, 2017
Do You See the Light?

C *hapter Four of* Of Mice and Men *opens with an in-depth description of the room belonging to Crooks, the stable buck. It's a small enclosure attached to the barn, and Steinbeck details the features of the room, the various possessions of the only African-American on the ranch. To start our discussion, I asked my kids to reread the first page and a half of the chapter, and we then brainstormed those things on the board. When we finished, I asked them to pick an item and explain what it tells us about Crooks' character. Kids noted that he has a tattered dictionary and a mauled copy of* The California Civil Code for 1905. *They surmised that those particular books suggest a man who wants to know his rights, who uses the dictionary to better understand the writing in the other. The fact that he has a big alarm clock told them that Crooks is self-reliant, unlike the hands on the ranch who depend on someone else to awaken them. His leather-working tools tell the story of a character who fixes things, whom the boss relies on.*

When the conversation's energy finally diminished, I looked back at the board. "I guess we know Crooks pretty well, don't we? I mean, we probably know as much about him as anyone else, right?" I looked around the circle and saw all sorts of nods.

"Or do we?"

"Uh-oh," said one of my girls. She knew something was coming.

I walked over to the board and stroked my chin. "Let's see," I said. "We have a character whose room is part of the stable."

I pointed to an item we hadn't discussed. "His bed is a box filled with straw. Hmm. . ." I heard a few titters around the circle. "What do we call a box like that in a barn?"

"A manger?"

"Hmm. . .a character who sleeps in a manger in a stable. He has how many visitors during the night?"

Now the kids were laughing. "Three!" they called.

"Hmm. . .it does appear that we have ourselves a Christ-figure." With Western literature, it's easy to look for that motif, and it can be a dangerous thing to try to impose one upon a story where it doesn't really exist, but there it was right in front of us. I mean, when Crooks asks Lennie why he has come to see him, the big man says, "I seen your light."

Now we had real work to do. I asked my students to confer for a couple of minutes and come up with gifts that the three visitors bring to Crooks. We decided that Lennie brings companionship. Candy, the dream of the farm and a chance to be independent. That was clear enough, but that left us with Curley's wife. What on earth could she give to the man? We struggled to find an answer, but in time, we decided that, for just a moment, when Crooks literally stands up to the woman, he feels a sense of pride and dignity.

Just like that, however, the gifts disappear. Curley's wife threatens to have Crooks lynched, and he immediately assumes a chastened, deferential posture. He tells Candy when the old man leaves that he isn't really interested in joining the men on the farm they plan to buy. When Lennie leaves with George, Crooks is once again alone, without company.

"What sort of a messiah is that?" I asked my class. I looked at the clock and saw that I had just a minute to bring the lesson to a close. I decided that for once I didn't have time to let my kids work out an answer. Instead, I told them what I thought.

"An ineffective savior, that's what he is," I said. "Crooks is described as a Christ-figure, but he doesn't have the power to help the other characters, let alone himself. What's the message behind that?"

A student called for the koosh. "They have to do things for themselves," she said. "No one is going to help them solve their own problems."

I smiled.

"I'm guessing that when you came to class today, you had no idea that we were going to find these things in the chapter, right?" The kids nodded. "But think about it. Why would Steinbeck devote one of his six chapters to an evening where four lonely people come together? We meet Crooks, but we learn nothing about Lennie, nothing about Candy, and nothing about Curley's wife. Could this chapter be about. . .theme?" With that, the bell rang, and my kids were off to learn other things. I took a deep breath and waited for my next class to come in, ready to see what they had found in their reading. Waited to shine a different light to help them see.

As we finish reading the book this week, this chapter will play an integral part in our understanding of Steinbeck's message. Let's see how well my students do that on their own. As for me, I plan to be very quiet on Wednesday. . . .

I loved the "uh-oh" that escaped from one of my students that day. I'm not sure how much thought she put into the utterance, whether it just slipped out of her mouth, or, like a robin that spots a predator in the yard and sends out an alarm, she was alerting her classmates that their brains were in peril, but the attention level in the room certainly spiked at that moment. We had been together long enough as a class for my kids to be adept at reading my moves. They knew that I was always going to give them time to notice things on their own, to ink in a rest or two in a measure of our score so they could predict what might be possible next. French composer Claude Debussy called music "the space between the notes." It is that space, that interval of time, that allows us not only to process what we have just heard but to also anticipate the note that is to follow. It is the tension created by that anticipation that sets up the heart-filling reward of resolution, whether it be from note to note or from the beginning to the ending of the movement or the piece.

That's music, and it is not only something that we can experience as we listen, but it's also something that we can experience as we remember. It is our memory of hearing a song that makes the wait for resolution all the more delicious, that makes our time within that space exhilarating. There were times in our class when we all realized at once that the music had started for us. It was a feeling that we were suspended within a space with the knowledge that in a matter of seconds, what we had known as a simple melody was about to be augmented by notes to create a much more richly-textured harmonic structure.

In this case, the "uh-oh" was a leading tone, a harbinger of something intellectually chordal about to be played. I could have sung that note myself, but for the sake of my students, it was more important that it was voiced by a classmate. The more my kids realized that as a collective they could create their own meaning and help each other understand its depth, the greater the analytical ability that each of us acquired. That is the power that a highly-functioning class owns that individualized learning does not.

So it was that we continued to compose our class symphony, note upon note, chord upon chord, developing themes and variations without a coda yet in sight. As for your own composition, whether you are a musician or a builder or an artist, it is crucial that you envision a structure for your classes so that they can become more than a collection of individuals. It will be up to you to create a channel for the synergy that your kids will develop. When they learn the value of learning together, you can always step in from time to time to crank up the energy level, but you'll find that a student-led class is much more effective than one that depends too much on the teacher to get things done. You'll also have a lot more fun watching your students discover that they have the power to do incredible things on their own.

What Steinbeck Said: Post #46
Wednesday, January 25, 2017
A One-Match Fire

I have been reading Of Mice and Men *with my classes for the past thirty years, and I have come to know a rhythm to my teaching of the novel. I know where I have to guide my students, and I know where I can sit back and let them take over. Chapter Five falls into the latter category. Today we began our circle discussion with my traditional question: "What do you think?" The kids needed no more prompting than that for this chapter. In each class, a student quickly called for the koosh and offered an opinion about Lennie's killing of Curley's wife. From there, comments ranged from empathy to sympathy to blame for different characters. I sat silent, enjoying the flow of the conversation.*

This went on for thirty minutes or so, and even when the discussion lagged for a few seconds, someone would ask a question of the class or make a comment that would take us in a different direction. In each class I waited until students stopped looking my way as they shared their ideas. Even though I did nothing but nod my head to let them know that I understood what they were saying, kids are so used to replying to their teachers, that it took a while for them to realize that the only people in the room who were going to engage in conversation with them were their classmates. Oh, I was listening, and it was killing me not to ask a follow-up question or add a rejoinder to their interpretations, but this discussion was in no way about me. Rather, this was a community of readers sharing ideas, spurring each other to go deeper or to build upon ideas that were coming from all parts of the circle. When the point came in the discussion that my students were ignoring me entirely by talking to each other directly, I slipped out the door, walked down the hallway to the fountain, and sipped a drink. When I returned to my seat, I found that the conversation had not skipped a beat. I had told each class in the fall that this would someday be a sign that they had arrived as a class, and sure enough, that's what I saw as I watched the discussion continue.

Each year, this dialogue absolutely delights me because it means that my kids have become independent learners. As I tell them once I do enter into the discourse, whenever we start a discussion, their role is to stack the firewood that is our reading with their own kindling, and my job is to light a match. Sometimes I have to add a little lighter fluid, but on this day, I just needed to create a little spark and sit back to enjoy the rising flames. Once the fire died down to coals, I took a time out.

"Are we good?" I asked. The kids seemed to think so.

"Let's process what just happened before we go any further." I asked them to take a minute and discuss with partners what they had just witnessed for the past half hour. When it came time to share, they reported that they were surprised at how many different topics they had explored, at the depth that they'd achieved on some of those questions. More than anything, they were surprised at how long the talk went without me interrupting. In each class, someone noted that they had finally passed the water fountain test, and there were smiles all around at that accomplishment.

There were still twenty minutes left in the class, and the discussion that had burned brightly was now smoldering embers. I stoked it again with an invitation.

"Would you like to go deeper?" In one class, two boys sitting beside each other immediately shouted "Yes!" in unison. We laughed, and I led them in yet another visualization of the setting of the chapter. That eventually led us back to theme, and as the kids once again grew excited about what they were discovering, I could at last join in the fun. Within minutes we had developed an even greater synergy, and as the bell rang, we all sighed. That feeling was in

part, I'm sure, an expression of satisfaction for what we had experienced together. As at least one student in each class remarked, however, it also represented a little bit of frustration in the knowledge that we won't be reading Steinbeck's final chapter until Friday.

Patience may be a virtue, but that doesn't make it any easier to wait for some things, does it, kids?

As active as I could be in the classroom, and it seemed I was always a moment away from bounding in and around the circle, it was days like that one that provided me with the most satisfaction as a teacher. Thanks to my students' high spirits, I was free to sit among those excited souls and in effect meditate on the experience unfolding before me. If our class had become a collective mind teeming with thoughts and emotions, then I played the part of the silent witness, distanced enough to appreciate the special nature of our class discussion. With my students in control, I had nothing to do except to sit back and to *be*.

Not that I wasn't doing my own thinking and feeling, but I distanced myself from taking an active role in the opinions and interpretations my students were expressing. What was I thinking? Something along the lines of, "This is it!" That was my hope from day one of class, to arrive at a place where I was not directing my students' learning or even providing a catalyst for it. Instead, I was a privileged guest at their passionate sharing. None of them seemed to mind.

What was I feeling? That might best be expressed by the Sanskrit word *mudita*, which translates as the joy that we experience when we witness the well-being or accomplishment of others. Sitting quietly in my desk in the circle that day, I was filled with mudita because my kids were completely in charge of their own learning. The spotlight was not shining me, but the room was ablaze with a glow coming from each of my students. For that thirty minutes at the beginning of the discussion, I basked joyfully in the light created by my seniors. Being able to join in the fun thereafter was an extra blessing.

It may not be easy at first for you to silently observe in your classroom. The pleasure that comes from maintaining the attention of a group can become quite addictive, and you may struggle to give up that feeling of power that comes when eyes and ears are on you. It's not that there's anything wrong with a teacher holding a class full of young people in thrall—I can remember the thrill of sitting as a student and marveling at the brilliance of some of my teachers—but in the continuum of my evolution as a teacher, I found self-taught classes to be quite a bit down the line from those days when I was the center of a lesson. Just remember, those moments are like tulips that you plant as bulbs in the fall. You will have to be patient and resilient as you teach your students to be self-reliant, not just as individuals but, more powerfully, as a class. Here we were, early in our second semester, and that was the first day that I could truly say that my kids had demonstrated the ability to ride on their own. We'd taken off the training wheels some time before, but this was a look-ma-no-hands moment. If you're a parent, you know the joy of watching your child pedaling away from your guidance and your grasp. As a teacher, you'll multiply that twenty-five times per class.

What Steinbeck Said: Post #47
Friday, January 27, 2017
Of Hearts and Minds

*T*he traditional American classroom has at times been referred to as "an emotional desert." The business of school, with all of its good intentions, has long focused on objectives and outcomes and targets, has taken a dispassionate look at the acquisition of knowledge and skills, has eschewed "touchy-feely" experiences for critical thinking, has favored the head over the heart. Of course, learning occurs every day in the absence of palpable emotion, and students excel every day by concentrating on logic and reason. Yet, what transforms a class period from a lesson to something truly memorable? I submit that emotion is that essential factor.

We created something to remember in our classroom today. We began by reviewing our reading Of Mice and Men, and I took my students through chapter

179

by chapter, starting each summary with its opening scene.

"Chapter One. The curtain opens. What do we see?" We talked about the river, the mountains, the highway. I asked my kids to see once more in their minds the first appearance of George and Lennie, to recall the discovery of a dead mouse, the fiery temper unleashed by George on his startled companion, the recitation of the dream. We moved on to the bunkhouse in Chapters Two and Three, to the introduction of characters, the threats to an old dog and a mentally-challenged man. We again envisioned the humble room of Crooks and its message of a helpless messiah and the tragic end of Curley's wife at the base of a mountain of hay. All prologue to our reading of the novel's final chapter.

We call it a guided reading. Almost any time I read aloud, I pause from time to time to ask questions, to facilitate discussions, to point out key features of the text. Today I prefaced my reading by telling my students that we would proceed "without commercial interruption." For some twenty minutes I performed Steinbeck's remarkable coda. I shared his portrait-like description of the scene, I spoke the poignant words of the final conversation between two long-time friends. I paused, I whispered, I shouted.

I touched emotions.

As we closed our books at the conclusion of the story, I let the moment settle for a few seconds. Then I rose and walked over to turn off the lights for a few minutes, to allow my kids to be alone with their thoughts and feelings. I learned long ago that my students think more effectively when they first have a chance to feel about an experience. The move from heart to mind has to be gradual, and so after our personal meditation, I invited kids to share those two minutes with a partner. As they talked, I opened the door to allow a little more light, and after we came back together as a class, we discussed how we felt about the ending with the shades still down, the lights still off. Only when we had expressed our hearts and were ready to examine the beauty of Steinbeck's craft, did I turn the switch on once more.

At one point, I told my kids that I had done quite well with my reading today, that I had made it through my performance without distracting from it by breaking down. That hasn't always been the case, I assured them. I told them of a day a long time ago in a classroom far, far away when I paused in my reading, took a loud, tremulous breath, and tried unsuccessfully to read without a quavering voice. As I tried to find my composure, a wonderful young man sitting across the circle said, "This is going to be bad, isn't it, Mr. Stemle?"

All I could do was nod and sniffle.

"It's OK. We know you can do it."

I think of that moment every time I read Chapter Six. On this day, I thought of all of you who have been in that circle with me as our hearts broke for George, as our thanks went out to Slim for his compassion. Unlike Carlson, we all knew "what the hell [was] eating them two guys." Our circle today was less than full, a number of students in each class off competing in activities far, far from home. One of my boys called for the koosh as the bell was about to ring. "I feel really bad for our classmates that aren't here," he said quietly. "They're going to read the ending by themselves, but they will never know what we did in here."

As I said, we created a memory today.

I can't say enough about the importance of silence in the classroom. Lord knows, it was often noisy in our room, bright productive sounds that I know passed through the walls into our neighboring classes, and it seemed that when we weren't doing something like sustained silent reading, there was always someone addressing the group or teams engaged in processing ideas. At the same time, I knew that there were occasions when we simply had to embrace the quiet in order to better hear the whispers from our hearts. On days like the end of *Of Mice and Men*, I wanted to give my students a chance to hear those murmurs, to reflect on the echoes of Steinbeck's shocking conclusion as it brought closure to themes that had sounded loud and sounded subtly throughout the short novel. Yet, I also knew that some of my students were uncomfortable dealing with their emotions in a public setting, even within the nurturing environment that we had created over the months we had been together. That's why I turned out the lights, not necessarily to darken the room, for the blinds never really kept all of the sunlight out, but to give us all just a bit of cover should we want to keep our feelings concealed. The sharing that followed was voluntary, though it seemed that almost everyone spoke to a partner in the few minutes I provided. As was the nature of my classes, I created choice for my students whenever I could.

As for me, I found myself caught between delivering a reading that would honor Steinbeck's vision without distracting my students' appreciation for his words and opening my own emotional core to my kids so that they could see just how important the moment was to me. As a professional, I felt that I owed it to my kids to perform in an artistic way in order to help them understand the beauty of the passage. Still, I wanted them to see just how passionate I was about literature, about our exploration of the human condition. To that point in the course, I had shown them how to write, how to present, how to argue, and how to collaborate. On that day, I wanted to show them how to cry. In the end, the performance won out, but there would be other occasions for me to let my emotions flow.

No matter what you teach, there will be occasions when tears show up in your classroom. They might be yours, and I hope that you do show emotion to that degree at least sometimes in your practice, but they'll more likely belong to your students. It will be tricky for you to honor those emotional moments without embarrassing their owners, but I did learn ways to do that. It's a little easier if the cause of the crying is your interaction with your content. We might find it hard to hide our feelings when we're reading a poignant piece such as *Where the Red Fern Grows*, but those in the room certainly understand why their teacher or their classmates are sniffling. You might think other disciplines might not produce such responses, but our son Paul once watched his math professor step back from the board after solving a complicated equation and remark with tears in his eyes, "To me, that is as beautiful as *The Mona Lisa*."

So, the tears may come, and sometimes unexpectedly. They might be the result of something happening far from the confines of your classroom, or they might surprise even the one affected. In our classes, kids sometimes broke down when telling stories about their families. When I was young teacher, I wasn't sure how to handle such situations. I didn't want to ignore the emotion, but at the same time, I worried that by acknowledging it, I might be making the circumstances worse. One day, faced with a particularly heart-rending sharing by one of my students, I found inspiration in how to deal with that uncomfortable silence that had shrouded the room. Rather than ignore the heavy outpouring of grief, I instead identified it as a gift, a moment of grace.

"I think we should thank Stacey for the present she has just given us," I said in a soft voice. "You know what she just gave us, don't you?" Their downcast eyes suggested that my students were unsure of what to say at that point, and anticipating that to be the case, I continued without waiting for a reply.

"How much trust do you think she has in this group, to be willing to share her sadness so freely with us?" It was a point of perspective that I had never considered myself, and I was pretty sure that Stacey and her classmates had never seen crying in that way, either, but there it was. Of course, her emotions were a gift, one that would extend itself when other sensitive occasions arose. No longer would we be unsure of what to do when someone showed feeling of any kind, no longer would we be afraid to open ourselves to our fellow travelers on that classroom journey.

As I have already told you, I always had a purpose for my moves in our classroom, and often I had several going on at the same time. While I discovered a way to help all of those Staceys and friends who found themselves in awkward moments, I also took an opportunity to remind my students to look at the benefits of any situation, as distressing as it might at first seem. Blessings will be all around your classroom if you look for them.

What Steinbeck Said: Post #48
Tuesday, January 31, 2017
We're Not Done Yet

*W*hile *we put a wrap on our reading of* Of Mice and Men *on Friday, we by no means completed our study of Steinbeck's novel. As I have told my students throughout the year, merely reading a piece, simply discussing it for a few days, is not sufficient for developing a deep understanding of its plot, its characters, its themes. It is not until we think through our writing* *that we can more fully comprehend the depth of a work. Today we took that next step.*

We began by looking more closely at Steinbeck's use of names, starting with his title. With apologies to Billy Connolly, Sean Connery, basically anyone with a hint of Scottish ancestry, I dusted off my best brogue and read aloud Robert Burns' "To a Mouse." Of course, this required a little bit of translating of the poet's dialect, but we made it to the end and the familiar words, "the best laid schemes o' Mice an' Men gang aft agley."

Eyebrows were raised.

We discussed parallels between the poem and the novel to discern Steinbeck's choice of titles. The kids decided that Lennie is the more fortunate of the friends because, in his mouse-like way, he is concerned primarily with the present, while George plays the role of the poem's narrator, casting his eye to the past and its "prospects drear" and to the future which he fears. We looked at character names as well. I told my classes that Lennie's name most likely comes from Leonard, *which means "lionlike strength," and they told me that his surname of* Small *could be ironic given his physical size or apropos in terms of his mental capacity. Then we considered* George, *a Greek name meaning "farmer." This one was definitely appropriate, we agreed. As for his last name, Milton, I told my kids the story of John Milton's 10,000-line poem about the great battle between the archangels that results in Lucifer's banishment from heaven. The poem's title? Why,* Paradise Lost, *of course.*

"I'm not saying that every author you read uses name symbolism," I told my class. "But Steinbeck did in this book, and Hemingway did in The Old Man and the Sea. *When we get to Dickens, well, you can bet we'll be checking out those names, too."*

The rest of the period was spent in teams organizing projects for our study of the humanities. Next week we'll watch Gary Sinise's film version of the novel, and we'll follow that by presenting to each other the natures of art, music, architecture, literature, religion, and philosophy. Finally, having examined the book, having learned about those disciplines of the humanities, we will combine that knowledge into an essay that explores one of the novel's themes through the lens of one of those aspects. More on that later, but if my students took anything away from today's class, it was that we have not stopped learning about Of Mice and Men. *The friends' dream may have eventually died at George's hands, but the story continues. . . .*

W henever I asked my classes to focus on a feature of a text such as name symbolism, a little part of me wondered about how many subtleties of other works I had been blind to for so many years. From time to time I would return to a book I had been assigned in high school or in college to read it again, not from a student's perspective but a teacher's, only to find that the piece was much different than I had remembered. Of course, the book hadn't changed, but my perceptions of it had because of a combination of my life experiences and my deeper knowledge of literary techniques. I remember reading *Romeo and Juliet* in ninth grade and being dazzled by Franco Zeffirelli's film version on a class field trip to the Campus Theater downtown, but the play's impact on me primarily centered on the tragic turns of the plot. It wasn't until I found myself teaching freshmen that I took a closer look at Shakespeare's craft, starting with the bawdy wordplay in the first scene of Act I. Perhaps my teacher had pointed out the sexual undercurrent that coursed throughout the teasing dialogue between Samson and Gregory as they discussed maidenheads and pretty pieces of flesh, and I was just daydreaming about baseball practice, but it's more likely that we had focused on other elements of the play's opening. In any event, reading that first scene with new eyes was a revelation.

When you were a kid, did you ever receive a message from a friend written with lemon juice? Maybe that was just something we did back when I was a boy, but when I did get such a note, I would see nothing but a blank page until I held the paper over a flame. Then the secret would be revealed as the brown letters magically appeared. Years later, as I watched my students struggle to discern the layers of meaning in complex texts, I often acted as a candle beneath their reading, shining a little more light on the subtle aspects of a work. Once they learned that the understated elements of a book did not have to remain invisible, that they could light their own wicks with their imagination, then they began to understand why classic works are so roundly lauded.

Nothing thrilled me more than when one of my kids shared an insight in discussion that took us all to a new level. We had a sense that the voltage of the circle had been turned up a notch, that we were suddenly able to experience a new dimension. Sometimes kids would stop by the room before or after school to tell me something that they had noticed in a book they were reading outside of our assigned one, and we would chat for a few minutes about the writer's craft. Those may be the moments I miss most about teaching, those few minutes where we could go beyond the noise in the hallway and share an intellectual confidence. It was like watching a moonflower bloom at sunset, and I so cherished the beauty of a young mind opening to new possibilities.

More than their minds, though, I saw the effect that literature had on my students' hearts. When they discovered that writers were doing more than just telling stories, they began to interpret on different levels, and they came to feel the power of figuring things out on their own. It was a private experience as well, just a reader and her author sharing secrets. That's why I was honored when my kids let me in on their discoveries. All I had to do was light the candle.

How exciting is it to think of yourself as an agent of change? Of course, you won't be responsible for the discoveries your students will make. If it was that easy, then teaching would be simply a matter of conveying ideas, but there will be a certain joy that you'll feel when you help your kids start understanding the world in a whole new way. In a sense, you'll be reliving a time when you realized your own sense of wonder, whether that came when you were in the presence of a master teacher or when you were alone in your room or in the hush of a library, suddenly seeing the light, not realizing that all the time you were in darkness. When you witness that dawning for one of your students or for a whole class at once, you'll find another source of light that only teaching provides. Just think of what you'll be able to see then.

What Steinbeck Said: Post #49
Thursday, February 2, 2017
The Servant Road

*O*ne *of my favorite books is called* The Servant as Leader *by Robert K. Greenleaf. In essay form, the author bases his commentary on Herman Hesse's* Journey to the East, *a novel that tells the story of Leo, a servant to a caravan who performs menial tasks but who also sustains the travelers "with his spirit and his song." It is only at the end of the group's trip that they discover that Leo is in fact a great tribal leader. Greenleaf's jewel was a gift to me from the members of a Choice Theory class I taught in Michigan some twenty years ago, and I have always cherished it not only for the group's thoughtfulness but also for the message they were sharing with me in giving me that present. I remind myself from time to time that while I often find myself leading, I am in many ways a servant first.*

The past two days have afforded me several chances to serve. The first came early on Thursday morning as I chaired our district's Elementary Reading Curriculum Study in its biweekly meeting. Our task is to examine research to further our understanding of the reading process so that we might effectively move to a districtwide approach to instruction. This meeting saw us determining guiding principles around reading fluency and vocabulary instruction. My job in each meeting is to facilitate, to structure the agenda and then monitor the flow of discussion. It can be tricky depending on the content of the conversations— some topics generate more heat than others—but I find that I am most effective in my role when I strive to serve rather than to lead. When I help my team arrive at consensus in a collegial fashion, we tend to achieve our tasks more efficiently. Thursday was one such day.

The rest of Thursday was devoted to serving my students. I shared a writing tip with them regarding essay conclusions, and then I reviewed their progress on our most recent paper. I explained that many of them had failed to properly address the prompt, and I advised them that this would not be a profitable exercise in their college classes. I did this gently but firmly, and then I turned our

187

focus to our next piece. That meant making sure that we clearly understood that upcoming prompt, a delightful assignment that asks writers to explicate a theme from Of Mice and Men *through the lens of one of the disciplines of the humanities. To that end, we brainstormed topics, converted some to themes, and then discussed how art or music or architecture might provide us with a perspective on that message. It's an abstract analysis, and my experience has taught me that if we don't lay this foundation, some of my students will have a hard time building beyond a ground-level interpretation.*

The rest of the class period saw a continuation of our team preparation for presentations on the humanities. Again, I sought to serve, and in meeting with each group, I either knelt or sat beside them to not only get closer to their eye level as they worked in their desks but also to signal that I was not above them in the process. I had two questions as I arrived at each station: "What are you finding in your research?" and "How can I help you?"

When school let out, I hustled out to my car and then drove to Casper for the Teaching Writing and Literature in Wyoming Summit *to be held the next day. For the past ten weeks, I have served on a committee that seeks to revise a document explaining the nature of college and university writing classes to high school students. That committee convened at Casper College on Friday along with forty teachers from high schools, community colleges, and the University of Wyoming to enlist their help in revising the work. My role was to share my perspective on several topics with the entire group and to participate in a small group discussion. I had a wonderful conversation with an English teacher who is looking to establish a senior project at her school. I shared our school's website information on our program, and it was fun to watch her excitement grow as she envisioned a number of possibilities.*

After five hours of driving, I arrived home around 9:00, weary but satisfied that in serving my three groups over a two-day span, I had also led them to success. I can't say that my work was in any way menial, but I did my best to share my spirit, my good humor. A servant at heart, I accept my leadership roles with gratitude. It is a journey I have long been fortunate to travel.

So often we seem to base our evaluation of professional educators on their leadership qualities. We look to department chairs to serve on committees because they are used to organizing and leading their colleagues. We look to principals to run those committees because they are used to making decisions that affect their schools. We look to superintendents to lobby legislatures because they are used to structuring their districts' direction. This seems to make sense at first glance, to leave an organization's decision-making to those best "suited" to do so, and yet in practice, schools often seem to narrow their possibilities for success by limiting the pool of contributors to the process.

I observed that phenomenon in every school I ever served. Whenever a committee was needed, it was inevitably the usual suspects who were invited. When we had options to send teachers to conferences to learn and report back to the faculty as a whole, it was quite often the same names year after year. Every once in a while, I asked my principals about including a wider range of participants, but on each occasion, I heard the same answers. "He won't help" or "She will just complain the whole time" or "I think there are people more deserving." I'm sure that there were legitimate reasons for excluding a few teachers from governance roles for our school, but it seemed that at other times it was a matter of personal differences. When that was the case, there were talented and intelligent members of the staff who were left out because the school's leadership was either concerned that they might cause trouble in meetings or believed that they did not possess the skills needed to help the organization. It wasn't my call, but there were days when I wondered whether I could do something to help to change the situation.

Of course, there were times when I thought the same sorts of things about students. "I don't want him in our class because he causes trouble." "She hasn't earned her way into this class." That certainly wasn't appropriate or professional, but exasperation can lead us to think and say things that we're not proud of later. The fact was, there were kids who tried my patience and tested my skills. The good thing was that I never took action on my complaints. I'd vent a little, cool off, and then find a way to teach those kids who challenged me, and all of us were better because of it.

Still, it bothered me that we limited opportunities to serve for a lot of our teachers. I knew there had to be a way to get more of my colleagues involved, and I finally received some encouragement from a remarkable organizational theorist named Elliot Jaques. I heard Dr. Jaques speak at a conference in the mid-1990's, and I was so intrigued by his ideas regarding work levels that I sought him out afterward and ended up speaking with him for an hour about utilizing our resources more effectively. In sum, he believed that companies often overlooked their talent because they viewed their employees as role fillers who had no value outside of their perceived lanes in the organization. He advocated studying the personal characteristics of individual employees and using them in situations that called for those abilities.

"Your best problem solver might be your head custodian," he told me, "but how often do we run ideas by our janitors or our secretaries?" At that moment, I had an insight that I could not wait to share with my principal and my superintendent. I thought of that person in our building, our head of maintenance. What were his responsibilities? He organized people's tasks, he monitored the system. He solved problems. Lights not working in the auditorium? Call John. Sprinklers on the football field on the fritz? Where's John? Yet when we were stumped on how to implement a new bell schedule, or we couldn't figure out how to raise test scores, we relied solely on certified personnel. Why didn't we present ideas to those who dealt with problems every day and see if they could detect flaws in our approach? They didn't have to necessarily have the answers, they just had to check to see whether our notions were sound, whether we were on the right track.

I never did have any success in convincing my school to bring in our non-certified staff into the discussion of academic and systems issues. Perhaps it was too much of a paradigm shift. Perhaps we just didn't trust that someone from outside the box could help us see beyond it. Maybe I just didn't push hard enough. I left teaching wondering whether Dr. Jaques' approach could have helped my faculty be more efficient. I had no doubt that we had missed a chance to let many people who served us well day in and day out also lead us sometimes. We were poorer for that miss.

How will you achieve what I couldn't? Perseverance will help. You'll never know when your next proposal might stir something inside of a decision-maker. Maybe another route to take will be to encourage those colleagues you have in mind to step up and volunteer to help. You can facilitate that by leading on your own. Involve those problem solvers with your own situations that puzzle you, and once they feel comfortable being part of your solutions, invite them to join you when you participate in larger contexts. It won't be much different than the way you will encourage your students to try new things, to take little risks. In providing chances for others to serve, you'll grace your school with a lasting benefit, one that just might spread farther than you could ever hope.

What Steinbeck Said: Post #50
Monday, February 6, 2017
The Well-Tempered Teacher

*M*usical tuning can be a tricky chore. In working with instruments of fixed pitch such as a piano, a harp, or a guitar, tuners often create "false" intervals so that songs played in certain keys do not sound out of tune. This problem is more easily solved by singers or players of instruments without fixed pitch such as violins because they can adjust their intonation on the fly. To the listener, the music of a well-tempered instrument flows. Only the trained musician knows what goes into the creation of that sound.

Temper was clearly a key feature in our classroom today. We began our viewing of Gary Sinise's 1992 adaptation of Of Mice and Men, and as I guided my students through the artistic elements of the film, we concentrated on the decisions made by screenwriter Horton Foote, the themes and motifs developed by composer Mark Isham, the varied light employed by cinematographer Kenneth MacMillan. More than anything, we studied the acting craft displayed by Sinise and John Malkovich in their portrayals of George and Lennie. We focused on the former as his anger flared and then subsided, as it suddenly hardened and then just as abruptly softened. It was a subtle performance, one *carefully created with the use of the actor's voice and gestures and facial expressions. We watched an artist in tune with his role.*

In my first class of the day, the music of my teaching started well, but when my DVD player started to stick, I was faced with some unexpected accidentals in the score. When the film paused initially, I figured it was just a glitch, but when the image eventually froze, I knew I had to do something and quick. I pushed the eject button so that I could check for dust on the disk, but for some reason, the tray wouldn't budge. Hmm. . .no worries. I asked my class to turn to partners and discuss what they had viewed to that point, and I walked to the library in search of assistance. I brought one of our techs back with me to the classroom, and though he eventually extricated the disk, the fix lasted but another minute before the image stuck again.

At that point, precious minutes were fleeing, and while my class seemed to understand the situation, the kids were nonetheless losing out on learning. Years ago, I would have been past frustration at that point, but one of the wonderful benefits of aging is the patience born of experience. As a younger teacher faced with a similar dilemma, I fretted and muttered and complained. Of course, none of that ever fixed a machine for me, but it was all I knew to do. Today, I knew there was a way if I just waited for it to appear.

Then I remembered iTunes. In less than two minutes, I purchased the film and switched modes from DVD to laptop. When I cued the action to where the player had left us, we continued our viewing, and we even noted that our newer version had upgraded us from standard to high definition. A lesson that had threatened to fall completely out of tune had been tempered by a veteran ear.

Teaching is experiential in nature. You won't come fully assembled from the factory, much as you will like to think you're ready to be amazing in your first years in the classroom. Instead, you'll learn as you go, and as you acquire new techniques and perspectives, you will not only become more effective in your practice, but you will also find more confidence. That's the tempering to which the previous post refers. It's easier for teachers to be relaxed when things don't go exactly as planned in a lesson when they've been through that sort of situation before. As you gain experience, you won't panic, you won't fear losing control of the class period. Deep down, you'll know that everything eventually sorts itself out, and you'll convey that sense of calm to your students. You know, don't worry kids, I've got this.

It's one thing to grow in one's profession, to refine skills and approaches. It's another to do so without regret for what could have been all along. Midway through my career, when I was immersed in all sorts of professional development, I couldn't help but feel bad for all the students who had been in my classes before I learned about cooperative learning, equity techniques, Choice Theory, and mastery teaching. Every once in a while I'd hear from kids I'd taught years before, and while they sincerely thanked me for what I had done for them, I wanted to say, "Oh, if only you could be in my class today." It wasn't just that I wished I'd known how to handle difficult circumstances more appropriately, but as I grew more experienced as a teacher, I found ways to help kids learn more. Those poor students who never got that chance!

It was my mentor Kathy Curtiss who helped me see things differently. "You don't have to beat yourself up for what you didn't know, Eric," she told me. "Just be happy that you know it now and can better help your kids from this point forward." And just like that, I let that guilt float away. I realized that my students had always appreciated me for who I was and didn't wonder who I could be. If that view had worked for them, it certainly could work for me. More than that, I began to teach my kids to see their own abilities in the same way. When some would say, "Man, I wish I knew how to write like this last year," I would congratulate them for the hard work they'd put in to learn more about composition and remind them that it wouldn't be too long before they'd be saying the same thing about our class.

In teaching and in life, we do well to honor the past and celebrate the moment. Don't worry about the future. It will surely take care of itself.

Eric Stemle

E very autumn, I bring a few pots of geraniums from home to add some life to my classroom. I water them twice a week and make sure that they enjoy plenty of sunlight, and while the plants remain dormant for most of the winter, eventually a bud or two appears. By the time the last final exam is graded, those geraniums are in full bloom, heavy with blossoms, ready to go home for the summer.

As I entered my room yesterday morning, I was greeted by some brilliant red petals at the top of one of my pots. Most of the geraniums were still a dense collection of dark green leaves, but at least a few flowers had decided to show their colors. Did my heart good.

After watering my pots, I made a cup of tea and settled at my desk to grade a few papers. It has been a long couple of weeks marking essays, and I haven't found a lot of middle ground on this assignment. My students have either nailed the prompt or completely missed it, and for the most part, my kids continue to follow a consistent arc. Those who came in as good writers have written well all year. Those who struggled in the past have improved over the past few months, but they continue to make the same errors from essay to essay. That's not unusual at this point in the course, but experience has taught me that it is also not unusual around this time of the year that a few students begin to flourish.

I watched one of my writers bloom this morning. Well, not in real time, but as I took purple pen in hand to read a young woman's short story essay, I quickly found myself entering into a delightful dialogue with her. She has worked hard throughout our first four papers, and her writing has been solid all along. Today, however, I saw a bud suddenly open, watched vibrant color unfurl itself across the pages. Here was an interpretation that burst with energy and creativity and wit. I had seen the promise of this emergence in her earlier efforts, but today I saw it flower in glorious fashion. With joy, I added comments. I celebrated her phrasing, exulted in her connections, lauded her for her wit. As a single blossom *can stir a deep emotion, her essay brought tears to my eyes.*

From time to time, folks ask me how I teach writing. I know that they're wondering how I structure my lessons or which materials I use. They're usually surprised when I tell them that nearly all of my writing instruction happens in those black and white and purple conversations. It takes patience to be the stem, but I know that as I send along the proper nutrition, my senior geraniums eventually bloom in grand profusion. I never know when a bud will appear or when petals will pop, but I celebrate each and every one. This was one of those special mornings because my classroom became just a little more beautiful.

Friedrich Fröbel might not be a name you are familiar with, but if we're going to talk about the essence of education, let's start with his story. Fröbel was a 19th century Prussian educator who based his practices upon the ideas of a Swiss theorist named Johann Heinrich Pestalozzi. Both men believed in allowing children to play in their learning and both sought to break down the learning process into its elements. The result for Fröbel was his development of an approach he called *kindergarten* that, in its original form, provided students not only the freedom to explore but also a progression of activities involving simple objects such as balls and cubes and cylinders that allowed the children to first perceive qualities and differences and then create by using those objects that Fröbel called *gifts*. His kindergarten encouraged singing and dancing and drawing in a stimulating environment. While Fröbel's original concept has been altered over the years to what we now have as early childhood education, the genesis of his vision was as simple as a garden designed to nurture its blooming students.

I certainly didn't see my classroom as a garden when I started out. In my early years of teaching, I loved the classroom moments, the discussions and role plays and storytelling. I knew the importance of teaching composition, and while I enjoyed sharing secrets with my students from day to day, I viewed essay evaluation as more of a chore than an adventure. There were so many papers to grade and so little time to turn them back around to my kids. There was the matter of squeezing comments in some sort of legible fashion in the margins because, before the advent of word processing, I rarely if ever asked my young writers to type their papers. That meant that there were times when I strained to find room to write something meaningful on a page that was crammed from left to right with handwritten words. Oh, and don't get me started on the grammatical errors and misspellings. For most of my career, I sought the perfect way to deal with those. Some years I marked every one and covered the pages with my own ink. Other years I ignored them completely and worked on those issues in class lessons. I even tried to find a middle ground by asking my kids to write at the top of their papers whether they wanted me to edit at all. Grading papers was work. Hard work. I came to dread it sometimes.

I don't remember exactly when I decided to take an organic approach to my students' writing. I had always made some sort of a personal connection with their papers, had always found ways to encourage them no matter what the grade ended up on a piece. Even though it seemed that I was always changing my focus in my quest for the holy grail of grading, what remained constant was my mission of guiding my students to become effective and entertaining writers, whether they were going to college or planned to enter the work force directly after graduation, whether they ever needed to write for their jobs or eventually help their own children develop skills to be assessed by English teachers long after I was gone. Even if it was only for the few months that we were together, even if they never wrote another sentence after we parted, I saw writing as a way that my kids could develop their thinking, their outlook on the world. Still, it was just so exhausting to deal with all of those essays. I finally decided that it wasn't the kids. It wasn't the assignments. It wasn't even my instructional methods. It was the way that I perceived my homework, those hours every evening that took me away from my family, that drained my energy, that simply wore me out both mentally and physically.

Eventually, I did see myself surrounded by beautiful blossoms, but another analogy also comes to mind. As I was once an infant in my own learning, in my teaching, so were my students when they first arrived in our classroom. No matter what previous experiences they'd had, no matter how gifted they were in their language skills, all were born into a new environment on that first day of the school year. As the early weeks evolved, my kids watched me as their model, witnessed how I wrote and read aloud, how I expressed my interpretations. I watched them as they learned to, in a sense, roll over and sit up, to crawl, to take steps while I held their hands, and finally to walk on their own, moving unsteadily but joyfully into my arms. I encouraged them when they wobbled, picked them up when they teetered and fell. I celebrated their independence, and I delighted in walking beside them, in sharing what we all learned together as we explored ideas and concepts. As their graduation neared, we found ourselves running side by side until they found their own pace, turning to wave as they sprinted far beyond me. Weary and yet fulfilled, I rested for a while and then made my way back to the beginning, welcoming a new nursery full of young minds.

If you teach high school, you'll find that, like toddlers, your students will be vulnerable. They will find it easy to sit contentedly and watch the world around them. To rise and take those early steps, to venture forth on unsteady legs, takes not only courage but also the trust that someone—a mother, a father, a brother or sister—will be there to catch them when they fall and comfort them when they land with a crash. When I began to feel more like a parent, arms outstretched as I read their essays and their journal entries, I found the secret to guiding student writing. I modeled, I cheered, I comforted. I embraced each little triumph. It was a race we all ran well together.

In loco parentis is a term that you'll hear early in your career. While I'm sure that you'll be reminded every so often of the responsibilities that you will assume when students are in your care, you'll also experience the joys of that role as well. That will be something to sustain you on those nights when you feel worn out, maybe even discouraged about whether your efforts are making any difference at all. Children will fall, but they will also rise and run. Flowers will blossom every spring. There will lie your reward.

Eric Stemle

What Steinbeck Said: Post #52
Friday, February 10, 2017
Resolution

*W*e finished our viewing of Of Mice and Men *today. Or should I say, our listening of the film. While my focus this week has ranged from the brilliant images brought to us by director Gary Sinise and his cinematographer, Kenneth MacMillan, to the subtle screenplay crafted by Horton Foote, today we concentrated on Mark Isham's score. My kids are practiced in interpreting visual symbols and parsing dialogue, but I'm not sure they have had a lot of experience in analyzing the role that music plays in expressing a film's themes.*

On Monday and Wednesday, we listened for two musical themes. The first we attached to Lennie. It starts with a harmonic structure played by strings. It's a pulsation, a heartbeat. In comes a slow, wistful piano melody, played in a minor key. Then we are introduced to that idea during the opening credits that end with the image of George riding solo in a darkened boxcar. From there, we hear the theme several times with the camera trained on Lennie.

Today we dug deep into Isham's art. First, we watched the film's conclusion until the screen went black and silent. Then I replayed the last two minutes so that we could follow the final moments of his score, and you can find that passage at the very end of the soundtrack. As you listen, you might identify the sadness of the film's situation, and while it's easy to assign that emotion to the composer's use of a minor key, in this instance, that interpretation is perfectly appropriate.

Here is where the images on the screen blend with the music. Sinise moves us from the haunting reprise of George's lonely train ride to a fantasy in which the two friends load one more barley bag before walking away from the camera in a slow motion shot that matches the tempo of Lennie's theme. George takes off his gloves, and Lennie, a half step behind him, places his hand on the small of his companion's back as if to guide him. Is this George's revised vision of his dream? Is there any hope for him now that the two are separated with Lennie's death?

The music clues us into what George is thinking and feeling. It's still Lennie's theme that we hear, but as he touches George from behind, a new instrument is heard. Isham adds a harp to play an arpeggio, a triad that brings a surprise. Our minds expect yet another minor chord, but as we hear the root, its third, and then its fifth, we realize that the film has resolved in a major key.

In the quiet of a somber discussion, my kids and I considered possibilities. In a story of unfulfilled dreams and constant fears, the music suggests that the film has provided an answer. Whether it's about Lennie, who has at last found his paradise (cue the harp), or George, who has finally accepted the responsibility that will help him move on with his life, we find comfort in that final note.

"You have read the novel," I told my class as the period drew to a close, "and you have talked about it. You have watched the film, and you've talked about that. In the next three weeks, you will create and present projects, and you will write an essay, both of which will give you an even greater understanding of the book. I truly believe that by the end of this month, you will know Of Mice and Men as well as you have ever known a story."

I'm not sure what my kids were thinking when they heard that announcement, but it was music to my ears.

Though, like everyone else, I guess, I loved songs as a boy, I didn't have much of a musical education growing up. This was not the fault of my mother, who tried to get me to take piano lessons, but as an eight-year-old, I was more interested in playing baseball. I did enjoy music, though, and so I tuned my radio to our local AM station and saved up my allowance to buy Beatles albums. What I didn't have was an artistic sense of what I was listening to. I knew that there were things I wasn't catching in the music, but I didn't know what to do about that.

I married the answer. It didn't take me long to realize the treasure that I had found in Teresa, but it went beyond her wonderful personal qualities. Suddenly, I had at my disposal an encyclopedia of music theory into which I could immerse my imagination, and I knew for a fact that learning from my bride was so much more fun than scanning the *World Book*. With her help, I started fiddling around with the guitar, and with her inspiration, I found confidence in my voice and began singing more enthusiastically in church and community choirs. More than anything, however, I had questions. Boy, did I have questions. I would usually preface them by telling her that I was wondering something about music, and she would take a deep breath and shoot me a look that told me that she knew she was going to have to do some thinking. I rarely asked her about simple things. Instead, I would ask something along the lines of, "What do you call it when two notes are played at the same time and then separately?" She didn't always have an answer for me, but she was infinitely patient in explaining to me how music works, and what really excited me were the connections that I began to make between musical theory and my teaching of English.

Over the years, the essence of my classroom was exploration. While it took my students a while to get the hang of looking beyond the horizon, beneath the ocean's surface, by February, they were not only seeing the world in different ways but hearing it that way, too. As we listened to elements of the soundtrack to *Of Mice and Men*, we added an aural layer to our interpretation of Sinise's film. Like our study of Steinbeck's use of symbolism and word play, Isham's musical metaphors gave my kids a chance to better understand what makes art. Sometimes I just let that realization settle in, but other times I would remind my classes that what we were doing together didn't happen for everyone. I was thrilled to learn it from Teresa, and I was always excited to pass on my love for making connections to my students. It wasn't the knowledge that mattered. It was the facility that we all developed for looking and listening.

And here's the catch. Delving into literature and film took time. Each level that we moved into took time to explore and to process. Of course, when we became good at interpreting in new ways, we tended to grow more excited and thirsted for even more depth. That took time if we did so as a class, but isn't that where the best learning happens? Isn't that what helps develop our love of lifelong learning? Isn't that our ultimate goal as teachers, for our students to leave us in a quest to learn much, much more on their own?

It seems not to matter to the powers that be that the answer to each of those questions lies in the affirmative. We find ourselves in a political climate that demands test scores to validate the worth of a teacher, a classroom, a school. Time may be money, as we've always heard, but in today's education, test scores are the bottom line. Still, the borrowing of a few minutes in a class period to invest in a lifetime pursuit of meaning always seemed a wise financial move to me. When we took the time to have fun with our analysis, to go far beyond what a curriculum might prescribe, the interest rate always seemed to soar.

I'm hoping that at some point in your career, the national obsession with test scores will lessen a bit if not fade away altogether. It might not, however. This concentration on data just might last for a long while, and with it, teachers will continue to feel pressure to help their students achieve numbers. When school goals are stated in terms of ACT scores and not in terms of what is to be learned, it's hard to ignore the importance that the those in power place on such measures. I'm not suggesting that you resist the expectations that your school and your district establish regarding performing and assessment, but I am encouraging you to find ways to go beyond what is required. Make your classroom into a beautiful movie, one that is more than lines of dialogue and colorful images. Find a way, every day, to bring music into your teaching: the melody of imagination, the harmony of collaboration, the rhythm that pulses with entwined hearts beating together toward a common purpose. When that music plays for each of your students, can their dancing be far behind?

What Steinbeck Said: Post #53
Tuesday, February 14, 2017
Children Will Listen

*S*ome *twenty years ago, my* Senior Humanities *class watched Stephen Sondheim and James Lapine's Tony Award-winning* Into the Woods, *a perfect story for those about to go out into the world for themselves. The kids enjoyed the interplay between Little Red Riding Hood and The Big Bad Wolf, Cinderella and Prince Charming, Jack and his mother and the Giant. As a teacher and the parent of young children, I connected with the Baker and his* *wife, but the songs that touched me most were sung by the Witch. Search YouTube, and you will find a concert version of Bernadette Peters reprising her Broadway role by singing "Children Will Listen," a performance that still chills me.*

Since those Green River High School days, I have often found myself humming this song, and it has become my companion as I model for my students. Because I want them to live their way through a piece of literature, I show them myself as a reader, an interpreter. Because I want my students to love writing, I share with them my own. Because I want my students to be eloquent, I speak in academic and artistic language. How can I expect my kids to be passionate about their learning if I don't share my passion for my own?

Every once in a while, my students remind me that they are listening and watching. I see snippets of my sample writing appearing in essays, and though that once bothered me because I wanted my writers to follow their own paths, I have come to realize that they are simply walking in my shoes before they eventually buy their own. A few years ago, a student told me that despite all of my instruction on public speaking, what taught her the most about presenting was listening to me speak to her class every day. I had never given much thought to my daily interactions with my kids being actual pedagogy, but there it was.

Today was the last before our humanities presentations begin on Thursday. My teams put finishing touches on their plans, and they once again found the synergy that infuses a collaborative effort. As I walked about the classroom, I thought back to that long-ago October when these same kids were frantic in their last-minute preparations for their initial presentations of the year. In this moment that is February, they are excited to perform, but they also possess a certain confidence. They have traveled a long road already.

As I made my tour from team to team, Sondheim's words and music walked right along with me, and I felt the responsibility that the Witch advises us to consider:

Careful the things you say,
Children will listen.

Careful the things you do,
Children will see.
And learn.
Children may not obey,
But children will listen.
Children will look to you
For which way to turn,
To learn what to be.

Tonight, I thank my students for watching, for listening. What a gift they are!

To learn what to be." In that one line, Sondheim encapsulates the hope I had for each of my students. I wanted them to learn to write at a collegiate level, but our class was about more than that. I wanted them to learn how to read and interpret and discuss their ideas about literature, but we were about more than that, too. In the end, it was always about *becoming*. Ours was a class where you came to find out who you were and who you were on your way to being. Of course, we all moved in that direction at our own pace, including me, and perhaps that's what made the challenge of teaching so rewarding. We were all seeds, embryos. We were all nurturing each other as we grew wiser in the ways of our culture at large.

While it may have been true that my students were watching and listening, even when I thought they weren't paying attention, it was also important for me to see and hear as well. At times I felt that I was falling back on my early teaching approaches, like I was acting on a stage or anchoring a newscast, performing for an audience with a barrier in between us. It wasn't that my kids weren't attending me, but there were days when I felt that they as well as I were doing nothing more than going through the motions, knowing that we had a responsibility to be respectful of each other but not really creating an authentic sense of collaboration. I was fortunate that those days weren't too frequent, but when they happened, I would go home and reflect upon the opening we had missed to be special with each other during that class period.

If you've ever tried forms of mindful meditation, you know that the practice allows you to be present in the moment. It means not focusing on the past or the future, not being anxious about what might come or regretting what has happened. Being aware of what is around you in the present moment is not as easy as it might sound, and it doesn't take long during a silent mediation for thoughts to arise that take you beyond the here and the now. That's just how our minds work, right? We're continually processing and evaluating, and yet, mindfulness teaches us to suspend judgment when a thought shows up. Instead of feeling guilty about losing our concentration on the present, we simply acknowledge the thought and return our minds to our breathing or to some other method of immersing ourselves in the moment.

The same practice can apply to your classroom. There will be days when everything comes together, when the connection between you and your students is palpable, and you wish that every lesson could have that same feel. Of course, that's about as possible as keeping thoughts from creeping into your meditations. There will be times that your teaching feels awkward, others when you sense that your students couldn't really care less about what you or their classmates have to say. Those aren't occasions to agonize over, however. They will happen, but they won't define the nature of your classes, especially if you use them as reminders that each day will give you a chance to experience something truly special, just as each breath can center you on the eternity of the moment.

That's why I took care when the bell rang to begin class, and I closed the door to be alone with my seniors. That's why I took risk after risk to reveal my thoughts and feelings with those young minds and hearts, to let them know that they could trust me to trust them and that, together, we could build a learning environment unlike any other. Thank God, they listened.

Yours will, too.

What Steinbeck Said: Post #54
Thursday, February 16, 2017
Cutting a Classroom Rug

*S*tep by step, my students have become more and more polished as presenters. Oh, they've had their stumbles, and sometimes they still grapple with avoiding inarticulate transitions or employing meaningful gestures in their talks, but they have come a long way this year. In the fall, they took their first steps in presenting to a college class as they collaborated to create business plans and then to convince a panel that their proposals were viable. They wobbled a bit as they tried to maintain their balance, but no one took a tumble, no one did a face plant on the carpet. They admitted to being anxious, but they somehow moved forward.

By December, as they taught short story lessons in teams, they stood tall and walked with purpose. Gone were the obvious nerves and mannerisms, replaced by confident openings and closings. They strolled through their presentations, engaging their classmates with humor and creativity. I smiled to see them find their strides. Since then, my kids have presented on their own in a class feature called The Daily Meditation. For ten minutes each period, a student shares a film, an artist, a book, a song, or a bit of humor. Those performances have built upon each other, as if we have walked hand-in-hand toward the goal of a masterful presentation.

Today was the first day of a round of team presentations centered on the humanities. Over the course of three days, my kids will share with each other ideas about the art, music, literature, religion, philosophy, and architecture of 1930's America. As they present, they will teach each other the manner in which the arts created a context for John Steinbeck's writing of Of Mice and Men. To that end, for the past two weeks they have worked in earnest to research and to structure twenty-minute lessons. As I came to school today, I was excited to see just how they would deliver their plans.

While my teams presented, I sat, rubrics in hand, observing and evaluating their performances. I was thrilled with what happened before me. I saw students *who at last understood the necessity of audience engagement, who had finally grasped a sense of the role that structure plays in communicating ideas that can with time become memorable. I saw them not just presenting ideas but enjoying themselves in the process. They couldn't wait to entertain and inform their classmates, couldn't wait to show off what they had created. These were no longer toddlers on unsteady legs, no longer children walking mechanically toward a nearby destination. Today my students transcended those earlier efforts as they delighted in their next steps. They didn't just walk their classmates through material. They went beyond the simple sharing of information.*

Quite simply, they danced.

Over the course of a school year, there is a moment when the spirit moves in a different fashion. A moment when kids start not only start to get it but to also realize that they get it. That moment happened today in each of my classes. I saw it in the graceful steps and spins and gambols that my teams were executing, and I heard it from their classmates who lavished praise upon their nimble colleagues when they provided feedback on each presentation. I heard laughter, and I saw knowing smiles. The best part of the day was closing my door on my way home, knowing that next week's lessons will be even more artistic, even more ebullient because today's presenters showed those who will follow them where the dance floor is. I wouldn't say I was Gene Kelly gliding down the hall toward the parking lot, but there was definitely a bounce in my step and, I do believe, a song in my heart.

As you know by now, the creation of a nurturing classroom environment does not come easily. It's hard enough to take a disparate group of young people and mold them into a high-functioning unit, maybe even a loving one, without all of the obstacles to success that are inherent in a public school. If you taught in a vacuum, without all of the moving parts that impact what you hope to accomplish with your students, it would still be daunting, but throughout my career, it seemed that beautiful moments like the one I experienced with my kids in the previous post were often achieved in spite of all the factors that seemed to get in the way. One such issue that made a difference in the way my students progressed as individuals and as a class involved our bell schedule. Before coming to Evanston High School, I had taught in a number of arrangements, ranging from a seven-period day of forty-five minute classes that met for the entire school year to a rotating block schedule where students had eight classes of ninety-minutes each that rotated on what we called "A" and "B" days. When Teresa and I moved to Evanston, I found myself in a new schedule altogether. Most classes met ninety minutes each day for a semester, while a few such as music and Advanced Placement courses met every other day for the year. As you might imagine, this setup was a headache for our counseling department, as quite a few students had schedules that included both rotating classes and semester ones.

At that point, my English classes were semester in length, and for the first time in my career, I was faced with working all of my lessons into four calendar months. I quickly discovered that my expectations for assignments had to change as well. While my sections still met the same time number of minutes over the span of a semester as they did when I taught year-long courses, my kids now had half as much time to read and write outside of class. I was used to reading four or five novels with a class, and now we were doing two or three. The same applied to our writing assignments. I couldn't help but feel that my students were missing out on learning.

Not all of my colleagues were displeased by the situation, though. Semester courses meant having fewer students at one time, and that meant fewer papers to grade. From the student perspective, that meant less homework to do, fewer tests to study for. I appreciated those aspects of the schedule, and yet, I missed having my students for the entire year. I missed watching them grow.

A few years passed, and as a school we decided to balance the schedule as best we could. That meant that some semester offerings would become rotators, and the English Department voted to make all of its classes year-long. Again, not all of us were happy with that move, but I was thrilled to have a school year back. On a day like the one I detailed above, I was particularly grateful for the time that my seniors had to develop their skills, to gain confidence when speaking before an audience. If we had met as a semester class, they'd have had fewer chances to practice and in turn to observe others to learn more about presenting. The pace of the class would have been faster, and I'm not sure that we would have ever felt as close as a group had we not the time to reflect and to share our musings with each other.

As you strive to foster your own culture, you will have control of pretty much everything that happens for you and your students within the confines of your classroom, but the one factor that you won't have influence over is the bell schedule. Your school will dictate how often your classes meet and for how many minutes, and it will be up to you to fashion what you can out of that scheme. Will it be aggravating at times? Surely, but that's no cause for despair. Rather than lamenting your lack of power over the situation, you can instead find satisfaction in being creative with your use of time. It's not likely that you'll find yourself smiling through all of your difficult circumstances, but it will be important to find perspective when stress starts to creep into your practice. Be sure to give yourself occasions to reflect upon your progress toward making your classroom a special place for your students. Be grateful for those bumps along the road because they will eventually make the journey that much more rewarding. Remember, nothing will be more crucial for you as a teacher than facilitating the growth of your students, whether that happens over a semester or a year, forty-five minutes per period or ninety. Whatever the schedule, you will have the power to help kids change.

What Steinbeck Said: Post #55
Tuesday, February 21, 2017
Eat Your Greens!

*A*bout a dozen years ago, I spoke with an alumnus who was home for Christmas break, and I asked how he was doing in college. "Fine," he said. "But I really wish I would have read more when I was here."
"I seem to recall assigning quite a bit of reading," I said with a smile.
"Yeah," the boy said, "but you should have forced me to read."

Well, if he really remembered being in my class, he would have known that I never force my students to do much of anything, but that's a blog post of another color. Still, after he left, I gave his assessment some thought and checked with a few other students from earlier years. All agreed that they hadn't read enough in my class.

The next fall, I instituted Additional Reading Opportunities *(ARO), a fifteen-minute sustained silent reading routine for every class period. Over the years, I have done a bit of tweaking to the demands of ARO, but the basic features have remained constant. My students read novels of their choice and earn credit for them by conferring with me upon completion. The fifteen minutes in class isn't designed to meet their reading needs, only to honor the need to read every day. Most of the pages are read outside of class.*

Years ago, when I taught freshmen, most kids wanted to tell me the plot of their books, some in excruciatingly minute detail, but my book conferences with seniors have been more conversational. We talk about character motivation and author's craft. I ask them how they came to read certain books, and I encourage my kids to reread at least one of their favorite novels during the year. There's nothing like visiting an old friend.

I had one such conference today with a student who had, at the begging of two friends, read a series in middle school that was written for adolescent girls. She came in this morning to discuss her second time around with the first book of the set.

"I've never read this book," I told her when I looked at its cover, "but I've certainly heard about it in a lot of ARO talks."

"I read it in seventh grade," she said with a frown. "Ashley and Rachel told me that it was amazing, and they kept bugging me to read it. I really didn't like it, but I read the whole series."

"To please your friends?"

"Not exactly. More like to keep them from hassling me about it."

"So, why read it again?"

"Well, I thought, I'm older now. I've changed a lot. Maybe I'll like it."

"And?"

"And, it was OK," she said with a rueful smile. "I still don't like it. Every chapter it sounds like she's trying to be J.K. Rowling. I might as well read Harry Potter, but I've read all of those three times. They did the same thing with The Fault in Our Stars. They said I had to read it or they'd never forgive me."

"Did you read that one?"

"Of course," she said and then laughed softly. "I can't help it. They're very persuasive."

"I see."

My student was caught in a familiar trap, wanting to please her friends but suffering a little because her sense of duty was interfering with her own tastes and desires.

"You know what?" I said. "There are so many good books out there. Great books. There's no need to get stuck reading one if you really don't want to finish it. I'll give you credit for the pages you've read if you ever decide to move on from a book that's not working for you."

The girl looked at me as if I had just commissioned a crime.

"No, really," I continued. "It's not like having to eat your vegetables in order to get dessert. You can quit a book anytime it's not working for you. I promise, I won't tell Rachel and Ashley."

She bit her lip and nodded. "I'll think about it," she said. I wrote my initials near the book's title on an index card that listed the books she had read so far in the year. Four books in a semester earns an "A," something she accomplished easily in the fall. Already she has read two this second semester, and as I handed the card back to her so that she could place it back with those of her classmates in a box we keep on the windowsill, she wrote down the next book she planned to read.

"May I ask?" I said as she paper-clipped the cards together.

She sighed. "It's the next book in the series," she said, her cheeks reddening slightly.

"Just can't get enough of that broccoli, can you?" I asked.

She smiled shyly. "It will make my friends happy." I smiled back with a nod.

"Don't worry, Mr. Stemle," she said as she grabbed her backpack and

headed for the door. "I'll save some room for ice cream."
"Any flavor I would know?"
"You'll just have to wait for a taste," she said.
Sweet.

I used to walk by math classrooms after school and marvel at how many students were there seeking help on their homework. I told myself that English was a different animal, that our students weren't searching for an answer to a problem but rather creating their own analyses, but still, I often wished that more of my kids would drop by to see me about their reading or their writing. When I instituted the *ARO* conference requirement, I suddenly solved two of my problems at once. I had long devoted some time during class for independent reading, but I had conferred with my underclassmen during the period, concerned that I would get few takers if I asked kids to come in on their own time to talk over their books with me.

When I began teaching seniors who were earning concurrent college credit for our class, I decided that I could expect a stronger commitment from them. Because most of my kids had their own cars or caught rides with friends and weren't restricted by a bus schedule before or after school, I set a policy that all reading conferences would happen outside of class time. One of my rationales was to help my kids develop more of a collegiate mindset, to prepare them for finding time to see their professors during office hours, but I also wanted more time with those conversations. The results were wonderful. With more time and without the distractions that existed during class period conferences, my talks with my kids took on a whole different tenor. No longer was I checking to see whether they had read the book. In fact, I told them when they sat across from me that what I really wanted to do was talk about what they had noticed in their reading. Sometimes we discussed literary elements, other times I asked them about their strategies for working through a book, especially a difficult one. Some students never came in to see me, some came in week after week, long after they had met their requirement for *ARO*. One thing seemed clear: once a student made the time to come in for his first conference, he was more likely to come back again and again. Each time I sat with a student, just the two of us, I had a sense that we might just create something special, whether it was an interpretation of what she was reading or a more refined draft of an essay.

Did I reach every student in that way? Sadly, no. Most of the time before and after school, our room was quiet save for an occasional visitor dropping by to ask a question or two. I made the most of my time alone, but my heart did warm a little every time I saw one of my seniors carrying in a paperback or a laptop. Often kids would start by apologizing for taking up my time. I had to assure them that there was no better use of that time than to engage mind to mind for fifteen or twenty minutes.

Your time before and after school, even during lunch, will seem precious to you, and it will often be captured by all sorts of outside factors. You will have faculty meetings, committee meetings, conferences with parents, or just visits from colleagues who want to talk a bit. And that's just what will happen if you aren't involved in extracurricular activities. If you coach or you sponsor a club, then you will have very little time at all to meet with students outside of class. While sometimes there will be little you can do to square your students' availability with your own, remember, it won't be the logistics of such meetings that matters as much as how you use that time.

To be as efficient as I could, I took care of each day's essential tasks during my planning period. It was unlikely that any of my students would drop in during that time, and so I used those minutes to run copies, make phone calls, or send e-mails. It was also during my planning that I met with my principals or other teachers with whom I was collaborating. If any time was left over, I'd grade an essay or two or do some reading in preparation for the next day. Those were also the activities that I reserved for my classroom time before and after school. I tried to be in my room whenever I could in the event that kids needed to see me, and while I was waiting, I graded or planned, chores that could always be done at home if I didn't get to them at school. Setting my time up that way helped me avoid the frustration of being interrupted while I was doing something that just couldn't wait, and without that irritation, I was free to feel more relaxed and welcoming with my drop-ins.

That will really be the key to building relationships with your students and your colleagues. It will be critical that when you interact with them, they feel that nothing is more important to you at that moment than being with them, than being able to help them. It's easy to tell a teacher to have a cheerful attitude, but it's hard to feel that way when the stress of mounting duties and diminishing minutes starts to build. You won't be able to control the amount of time you'll have, and you won't always have much power over your responsibilities, but you can set priorities for your work so that on those occasions when your attention is requested, you'll have both the time and the energy needed to focus on the moment at hand. By putting last the things you can do outside of school, you'll put first the needs of those folks you can't take home with you.

What Steinbeck Said: #56
Thursday, February 23, 2017
The Play's the Thing

*T*oday brought our third and final round of presentations. As I wrote last week, it has been fun to sit on the side and enjoy the creativity of my teams, and I have truly appreciated the participation of classmates when they have asked to interpret Of Mice and Men *through the perspective of the humanities. The atmosphere in the room has been upbeat and supportive, and I can't imagine a more nurturing learning environment than we have in all three of my classes. We have really found our niche as a community of learners.*

The presentations for my first two classes finished close to the end of the period, and in our remaining time, we discussed what's coming up next week and beyond. My third class, however, some twenty minutes to spare, and so I decided it was time to pull out a couple of old activities. I hadn't done either one of them in years, but as I was walking from the office to my classroom yesterday, I came across a good friend leading one of her classes in playing "Elephants, Giraffes, and Crocodiles" in the foyer.

"Look familiar?" she said. I nodded.

213

"We've been playing theater games the past week, and I realized that most of them I learned when I student taught with you." She listed some of the games, and I laughed because they had played a big role in my classroom when I taught younger students. In the past nine years, as I have taught College English 1010/1020 *exclusively, I have drifted away from learning games. We still have fun every day, but seniors seem to be OK with not playing so much. At least that's what I thought.*

The first game we played today was Imaginary Toss, a cooperative learning activity that starts with students standing in a circle. I began the game by announcing that I would be tossing an "object" to one of my students, and she in turn called out another name. After the last student's name was called, I let her know that she would come back to me. Sounds simple enough. We started with an imaginary koosh ball. "Taylor—koosh!" I said, and pantomimed a toss. Taylor "caught" the ball and then called out to her partner, "Audrey—koosh!" I let the ghost ball travel around the room before Rhys threw it back to me. Then I looked once again at my receiver.

"Taylor—paper airplane!" I sent the imaginary plane across the room, following its flight with my eyes. Taylor caught it just above her head and sent it to Audrey. A few seconds later, I tossed a frisbee to Taylor, followed by a beach ball, a bowling ball, and a raw egg. Squeals of laughter. I looked about the circle as much as I could when I could see that Rhys wasn't returning an object my way. Some kids were marvelously dramatic in their actions. On the other hand, some made the same motions no matter what the object. I remember using this activity early in a school year to get an idea of my students' creativity or to see who was inhibited. Because I have known these kids since August, there weren't a lot of surprises today.

I waited until the raw egg was almost back to me before tossing one more item.

"Taylor!" I cried, waving my arm frantically above my head. "Live chicken!" Oh my. Even the kids who had ho-hummed their way through the game were into it now. Because the chicken was the last object, we all followed its progress, and the theatrics were a pure delight. When I at last caught the final toss from Rhys, I

looked down at my hands.

"Guys, I don't think this is a live chicken, anymore."

Those five minutes felt so good. For the past week, my kids had worked hard, delivered solid presentations, served each other as a helpful audience. Imaginary Toss was a great release for us all.

We returned to our desks, and I went deep into my bag of tricks for something we used to do long ago: mind games. That involved a scenario and a question. The first was, "A man lives in an apartment on the twenty-fifth floor of a building. Every morning he leaves his room at precisely 7:30, takes the elevator to the first floor, and goes to work. Every afternoon, at precisely 5:15, he comes back to the elevator, and takes it to the fifth floor. There, he exits the elevator and walks the remaining twenty flights of stairs to his room. Why does he do this?"

The kids can ask me any questions they want, but the only answers I can give are yes *and* no. *We worked on the riddle for a few minutes before I gave a clue: "When it rains, he goes all the way to the twenty-fifth floor." Well, this didn't help at all, but finally, someone asked, "Does his size have anything to do with it?" Ah. Immediately several hands went up.*

"Is he too short to reach above the fifth button?" There it was. What pleased me most was the way my student asked the question. She could have said, "Is he a midget? A dwarf?" Instead, she avoided labels and still got the information she needed. Pretty cool.

With a few minutes left, I started another mind game, but class ended before we had narrowed down much information. The class groaned at the sound of the bell.

"Guess you'll have to wait till Monday," I told them as they waited for the answer. I heard a few whimpers, but the kids appreciated being given the chance to figure out the riddle next week. In the meantime, they have an essay to finish this weekend. If they work as well on it as they worked together this week to teach and learn from each other, I'm going to have a great time grading papers for the next two weeks.

Something tells me that I'm going to smile a lot with pen in hand.

I read once that in a given class period, no more than sixty-five to seventy percent of the time should be devoted to executing the curriculum. In an eighty-five-minute period like ours, that worked out to approximately an hour of instruction or practice. That might not sound like the most effective use of time, but when you consider administrative activities such a taking attendance or passing out materials, then those minutes do add up. In our classroom, that sixty-minute number might have even been high on a typical day. We took two minutes or so discussing the quote of the day, and that was followed by fifteen minutes devoted to *Word of the Day* and *ARO*. I suppose that anything else that was not directly related to the state standards would qualify as non-curricular. To some that might sound like we were off-task for a third of our class time, but nothing could be farther from the truth. It was just a matter of how you defined *task*.

It should be clear to you by now that our classroom was purpose-driven, and those purposes were many and varied. Naturally, there were all sorts of objectives to be met as I helped my students refine their language skills, and rather than employing direct instruction to most standards and benchmarks, I embedded them in almost everything we did together. Every daily presentation gave one student a chance to practice speaking and allowed everyone else to work on their listening skills and their critical thinking as they posed questions of their classmate. Each journal entry gave kids a shot at on-demand writing that they would be doing in college, each discussion an occasion to practice supporting their ideas with evidence and reasoning. And our learning games? Well, if each benchmark was a brick for building their fluency and their facility with language, then games and collaboration and personal sharing about our lives were all mortar to make that learning solid.

If I was the architect of my class' development as a community of learners, then I surely needed a blueprint for the foundation and walls of our structure, and that would be the curriculum. As Teresa and I walk around our neighborhood in the evenings, we see house after house after house designed by the same builder, and with some variation, they all look pretty much the same. It's not until you walk through the front door that you see what makes each home unique. They

216

might have similar floor plans, but it's the way in which the owners decorate and furnish their rooms that influences the personality and the function of the house's interior. My interactions with my students from day to day, the creative ways that I challenged them to think deeply and critically, the various ways that I inspired them to take risks, to open themselves to new ideas, all essentially defined the interior decoration of my instruction.

I can't say that everyone shared my perspective on time in the classroom. I had some evaluators who wondered whether I was pushing the kids hard enough with drills and assessments. Sometimes we simply agreed to disagree on how best to use resources, but what it really came down to was results. When those principals and curriculum directors read what my students wrote and listened to what they said in discussions, when they observed the excitement in our classroom that arose purely from the joy of learning together, they put away their stopwatches and left me to my own devices. I couldn't have planned it any better.

Results. If you are going to enjoy the freedom to do things the way you want, you're going to have to deliver evidence that your students are learning. That's only fair, right? While anyone visiting our class could see that my kids and I loved being there with each other, it was always about the learning. Kids have fun playing games and teasing with each other, they enjoy stories and films, but what really held my classes together was the understanding that we were learning together, that being in that class meant that all of them could grow stronger in their reading and in their writing, in their speaking and their interpretations. Just keep something in mind, however. Happy people aren't that way because of what they accomplish. They find success because they're happy, and that feeling affects their efforts. You won't get those desired results early in the school year because learning takes time, but you can build that good feeling in your classroom from day one.

Blooming

A t last, the petals had opened! Learning was now fully public, and my students' beautiful ideas were calling out to others in a chorus of color. And with that display, pollination also occurred, ideas begetting more ideas, those ideas blossoming into concepts. As my gardener nature became less involved in students' learning, my stem nature became more important than ever because the blooms required more help from me to hold them up. In addition, the sensitive petals were now exposed to wind and cold that they had not experienced as embryos in the warm protection of the soil. They were now buffeted by their preparations for college, by the scholarships they were pursuing, by the winding down of the winter season interscholastic activities that required even more of their time and attention. Life had become harder in our garden because its flowers were starting to droop, weighed down by all of the responsibilities that they had taken on. I provided a remedy in the form of my support, my love and humor, and somehow, despite the stress, my kids continued to amaze me with the beauty of their thinking and their sharing each day. Then there were those days when the sun's gentle shine warmed us all, gave us hope. Through it all, buds continued to unfurl, and with each new blossom, our garden was all the more beautiful.

What Steinbeck Said: Post #57
Monday, February 27, 2017
Now for Some Real Drama

*T*oday we began reading Our Town, *and not only do I love the play, but I also love the fun my kids have as we explore Grovers Corners, New Hampshire. As the Stage Manager fills us in on the particulars of his town, we pause and talk about our town. We discuss the way our town is constituted, the way we act toward each other. We talk about the makeup of our town versus their town.*

In his opening monologue, the Stage Manager lists the specific churches found in that little New England town in 1901, and we today we paused to compare that with our own denominations. He talks about the old names that mark their cemetery's tombstones as well as the homes of the village. We identified our town's old names: Barker, Welling, Lester. Each of those surnames appeared in my classes today. The Stage Manager says that "in our town, we like to know the facts about everybody." We discussed the incidence of gossip in a small town such as Evanston, and I asked students who have lived in bigger cities whether rumors played as important a role there. Each laughed and said that folks tend to mind their own business in a larger place. We decided that in a small town, there simply isn't as much to do. We talk about each other for entertainment. That brought plenty of grins around the circle.

Once we reached the point in Act I where Wilder introduces the Webb and Gibbs families, we laughed a lot at the foibles of his characters, more for their familiarity to us than anything else. Here are people over a century removed from us, 2,000 miles distant from our classroom, and yet, the parents interact with their children much as ours do today. Siblings argue with each other and express their jealousies much as we do today. Following our unit on Of Mice and Men *that examined the human condition, this is a unit that examines the* self. *To that end, we used this class period to build a device for looking inward. Before our study concludes, we will find that what each of us stores inside is but a part of that universal condition. We will touch on transcendentalist concepts, and by the end of Act III, we will glimpse an appreciation for the transitory nature of our existence in this world by speaking and listening to the moving words of Emily.*

Oh, and on top of all that, we will simply have a ball reading aloud to each *other. A drama unit is quite different from one for a novel. The primary difference is that we share the reading, and that gives us a chance to pause whenever we want to discuss, to wonder as we wander through the scenes. True, we do that when I read excerpts from books to the class, but when everyone is reading aloud, there is a certain energy that extends across and around our circle, and it was evident today as we read in a round-robin fashion. The more we read, the more expression we used. That's why our introduction to* Our Town *made me smile, and that's why I look forward to Wednesday's continuation of our reading from today. We are going to learn a lot about who we are as a community. We'll imagine Wilder's town in our minds, but we will feel our town in our hearts.*

F unny thing about *Our Town*. My connection with the play goes back to my fourth year of teaching, when I chose Emily's closing speech as part of a long commencement speech that I delivered at the request of the senior class of Pennfield High School back in Michigan. Though I knew of Wilder's work, I had never seen a production or even read the script, and still I used a passage to encourage the graduates sitting before me to find life's lessons in literature. With great sincerity, I read to them about the wonderfulness of the world through the heroine's eyes. Had I left it at that, I'm sure my address would have been more warmly received, but seeing that I included two other excerpts, there was some well-deserved laughter when I at last sat and our principal announced it was time to recognize the seniors. "It's about time!" came a loud voice from the balcony. It hurt to hear that complaint at the time, but in retrospect, I truly earned it.

Just like me, you're human. You're fallible. Early in your career, and maybe longer than that, you're going to say something that gets you in some trouble. You're going to do something that brings criticism your way. It's not going to be pleasant, but you will learn from those experiences, and eventually you'll be a better teacher because of your stumbles. I delivered a number of commencement speeches after my debacle in Battle Creek, and each one was tight and time-appropriate. Perhaps that was because there was never a talk that I made without a little Thornton Wilder sitting on my shoulder telling me, "OK, that's enough," as I drew near to my conclusion.

To bring my story full circle, many, many years later, I finally did read *Our Town*, and that's when I chose it as a class reading as well. As I delved deeper into the play, I realized that the playwright's brilliance lay in his commitment to simplicity. Wilder's dialogue is not dazzling. The plot is not fascinating, most of the characters are not inspirational. It's simply simple, that's all. *Our Town* educates us well because it reflects who we are, and it asks us to reflect on that reflection. It does not so much show us how we should live as it teaches us the importance of being aware of how we do. It is a window into mindfulness as presented to us by a young woman whose life ends much earlier than anyone expects, and it is narrated to us by a man whose life is never really examined in the story. It is about *us*, you and me, and it is about taking time to appreciate today instead of dreaming about tomorrow.

That would have been a fine message to an auditorium full of eighteen-year-olds and their families. I could have delivered it in a concise and elegant fashion, too, but I was awfully young and inexperienced on stage that night. My audience never got to experience that moment so many years ago, but in my final year of teaching, another group of seniors, circled and enjoying each other's company, did. Want to know why I smiled so? Listening to my kids read to each other, knowing that while they were enjoying their discovery of the play, they couldn't really know what I knew. I had finally understood Emily's message: Oh, *Our Town*, you're too wonderful for anybody to realize you.

Eric Stemle

What Steinbeck Said: Post #58
Wednesday, March 1, 2017
My Favorite Sound

*A*s we continued our reading of Our Town *today, we began by writing a journal entry entitled "Daily Life." That's the name that the Stage Manager gives to the opening act, and as we sought to connect our selves to characters in the play, the entry gave us a chance to consider our day-to-day habits, routines, and rituals. I took the opportunity to think about my own habits, and with a few exceptions, I found that my daily life during the school year has not varied much in the past, oh, twenty years or so. I still eat the same breakfast (a small bowl of cereal and a cup of tea), and the same lunch (a ham and cheese sandwich, an apple, and a banana, though I do get a little wild maybe once a week and substitute a peanut butter and jelly sandwich). While for decades I awoke at 6:15 after Teresa had taken her shower, for the past two years I have set my alarm for 5:45 to head to the family room to do some yoga.*

Today, the fun part of our journal writing lay in the processing as we shared our practices in the circle, including our waking and retiring times, our eating routines, and our study habits. Some of these revelations were quite surprising to the group. For instance, two of my students told the class that they customarily go to sleep around 2:00 am. They both work at McDonald's till closing at 12:30, and how they seem so chipper in the morning with us is a mystery to me. I know that I will view both students a little differently the rest of the year, and I'm sure I won't be the only one.

Of course, I enjoyed sharing my own routines with the class, and they got a kick out of my regularity. I told him that I wasn't really stuck in a rut. For instance, sometimes I eat my breakfast right-handed. Good for mental discipline, you know. I also told them that in recent weeks my early morning habit has evolved from yoga to snowga. *They looked puzzled until I told them that I have been meditating by shoveling our driveway.*

More and more, I see affection being shared around our circle. The more we learn together, the more we share with each other and reflect with each other, the

222

more we seem to appreciate each other. Today we laughed a lot, and I saw knowing looks flying across the room. We are definitely growing tighter, and we are functioning more closely together. That makes the ringing of that bell at the start of each class my favorite sound of the day.

If I had to choose a single word to describe my teaching approach, it would be *organic*. In one sense that adjective indicates that my lesson planning and its execution relied more on how my classes were growing as a community of learners or how their collective understanding was evolving. I definitely had an idea of the skills that I wanted my seniors to leave with at graduation, and I knew a clear and effective sequence for helping them develop those abilities, but I also paid close attention to how everything was developing, and I made teaching moves intuitively depending on what I felt was best for my kids. In that way, my personal language arts pedagogy was animate, not mechanical. I was never one to follow a paint-by-number curriculum, and while that may have dismayed my principals at times, I simply believed that my students' cognitive development was too important to leave to a plug-and-play mentality. In that way, my teaching truly was organic in nature.

It went beyond instruction, however. The beauty of whole-class learning is that those many individual parts can help build a dynamic system that benefits each member. I have already described my students as newborns when they entered our class in the fall, and the same analogy can apply to my classes as whole. If a class was a zygote in late August, day by day growing into an embryo and, then a fetus, there came a time, usually near the end of the first semester, when the water broke and, wouldn't you know it, a viable baby class arrived, suddenly able to breathe on its own, ready to continue its growth and development. Once that blessed event occurred, it became evident to us all that we had become more than a class, more than a group or an organization. We were an organism composed of independent parts that had learned how to function together not only for the good of the body but of those parts as well. Some kids created our emotional center, showing empathy for their classmates when things got tough, joy when things went well, and love, well, love all the

223

time. Every class has a few students who are the heart of the group, who everyone relies on for support and circulation. Other kids were the lungs of our body, the very spirit of our efforts. They breathed life into us on days when we were listless. Still others played the role of the mind, directing our learning by their questions, in the way that they pushed each other to get things done. Of course, there were kids who listened more than they spoke, who took in what we discussed and digested it, providing a valuable audience for ideas to be absorbed and converted to more energy for our learning later on.

Not every one of my classes grew to be a strong and healthy entity. Some crippled themselves with petty disagreements, others were afflicted with laziness and apathy. As I grew more effective as a teacher over the years, though, I found ways to nurture my classes early on so that by March, heading into the final quarter of the school calendar, the organs were in sync, the body ready to run and jump and play. Most importantly, they were closer and closer to being weaned from my guidance. As a team of learners, they were ready to excel on their own.

If you're lucky, some classes will evolve just as mine did late in my career. The stardust will mix just right, and you'll find yourself marveling at how well all the pieces seem to fit. But once you have the good fortune to work with such a wonderfully thriving group, you'll want to find ways to replicate that experience. That's when you'll have to be a little bit of a chemist or a biologist, my friend. The more you understand about the essential elements of a great class and how they interplay to support and to drive each other, the more likely you'll help create magic with your students. It will take more than an intelligent design on your part. It will require an emotional one as well, and it while it may take you years of effort and faith in yourself to learn how to meld those two together, when you get the hang of a class creation, you will have a classroom that kids can't wait to enter every day.

What Steinbeck Said: Post #59
Friday, March 3, 2017
Speaking of Time

*T*oday's classes were shortened to forty-five minutes to accommodate an afternoon in-service, and as always, I tried to squeeze as much out of that time as I could. We had the last of our daily meditations in two classes, and while they both took a little under fifteen minutes, it made a difference in our progress in Our Town. Those two periods read enough of Act II to learn that Emily and George were about to be married, and we talked a little about the tendency for Grover's Corners youth to wed shortly after graduating from high school. We compared that practice to life in Evanston, and we noted two differences. One, with a few exceptions, most of our alumni wait a few years to marry. Two, while Thornton Wilder suggests through the Stage Manager that nearly all Americans "go to their graves married," we noted reasons for a much higher divorce rate today. In each class, at least one student suggested that the role of women has changed in our society since the play premiered, and most kids agreed that women no longer feel the need to be married in order to be fulfilled.

My other class enjoyed additional time to read, and they reached a delightful conversation that takes place between George and his soon-to-be father-in-law. The kids chuckled when they read the advice that Mr. Webb had received from his father: as soon as you're married, give an order so that your wife will learn how to obey; when your wife says something that you disagree with, remain silent but leave the house immediately; and above all, never tell your wife how much money you have. While Mr. Webb then tells George that he did just the opposite in his marriage, my students still found the approach rather out-of-date.

At this point in our reading, we're observing a generation gap. Of course, we see ourselves as more progressive than the characters in Wilder's play, much as we tend to think that our time is in many ways superior to the past. By next week, I'm guessing that my kids will have a different perspective as we read Act III. It's easy to confuse advancements in technology with human development. Kids think *that an America that had yet to see the advent of the automobile was charming but perhaps a bit unsophisticated. When they read Emily's speech in the play's last pages, they will come to realize that human nature hasn't changed much since* Our Town *opened. I'll ask them if it has even changed all that much since* The Odyssey. *All in good time.*

As much as I loved whole-class instruction and its many benefits, I always knew that what I took away, perhaps what many of my students took away from a discussion or an activity, was not always what some other kids perceived. There were many reasons for that lack of unanimity. It's part of human nature to lose focus from time to time, to miss out on a key point, perhaps. It's also in human nature to frame our perceptions within our own mental schema, and even if we all hear the same words being spoken in a conversation, we might not interpret their meaning or their import in the same way. That was critical for me to understand as a teacher, for I was never privy to what all of my students were thinking or feeling during any particular class period. Even on a day that seemed spectacular to me, it's likely that I had kids who left class without much appreciation for what the group had achieved.

The opposite was also true. There were days that seemed mundane to me, where the learning was predictable and nothing truly earth-shaking seemed to take place. Just an average day of processing information, of practicing our skills. Yet, it might have been on one of those days that one of my students had a wondrous epiphany. Who knows how and when the pieces come together for us in the course of a yearlong study? Who realizes just what the catalyst is for someone else's sudden understanding? It's a lot like the humor of a punchline dawning on us long after a joke is told, and I'm sure that I had students who giggled years after our time together when they at last grasped something that we had experienced in class.

My students' perspectives on human development were informed that day by their life experiences to that point, and it would have done me no good to tell them that they weren't so different from the turn-of-the-last-century characters that they were observing. They saw themselves looking through a tunnel rather than into a mirror, and all I could do was listen to their interpretations and ask them at times to elaborate or support their ideas. It didn't matter that they didn't see things the way I did. It only mattered that I gave them the chance to look and to tell each other what they saw. It also mattered that I had the patience to let my students adjust their vision because the years had taught me that while at any moment we may have seen through a glass darkly, in time, in good time, we would discover the light. Our light.

That can be the beauty of your classroom, my friend. I retired an old school teacher, and while I may have embraced each iteration of technology that came my way, I was till the end, an advocate of the acoustic approach that favored students learning with and from each other. You will most likely be blessed with a school that can facilitate online learning in a variety of ways, and that capability will provide your students with ample opportunity to explore beyond your classroom walls. Believe me, as a boy whose learning materials were confined to what I could stuff into my book bag and my teacher could fit onto her shelves, I am amazed at the power I now have sitting on my lap and in my pocket, but I urge you to never lose sight of that light that emanates from a room full of bright minds who have found a way to share with each other. When your students return to see you after moving on from your class, may they come back to where learning was more than just information back to a *place*. Their place with you forever.

What Steinbeck Said: Post #60
Tuesday, March 7, 2017
Stepping Outside of Ourselves

*W*e had ourselves a moment today, one of those shivers-down-the-spine occasions. I love when that happens. We were finishing our class reading of Our Town, and we paused to understand an intricate portion of the play. Having died in childbirth, young Emily has requested to return to her life for one day. Despite the warnings of her mother-in-law and *others who now share the cemetery with her, she asks the Stage Manager to take her back to her twelfth birthday. He explains that she will not only be in the moment but will also be able to observe herself in that moment. "You'll know the future," he tells her.*

Emily sees nothing to fear from that situation but later regrets her decision. Before we read that section, I asked my kids to think for a minute and consider that possibility for ourselves.

"What if, as we sit here today, we could step outside of ourselves and stand behind the circle looking in? Let's say we were looking back on this afternoon from twenty years in the future."

My students nodded and smiled.

"Perhaps one or more of us has died. Maybe one of us has become famous."

"Maybe somebody stole my boyfriend!" said a girl across the way.

"How would you look at this conversation if you knew what happened afterward? How would your perspective change?"

I gave the class some time to discuss with partners, and when we came back together, one of my students asked, "Mr. Stemle, what if that really is happening? What if we are already being observed by ourselves, and we just don't know it?"

Cue the eerie movie music. I felt a shudder.

I smiled at my student. "What if, in reality, we have been observing ourselves all along?"

For seniors and their parents, this is a reflective time. The door leading to adulthood is gradually opening wider and wider, and though the kids still can't see what's on the other side, they know that when they take their first step through after their graduation, there will be no coming back to this life they have known as high school. Whether they have felt comforted or tormented, this has been what they have known for four years. What lies ahead? There's no way to really know, but we do know what Thomas Wolfe told us: "You can't go home again."

Well, unless you can find a stage manager to let you in.

L   ooking back on that special moment in our class, I have no recollection
      of who asked me the question about us observing ourselves. I can't even
      remember which class period the student was in. While those little
bursts of energy that coursed around and across our circle were something that
we could never predict, whenever we began a discussion, there was always a
chance that we would thrill each other with an insight or a provocative question.

What I loved about those happenings was that they didn't always involve my
highest achieving students or even my most vocal ones. Sometimes it was the
quiet kid, the one who listened intently day after day, the one who shared
intellectual secrets with me in essays or journals, who ended up surprising the
group with a gem. There was nothing like the few seconds that then followed,
when the class showered praise on a classmate not used to standing in the
spotlight. If I was able to make eye contact with the speaker, maybe send along a
wink, then all the better. I knew an instance like that could be a spark to ignite
that student's participation for the rest of the year. If nothing else, it could inspire
the rest of the group, even the reticent ones, to share.

One year, I had a student who was easily my best writer, one of the best I had
taught in the course of my career. I couldn't wait to read her papers, and I had a
ball writing notes to her in the margins. Every reading taught me something,
whether it was an analysis that I had never considered or a clever turn of phrase
that I wished I had written. As profound as her writing was, though, we rarely
heard the girl's voice in our circle. In fact, if her countenance was any indication,
she was perfectly disinterested in listening to what her classmates had to say. I
waited as patiently as I could for her to open up in discussion, and while I
continued to encourage her to speak up in my comments at the end of each paper,
I never found a way to have a face-to-face conversation with her till late in the
year. She was an inveterate reader, but she chose not to come in for book
conferences, and so I wasn't sure that I was getting through to her about sharing
some of her remarkable ideas in discussion.

The change came when I offered her some options on her papers. I wrote to
her that she was really not receiving any benefit from practicing conventional
essays, and I suggested that she might have more fun experimenting with

different formats. I told her that she could choose to continue writing the best papers in the class for the rest of the year and really never grow as a writer, or she could try something new, something that would challenge her imagination. When her first such effort produced a dialogue between John Steinbeck and Dante Aligheri, I knew that we had something. The next day, she stayed after class, wanting to know whether I had read her piece. With a nod and a grin, I pulled her paper out of my folder, and we reviewed what she had created. For those few minutes, I delighted in seeing her smile. She thanked me for giving her an opportunity to expand her possibilities, and though I wanted to take a second to exhort her to share that sort of creativity with her classmates, I decided to let her take that one step before I suggested anything more.

The next day in class, she called for the koosh and offered an intriguing interpretation. The rest of the kids smiled around the circle, for they had always known they could learn a lot from her if only she chose to share. After class, she waited till everyone else had left and then stopped beside me as I stood at the door.

"I want to thank you for letting me love English class again," she said with a blush.

"My pleasure," I said, though I told her I wasn't sure what I had done.

"I've been bored for years," she continued. "Now I feel as if I can really do what I want to do, to learn in my own way. Thank you for that opportunity."

I told her that I looked forward to her sharing more in our discussions, and she assured me that she would indeed be contributing more. In fact, she delivered quite a few more of those spine-tingling moments before the year was out. I was always happy to be there to learn from her and from her classmates because I always thought that a teacher was nothing more than the oldest student in a class. You will never stop learning if you adopt that approach to teaching, my friend. See it all as a creative process rather than a transfer of knowledge, a way for you and your students to pull together to make meaning by bringing all of your gifts to the party. Once you get that going, there's no telling how many surprises you will enjoy.

What Steinbeck Said: Post #61
Thursday, March 9, 2017
The Effects of Thinking Critically

*A*s *I came into my third period class today, I counted heads and came up with eight, precisely half of our class roster. This came as no surprise because I knew that several kids were in Casper for state competitions. No problem. I've had classes with fewer students, and no matter how many kids are present, we go on with the plan for the day. We went through our basic routines of* Word of the Day *and ARO but before we began our discussion, one of my girls asked if we could move desks into a smaller circle.*

What a difference! Instead of hucking the koosh ball all the way across the room, we sat close enough to lightly toss it to each other. Kids who tend to speak softly were suddenly audible, and the whole arrangement just seemed more intimate. As a result, each student contributed significantly to the conversation, and conversing was the operative term. This wasn't seniors throwing out comments into the open air. These were friends looking each other in the eye and talking with sincerity and appreciation. It was lovely.

As for me, I was an observer. Well, for the most part. I listened while my class began their discussion of The Effect of Gamma Rays on Man-in-the-Moon Marigolds, *and as they put together the puzzle that is Paul Zindel's play, I sat in the circle and took notes. I had two reasons for doing this. First, I knew that my class was ready to lead itself. Second, I was looking ahead to Monday and hoping to provide my absent students with a recap of what their classmates shared today. If our continuation of the discussion is to be smooth when they come back, then we had to lay that groundwork today. Because I took careful notes, we can roll next time.*

What I heard this morning was a lot of fun. My kids had some emotional interpretations of Beatrice, the caustic and abusive mother, and they made some solid connections with her daughters Tillie and Ruth. When they dipped into symbolism, the energy in the room rose. I tried not to smile too much as I transcribed their ideas because I wanted my students to concentrate on

231

informing each other and not on pleasing me, but when they couldn't reach consensus, I could keep quiet no longer.

The debate centered on Zindel's controlling metaphor, the science project that lends its name to the play's title. The kids had decided that the marigolds represented characters, but they couldn't figure out who.

"Would you like a little guidance?" I asked. Of course, they did.

"How many characters live in the house?"

"Four."

"That means three marigolds and Cobalt-60, the source of radiation. Let's start with that last one. Who has the most influence?"

I thought this would be easy, but the kids had several ideas. Here is where I had to be careful. It would be easy to share my interpretation, but that doesn't help my students think clearly or deeply.

"Do you have a character who has identified herself as the source?" This was a neutral question because all four of the characters are female. The kids seemed stumped before the quietest of the group piped up.

"Beatrice says she has a half-life," he said. Ah. He was right, and the kids immediately realized it. The question now became, who does she affect lightly? Moderately? Greatly? To facilitate this discussion, I drew three pots of marigolds on the board and labeled them by their intensity of radiation. Now all the class had to do was match character names to the pots.

So simple.

Well . . .

The kids couldn't agree on the labels, and as they approached a stalemate, I guided them again.

"There are two ways to approach this problem," I said. "We can look at the radiation as the cause and decide which character gets which dose. Or, we could look at the flowers as the result, and figure out the dosage based on how the marigolds turn out."

Still pretty simple.

And still, we couldn't agree. As the end of class neared, my kids were looking frustrated.

"From the look on your face," one girl said, "I'm guessing we're not close."

"Oh, I wouldn't say that. I'm just enjoying watching you struggle."

These are students who don't do much of that as a rule. They looked less than amused, but they know I love them.

"Maybe our classmates will have an answer when we come back on Monday," I said with a smile, "but in the meantime, if you come up with something tonight, come see me in the morning."

I sure hope someone does. Maybe I'll even tell that student my take on the situation. Then again, maybe I won't. Either way, kids, it will be worth your while to drop in!

I wasn't taught that way in college. My literature classes sat in rows, all desks facing a podium behind which stood a professor, in each case a man, holding court. When we discussed a book, my classmates and I listened and took notes as our good doctors expounded on their interpretations. In some classes, we were encouraged to engage in a dialectic with our instructor, but I rarely participated because I felt inadequate competing with my superiors.

The term *professor* is honorary, and it is customarily earned through academic scholarship and longevity. I didn't often consider my professors to be teachers for they rarely seemed to employ a pedagogy. Instead, they professed, they told us what they thought and believed. Granted, there was much to be learned from paying attention to a learned mind, but if my profs were interested in helping me develop my thinking skills, they used rather indirect methods. For the most part, I played the part of the empty vessel, waiting to be filled with their knowledge. If I learned how to analyze in the same way as those folks standing behind the lectern, then great. My midterms and finals seemed designed as nothing more than to see whether I comprehended what I had been told. Of course, a well-written exam involved more than recapping lectures, and the prompts demanded skill in integrating ideas, but my point is that while I was expected to think deeply and critically on my assessments, my professors did little if anything to teach me how to do that. That is no indictment of their performance—they were merely following precedent. They were basically hired

233

to dispense knowledge, and they did that quite well.

My education professors, on the other hand, taught me how to teach. In order to do that, they modeled strategies and techniques so that I learned ways to help my students develop their cognitive abilities, their collaborative skills. It took me years of classroom practice to reach the point where I had pretty much eliminated any of my professorial tendencies, any of my need to tell my students what to think or believe. I know that at times my kids were hoping that I would just tell them what a poem meant or how to phrase a thought more elegantly, but by the time my career was drawing to a close, I felt that I had at last mastered the art of helping young minds accomplish more than they had ever achieved in their classes before. Part of that success involved taking them down roads they had never traveled to lands they had never envisioned. I may have been at their side, but it was they who looked and listened and learned.

Be patient with yourself as you develop your instructional methods. Teaching is experiential in nature—you learn some basics in your collegiate classes, but it won't be until you try those techniques and reflect and adjust that you will be competent in executing your lesson plans. As for polish, well, that will take you years and years. That's the sad part of statistics that tell us that nearly half of all teachers quit the profession before they have taught for five years. Think about that. What happens to a cake that you take out of the oven too soon? A pot that you remove from the kiln before it's fully fired? A novel that you put away before reaching its conclusion? The same applies to teachers. While you will always seek to improve your skills, even late into your career, you won't know if you have what it takes to excel in the classroom unless you give yourself time to get settled.

Of course, that means that will experience a lot of growing pains, a lot of doubts and a lot of frustration, but there is a reward waiting for you once you become accomplished at more than just professing. When you finally realize that you have become a true teacher, each school day will dawn with the promise that your students just might learn something that will change their lives before the sun goes down. Isn't that worth waiting for?

What Steinbeck Said: Post #62
Monday, March 13, 2017
Morning at the Improv

T oday, I improvised. My lesson plans called for a continuation of our
discussion of The Effect of Gamma Rays on Man-in-the-Moon
Marigolds, but after checking my long-range plans, I decided to shorten
*that conversation and move up an activity scheduled for Wednesday. This was
done in an attempt to provide my students with a more manageable reading
schedule for* A Tale of Two Cities. *A good decision, as it turned out.*

*Following a review of our circle from Thursday for the benefit of a large
number of kids who were absent that day, I asked my kids to pair up, and then I
presented them with three scenarios, each one involving a conversation between
a character from* Marigolds *and one from* Our Town. *The situations were
whimsical, but each one gave kids a chance to further explore the characters. I
loved the ensuing energy.*

Scenario One described the ghost of Emily from Our Town *visiting Ruth from*
Marigolds, *seeking to help the girl who is so troubled in her life. In Scenario
Two, George was plowing his field when Tillie arrived in a time machine that she
had invented. He wanted to brag about his farming, while she endeavored to
share news of future technology. Scenario Three saw Wilder's Julia waiting in
line to meet St. Peter at the Pearly Gates, trying to be helpful to Zindel's
Beatrice, who was characteristically impatient and wondering if she was even in
the right line. Each skit gave my kids a chance to interact with characters, to
find common ground between the plays, to touch on shared themes.*

*Did every pair create a brilliant improvisation? I'm pretty sure they didn't.
Did every pair even stay on task? I have no idea. I sat to the side and
watched and listened, not as concerned with the content of their dialogues as I
was with with the fun they were having. This activity was a departure from our
written analyses, and the kids really seemed to enjoy getting into character. We
processed each scenario afterward, and that gave me at least some idea of what
had transpired in the two-to-three minute duets. It was a nice way to end a short*

unit, a healthy diversion at the end of the hardest nine-week marking period. We
needed to let loose a bit.

As the bell approached, we had time for one final improv. I called for
volunteers to perform in the middle of the circle for the entertainment of the
group. In my first class, two girls leaped to the invitation. One portrayed the
Stage Manager from Our Town, *the other, Nanny, the non-responsive boarder*
from Marigolds. *The scene was set at a Starbucks, where the Stage Manager*
sought to explain the surroundings to the old woman who wanted nothing more
than to tell him all of the thoughts and emotions that she had been holding in for
so long. I couldn't have asked for better ending to the class. The girls'
performance was funny, insightful, and spirited. Their classmates filled the room
with laughter.

I joined them.

Now it's on to Dickens. . . .

I have heard it said that teaching is a lot like making soup. That sounds about right, but there are at least two ways to prepare a pot. One seems easy enough, just a matter of following another's directions by opening a can, pouring its contents into a pan, adding water, and stirring over a low heat. Well, wouldn't it be great if that's all we had to do? Open the curriculum file, find a lesson in the sequence, and present it to your students. Check to make sure every once in a while during the period that the learning is simmering well and serve it with a side of assessment. Of course, another method is determined more by the imagination and the artistry of the chef. The desired outcome is the same, a hearty, healthy, and delicious bowl of nourishment, but the second approach involves creating a meal suited to the eater. In that case, the cook keeps in mind the dietary requirements of those being served as well as their preferences in taste. As ingredients are added and stirred together, the chef worries less about a recipe and more about the aroma, the flavor, and even the appearance of the soup as it heats.

My improvisation in the lesson above was a perfect example of my day-to-day efforts in my kitchen classroom. Sampling our soup told me that a little more flavor was needed. I'm sure I could have proceeded with my original plan, but why would my kids want to eat a bland bowl, especially if I was going to serve it at least a few more times? I decided that treating their taste buds would not only make the lesson more satisfying, but it would refresh their desires to ask for seconds and thirds.

With no disrespect to Andy Warhol, it's easy for school to seem like a can of Campbell's. Teachers can fall into a lull of convenience, opting for preparing quick and easy lessons instead of the time and effort that it takes to gather and clean and chop vegetables, to season the broth, to make decisions while the pot cooks. But it's not just the teacher as chef who bears responsibility for a lackluster serving. Students have their own culpability if they merely show up to the table and dutifully eat whatever is served them. They don't need to whine about the situation, but there comes a time when the customers need to make their voices heard.

That isn't easy in a fast food classroom where you don't even place an order. You take what is served, no substitutions allowed. Students who ask for something different in their learning in those classes are often labeled as malcontents or problem children. And really, a classroom that is set up according to a strict curriculum really doesn't function well with variation. Can kids get a good meal in that sort of restaurant? Sure they can. I just never wanted to put on an apron in one of those places. It will be up to you to create the sort of establishment that you want your students to experience, but the key is simple. Whatever way you decide to teach, be courageous in implementing your approach. You'll still have a curriculum in place, just as most restaurants have a set menu. Just feel free to offer a daily special once in a while to spice up your units. Your kids just might like the taste of that.

Eric Stemle

*T*oday, we began our final literary unit for the year. Hard to believe that happens in mid-March, but if we're going to truly appreciate A Tale of Two Cities, we have to carve out some time. We started by listening to some musical metaphors for the four major works that we read during the year. I chose "This Nearly was Mine" to pair with The Old Man and the Sea, "The Theme from Superman" to go with The Odyssey, "This Land is Your Land" to complement Of Mice and Men. To introduce A Tale of Two Cities, I played the opening strains of Beethoven's Ninth. As the music swelled in intensity, I held up the Dickens' novel and announced, "This is Beethoven." I talked about complexity and dynamics, both hallmarks of the book. It doesn't really matter whether my kids understood the analogy completely. They'll get it eventually.

As we previewed the unit's guidelines, we took a look at its focus on inter-relationships. In the next few months, we will concentrate on the impact that our actions have on others, and to get a better feel for that idea, I had my classes sit in a circle on the floor. I began by holding on to the end of a ball of yarn and then tossing the ball to a student while making a connection to that person. My connections included being left-handed, a baseball player, and a class president in high school. The ball flew back and forth across the circle, eventually forming a web of sorts. We learned that two classmates had the same birthday, two were adopted, one boy's grandmother liked one of our female classmates more than she like her own grandson, and one girl's mother's brother's wife was related to a classmate's grandmother. Who knew?

When I could, I asked the kids questions about their connections to give us more ways to learn about each other. We found out where classmates attended elementary school, where they worked together after school. When the last student tied back to me, the ball went in reverse, the class identifying the connection each time until the ball was whole once more and in my hand.

This is just one exercise, but we'll refer to it throughout our reading of A Tale *of Two Cities, and we'll create a two-dimensional web to link characters in due time, all leading to a final essay which details those relationships. Let's just hope we don't get too tangled. . . .*

H ere we were, beginning the fourth quarter, and my kids and I were still learning about each other. Some of them had known each other since kindergarten, and some had met in our class. No matter when they first came to be in each other's lives, an activity such as "Knit One, Know Two" helped us all see how incredibly tied together we all were, and no one even mentioned Kevin Bacon. As the ball of yarn crisscrossed the circle, I wondered how many of my students were aware of the different levels of connection that were playing out before them. The spoken relationships were easy enough to understand, but when a classmate mentioned being in fourth grade with a friend in the circle, how many of us thought of those people who were with us then? I instantly thought of Sister Davidica and classmates such as Bob and Mark, Richard and Linda and Phyllis. In those few seconds, our web spanned time and distance, both much greater for me than anyone else in the room, but think of the effect that single utterance had on the ether. How many hearts and minds were touched at a subconscious level when those memories were stirred?

Beyond that, the web was our first true metaphor as we began our journey into Dickens' masterpiece. In the coming weeks, we would continually make connections between characters, between those characters and ourselves, between their lives and our own. The fact that we were using yarn instead of string was, of course, a nod to Madame Defarge and her sisters of the traveling knitting, but it would be quite a while before we witnessed that in our reading.

I paid close attention throughout the twenty minutes that it took to toss and retoss the ball because I wanted to be able to reference that personal information for the rest of the year. There is something empowering about your teacher knowing enough about you to share it with the group, caring enough to imply, "See, I was listening when you spoke to us." Each child in every classroom deserves that attention, the honor of being recognized for something outside of what happens in class. It's a little thing, but it means so much.

One year when we were throwing the yarn around, I was being observed by someone who had been in my room many times. We had teamed to deliver professional development to my staff and to others over the course of a few years, and he knew my teaching well, knew how important time was in my work. As the minutes unfolded, I glanced his way to see whether he was squirming a bit, uncomfortable with how long it was taking us to work through the activity. I never caught a sign, and we didn't talk about it afterward, but if he did question my decision to devote twenty minutes or so to telling stories about ourselves, he wouldn't have been the first visitor to wonder whether there was a method to my madness.

There will be visitors to your classroom. Some will be mandated by policy such as your principal's scheduled evaluations of your instruction. Some will be simple drop-ins, colleagues who need a quick favor or students who just can't wait till school is over for the day to come ask you something. You can see those arrivals as interruptions, or you can take delight in the opportunity to share your practice with someone besides your students. Even if they merely want to pop in for a few seconds, invite your guests to stick around for a while, to experience what happens in your classroom. Who knows, folks might see or hear something that will have an impact on their teaching, and when that happens, your school will suddenly be just a little more effective. When my principals came to observe me, I often invited them to join in whatever activity we were doing when they walked in. I involved them in our discussions, asked them to share some knowledge with my students. I wanted them to understand that I was proud of what my kids and I were doing from day to day, and I welcomed them to stop by any time they found themselves in my neck of the building.

You might fear those visits early in your career. A lot of teachers never get comfortable with them, but when you get to the point that you view your teaching as a garden show and not an act of secrecy, you'll be one step closer to helping create success for not just your classes but for your school as a whole. Word will spread that there are good things going on in that room of yours, and before long, you'll have colleagues asking for your opinion on teaching matters. That's a good thing. It will mean that your sphere of influence has grown beyond the collection of desks in your classroom. That will be a very good thing.

What Steinbeck Said: Post #64
Friday, March 17, 2017
Here's a Taste

F riday saw another shortened schedule as teachers were afforded the afternoon to work on their end-of-the-quarter grades. That change gave us just enough time to finish reading Chapter One of A Tale of Two Cities *together. I know it sounds odd that it would take us parts of two class periods to read three pages, but reading the beginning of a Dickens novel is a lot like eating chocolate mousse. Something that rich, you don't wolf down. Rather, you take small spoonfuls and savor the subtleties of flavor.*

There is so much to set up at the outset with this piece. First of all, there is the matter of the historical background that the author provides. I paused often to check my students' familiarity with the political context of 1775, to make connections with the American colonies and their situation as the chapter explains the state of affairs in England and France just prior to our revolution. There is also the perspective of the period that the book was published, as Dickens continually compares that to the 18th century setting of the plot.

Second, we began our long exploration of Dickens' style. Kids usually struggle to discern understatement, whether its Harper Lee describing her father's law practice in To Kill a Mockingbird or Dickens commenting on the "humane achievements" of the church in France as it tortured and killed a youth for not kneeling at the distant sight of monks passing. Yesterday, this is where I gave them just a dab of dessert as I explained the satire of the passage. I want them to know what to taste for as they read. Otherwise, they'll gobble all of that deliciously intricate phrasing, completely missing layer upon layer of nuance. As a group, we might never truly appreciate the depth of Dickens' genius, but at least we can move beyond being oblivious to the gifts he offers us.

We ended the period by discussing the divine right of kings, and, speaking of being clueless, the failure of the royalty, particularly the French, to perceive the growing unrest among the populace. On a broad scale, my kids know the outcome of the coming insurrection, but they know very little of the complexity of the art they are about to enjoy. I'm licking my lips just thinking about it!

I was never much of a survey-style teacher, but many of my colleagues were, and they worked hard to expose their students to as many literary works as they could. There has always been a school of thought that suggests that breadth is more important than depth, and so, in some classes, students read a high volume of poems and short stories and novels in order to be better versed on the span of literature. That approach goes hand in hand with the idea that the primary learning in a literature course is the piece as content. In that case, what happens in *A Prayer for Owen Meany* carries more weight than the reader's interpretative experience. John Irving's use of symbols and his thematic layering are critical to the teaching of that novel, more so than the reader's ability to discern them. In other words, the focus in a survey class is on the literature itself, and quite often the literature is presented in terms of what the teacher or critics of the piece see as its meaning. For that reason, objective assessments are often used to measure student understanding of the content. Multiple choice tests do the trick if the purpose is to determine whether the reader has followed the path laid out by other interpreters.

I never wanted to go down that road, myself. Perhaps it was because my teacher training at Michigan State came at the height of the reader-response criticism movement, where I studied the work of I.A. Richards, Stanley Fish, and Louise Rosenblatt, among others. Their ideas helped to inform my approach to teaching literature, and as a result, I concentrated on teaching my students how to engage with a text rather than on the work itself. Of course, that meant spending a lot of time discussing the validity of one's analysis, and there were many occasions early on where I had to convince my young friends that a story's meaning couldn't be just anything that pleased them as readers.

"Hey, it's possible," my seventh graders liked to say, suggesting that the answer to a Poe mystery might lie in alien interference. Working through those issues was messy at times, much more so than lecturing on the conventional interpretation. It was also time-consuming. Over the years, I learned that if my kids were going to become effective analysts, clear thinkers, then I was going to have to invest quite a bit of time in letting them experiment, in guiding them and providing them with feedback on their efforts.

Want to know why it took us two class periods to read three pages of *A Tale of Two Cities*? Simple. We were doing a lot more than reading. My seniors may not have left our class in May having read a lot of books or stories or plays, but they did take with them skills in interpreting the long list of works that they would read for the rest of their lives. I'd say that was a much better investment. As you begin your career, you might find yourself overwhelmed with the implementation of your prescribed curriculum because, in most cases, you will encounter the survey approach. There are so many standards and benchmarks to address, and so few days to do so when you consider the time taken away by testing, assemblies, and student absences for school activities, not to mention the time you will need to reteach concepts that your kids don't catch right away. You might try doing the math to determine just how much time you will really have to help your students master or at least achieve proficiency on any curriculum. Then you might want to go take a long walk in order to figure out just how you're going to make it all work.

Or you might just do what I did. First, accept that you can't teach it all. Your kids cannot learn it all. Any curriculum, especially something like the Common Core State Standards, can only realistically be viewed as guidelines. Would it be great to come to the end of the year and say that a majority of your students were proficient or advanced on each standard? Of course. Truth be told, that is unlikely, though, and it leads us to the second thing you can do. Study the curriculum and then determine what is truly essential to your students' learning of your discipline. That might be a step you take with your department or with grade level teams across your district, but even if it's just you, it will be critical that you decide what is absolutely required for your kids to know and do in order for them to have control of the content and the skills that your class presents. When that's done, devote most of your time and energy to concentrating on those topics. You've heard that less is more? Believe it.

Let me give you an example. The Common Core State Standards for writing for grades eleven and twelve contain ten standards and eighteen sub-standards. Those include guides for organization, research and documentation, idea development, and word choice to name a few. Of course, each of these standards and its benchmarks plays a key role in the development of strong composition. I can't look at the list and say that a college-worthy paper does not include each of those prescribed elements, but can a writer create a functional essay that does not "use precise language, domain-specific vocabulary, and techniques such as metaphor, simile, and analogy to manage the complexity of the topic"? (CCSS.ELA-LITERACY.W.11-12.2.D) Sure she can. Would it be the best paper turned in to her teacher? Probably not, but you are going to have to decide whether it's better for your kids to do the essential things well and some of the supplementary elements not so well, or whether it's better for them to be mediocre but acceptable on all of the standards.

Sometimes you will simply pull off a miracle. The conditions will be right, your teaching elegant and effective, and your group of students well-prepared and open to instruction. When all of those aspects are present, you just might get to the end of the year and read final papers that take your breath away. If that happens, then find a wonderful way to celebrate. If it doesn't, just realize that it's downright difficult to get your students to a high skill level for every aspect of your curriculum. That understanding might save you a long walk or two.

What Steinbeck Said: Post #65
Tuesday, March 21, 2017
Encountering the Mist

*T*oday *before we began our guided reading of Chapter Two of* A Tale of Two Cities, *I led my classes in a series of exercises to get their circulations pumping. I got them up out of their seats and we touched and tapped and rubbed our arms and heads and legs till our skin was tingling.*

The smiles on our faces told me that the kids were ready to dig into Dickens.

As we opened to the chapter, we were taken to a setting shrouded in the cold and mist of an English November. I paused from time to time to help my kids visualize, maybe even to feel in their imaginations the harsh conditions as we were introduced to our first character of the novel. At this point in our reading, my students always find Dickens' prose nebulous. I go into the novel knowing that they will experience this, and as I guide them in identifying the setting, I push and yet, at times, I pull.

One of the features of the novel that I want my kids to start noticing is wordplay. Dickens' puns are exquisite, and none exceed his description of Jerry Cruncher, the runner for Tellson's Bank. For this errand, he has ridden his steed to catch the mail coach that carries Jarvis Lorry to Dover and his meeting with Lucie Manette. The coachman, the guard, and the three passengers dread his approach, even as his figure emerges from the fog. He is a rough character, a raw-voiced man whom the author identifies as a "hoarse messenger." For my first two periods, I paused and threw my hands into the air.

"Did you catch that?" I said. "Oh, that is so good."

"What?" kids said. I explained the pun, and as it dawned at different times on kids, giggles popped up around the circle.

When my last class came to that point, and I read that sentence aloud, one of my boys snickered nearby.

"What's so funny?" I asked as if I didn't know.

"He's a hoarse messenger!"

"OK."

"Come on, it's funny. He rides a horse, and he has a hoarse voice." As they began to catch on, the rest of the class looked at their classmate with admiration. It was so much better to have him explain the joke than to have me point it out. I remind my students from time to time that we are all teachers in this class, and here was a wonderful example.

By the end of the chapter, I wanted my kids to understand one thing: the brilliance of Dickens lies in his layering. We have a hard time seeing that clearly at first, just as the guard and the coachman and their passengers are unable to

see who is calling to them through the mist. We, too, are passengers in this fog.
Soon that rider will emerge, as will our understanding of the book.

Throughout much of my career, my colleagues and I lamented the failure of our students to concentrate on what we thought to be simple tasks. Following a short series of instructions, engaging in a discussion for five or ten minutes, reading several pages and summarizing their contents. Those chores were always daunting for most of my middle school students who seemed to have the attention span of a Scottish terrier, but even my seniors had lapses where they appeared to lose contact with the moment. Perhaps they were ruminating over something that had happened in the hallway before class. Maybe they were thinking of what they planned to do that evening. Their phones could also take their attention away from the task at hand. No matter what the distraction, their ability to learn was compromised by the fact that the work before them was not their first priority at that moment.

And what did I do to bring them back into what we as a class were doing? I did what my fellow teachers did, what my own teachers had done throughout my schooling.

I asked them to pay attention.

Well, when I was in a good mood, I asked them. When I felt irritated or at the end of my patience, I would demand it. Yet, wasn't I the same person who would lose track of the conversation in a faculty meeting? Miss a salient point in the Sunday homily? Have to reread countless pages in my college texts because I couldn't remember a single word I had seen? Here I was, expecting my students to do what I rarely did, totally concentrate for an extended period of time. Worse, instead of helping them stay with a task, I merely insisted that they do so.

One night, listening to a favorite album while grading papers, my old friend Stephen Stills finally got through to me. "Sit yourself down," he sang over and over. "Take a look around." How many times had I heard that song and only nodded at the singer's instruction? This time, however, a meaning shone through. Maybe I was just ready to hear it, or maybe I really needed to understand it, but his message about slowing down and taking things in suddenly made sense to me within my own context. I had been pushing and pushing my classes, and when I hit a wall, I had grown frustrated because my kids didn't seem to have the same interest in the material as I did, didn't exude the same enthusiasm. And what did I do? I tried to force them to feel it.

Now, isn't that silly? It's not much different than asking them to read my mind. Why don't you know what I know? Why don't you see what I see? I just told you that—why can't you understand?

I remember having a conversation with a parent who complained that her son was faring poorly in my class because he suffered from a learning disability and couldn't concentrate. That made reading and writing hard for him, she said. I agreed with her that her child had trouble keeping up with our assignments, seemed bored in our discussions, but then I asked her a question. Was there anything her son did that showed his ability to focus? For instance, did he like to play video games?

Sure, she said. He loved them. Could play them for hours.

I smiled. "So," I said gently, "we know that in certain circumstances, he can concentrate."

She smiled back. "I guess we do."

Now all we had to do was figure out how to help the boy transfer that ability from one situation to another. You know what? That's true of almost all of us, whether we have a diagnosed condition or not. If an event or an activity catches our fancy, we can lose ourselves in the moment. Time seems suspended, doesn't it? We lose track of the hours, forget to eat or stretch our limbs. We are engrossed in what lies before us, and we worry not about the past or the future. As Jon Kabat-Zinn puts it, we are mindful of the present.

Tired of complaining and even more tired of not getting results, I followed Stills' advice. I sat myself down. I took a look around. Before long, what I saw was an answer. If my students were ever going to see beyond the ordinary in their reading, we would have to slow down and look deeply. That meant that I was also going to have to help them with that looking, give them new lenses, so to speak. And the result? When we started considering our readings at a finer granularity, we started to have more fun with our analyses. It was a little like playing "I Spy," and the kids started challenging themselves and their classmates to find subtle allusions and puns. It took more time for us to do that, so I started assigning fewer books, and I looked for works that were richly layered. It wasn't easy work for any of us, but there were moments, "hoarse messenger" moments, where a student's discovery spurred the class to dig even deeper. Sometimes we had to wait until March before that happened, but I welcomed it just the same.

If, as I told you in the previous reflection, less is more, then a corollary is that slow is better than fast. Take your time when you're leading your students to think in a deep fashion. I'm not saying that you have to dawdle and bore your kids, but if you find that you don't have time to go deep beneath the surface of some concepts, then maybe you need more time rather than less. Intellectual discovery may come in a flash for the Newtons and the da Vincis of the world, but for the rest of us mortals, making complex interpretations takes time. We often have to mull things over before we see connections at a different level. Not every lesson that you teach will require you to proceed methodically because a lot of your content will be accessible to your kids without too much heavy lifting. There will, however, be ideas that just won't seem clear at first. When you come to those, find a way to slow down so that your students can assimilate and explore at their own pace. It's a lot like hiking an easy path and suddenly coming to a creek deep enough that you have to traverse a log or a series of stones to keep your boots dry. You can hustle your way over and hope you don't slip, or you can take each step deliberately, testing to see if the footing is secure so that you can maintain your balance.

Your classes might trek along for a while, seeming to understand things without exerting too much effort, but eventually, if they are going to truly grow intellectually, they are going to have to cross a few streams. At first, they will need you by their sides to guide their passage, and in time they will find their own way to the next fording without your help, but even if they do fall head first into a river, they'll dry out soon enough. In the meantime, they'll get a better idea of just how deep the water is.

What Steinbeck Said: A Special Post
Wednesday, March 22, 2017

F orty-one years ago, I entered a classroom for the first time as a contracted teacher. Fresh out of Michigan State, nervous and not really sure about what I was getting myself into, I spent that first year as a writing instructor at Navajo Community College in Tsaile, Arizona. In that year, I learned a lot about what I didn't know about teaching. The following year, Teresa and I moved back to Michigan, and I began a four-year stint as an English and reading teacher at Pennfield High School in Battle Creek. Those years were my introduction to classroom management as I learned how to create independent learning experiences for my students and how to appreciate a spectrum of teaching philosophies.

A major change came into our lives as we moved to Green River, Wyoming, where we taught for nineteen years. I began that period as a junior high and middle school teacher for seven years, and that position changed my approach to instruction. I taught language arts and American history and too many exploratory courses to mention. I coached basketball and football, and I made friendships that continue to this day. I faced a difficult decision when I was invited to move across town to Green River High School, but the dozen years I spent there shaped my teaching forever. In 1985, I began teaching a variety of professional development courses for the district, and in time, I became a staff developer, splitting my daily time between students and colleagues. I was also blessed to study under some of the greatest theorists and practitioners in the profession.

In 1999, our family made one final move, this time just down the road a bit to Evanston. Teresa had the opportunity to return to teaching elementary music, and she became and remains the best kept secret in our district. I have had the honor of continuing to work with students and with teachers for the past eighteen years, and I have continued to hone my craft. None have been touched more than mine as I have been surrounded by remarkable people.

Two weeks ago, Teresa and I made one more decision: this will be our last

249

year of teaching. We feel that we have fought the good fight (more often than we may have liked) and soon we will have completed the race. By all means, we have kept the faith that there is no greater calling for us than to teach. Our deepest thanks to all of you who have walked beside us these many years.

In the meantime, watch this space!

I have always thought that there are three pieces of news that people should be allowed to share with everyone on their own terms. Not through the rumor mill, but one-to-one or as an announcement to a group. Those three are a wedding, a birth, and a retirement. It's fun to share those joyful tidings, and nothing seems more deflating than going up to a good friend, saying, "Hey, guess what?" and hearing, "Someone told me you're having a baby!"

Yeah. We are. Gee.

Teresa and I had planned on teaching another year, had agreed to make a decision before the school year started, but like a lot of our older friends, when the time came to leave, we knew it. We were tired. Simple as that. We could have taught that one more year, but we worried that our energy would continue to ebb, and eventually, our teaching would suffer. We didn't want that to happen for our students or for ourselves, so we slept on things for a few weeks and then made it official.

What I said about announcements? That goes both ways. Not only was it important for me to deliver the news, but I felt a certain responsibility to my colleagues. I considered a hierarchy of folks who I wanted to talk to before the general faculty and my students learned. I felt I owed it to my principals to tell them first. They would be directly affected because they would have to find a replacement, and the sooner they knew, the quicker they could put those wheels in motion. Next, I wanted to tell my department, and not en masse. I had taught with some of them for nearly twenty years, and I wanted a private moment with each. I figured that word would spread quickly, and so decided to I announce my retirement at faculty meeting the next Monday. As it turned out, most of the group was surprised to hear the news, and so I guessed that my English family had kept things to themselves. I was grateful for that consideration. Later that day, I told my classes. I figured that my leaving wouldn't make much difference to them because they were heading out as well, but many of them had brothers and sisters coming behind them, and I knew that would bring some disappointment.

"Couldn't you just wait another year?" a couple of juniors said to me in the hall. "We've been waiting so long to be in your class."

I nodded in sympathy. "I would have loved to teach you," I said.

"Then stay one more year! It's not that long!"

I smiled. "You know, there's never really a good time to retire if you think about it that way. There's always one more year in somebody's mind."

They agreed, but I knew they weren't happy. I had a parent come up to me a few weeks later. I had taught three of her children and adored them all. "I was hoping you would hang on until my youngest came through," she said with a frown.

"What grade is he in?" I asked.

"Sixth."

I widened my eyes. "I'd be seventy!" I said in mock horror.

"Well. . . ."

The decision made and announced, I felt a certain lightness. I knew that though a lot of work remained till school was out, I had entered into a finite universe. Every year I had pushed myself beyond what I thought was my limit, but this was different. I knew the end was within reach. I loved teaching in so many ways, even though it tired me out, but when I was finished, I went on to the next phase of my life.

"How's retirement?" I've heard many, many times.

"Highly underrated," I have replied. I hope to be retired as long as I taught.

As you read this, I expect that you are many years from even considering retirement. It might not be forty years out, but there is so much ahead of you, so much learning about our profession, so many rewards for devoting your life to the learning of others. For loving young people. Can you understand how amazing that last part is? No matter how we define teaching, no matter how we break it into its constituent parts and try somehow to improve on it, in the end, what will make you special as a teacher will be your love. The love you have for your students, the love you have for the content you share, the love you have for learning. If that's what you bring into your classroom every morning, nothing else will really matter. If you ever find any of that love missing, well, there are always other occupations available to you, and there's always retirement. Somehow, I don't think that you'll have to worry about either. If you did, you wouldn't have read this book.

What Steinbeck Said: Post #66
Thursday, March 23, 2017
Defying Gravity

We have come to the end of the third quarter, the "black hole of education," as one of my former principals used to call it. He was referring to a psychological theory that states that the most daunting part of any task comes just after its midpoint. If I go out to run four miles, then I'm most likely to feel discouraged right around the completion of mile two. That makes sense, doesn't it? We we work hard to get halfway to a goal, but when we do, we realize that what he have remaining is exactly as much as we have achieved. I think that what my principal meant was that as we teachers put a lot of energy into our work at the beginning of the second semester, we often see little reward. The kids are mentally tired, and they have so many activities going at that point in the year that distract them from giving their all to their studies. Teachers are also tired, and spring break seems a light year away.

What can we do? My choice is always to change things up, to lighten the emotional load for my students. On Thursday, that meant presenting my classes with an extra option for their next essay. The directions call for kids to identify and describe a real-world problem and then propose in detail a possible solution. This is something that my students have done a number of times in high school, and that familiarity can certainly breed contempt. And really, who wants to read seventy contemptuous papers?

252

To provide my students with a different avenue of expression, I shared with them Jonathan Swift's delicious satire, "A Modest Proposal." Dismayed by the lame-brained schemes proposed by the British parliament to solve the poverty in his native Ireland, Swift responded with a counter that prescribed the eating of children. It is a brilliant excoriation of the treatment that the Irish resented in the early part of the eighteenth century, and it initially took my kids aback with its flippant call for such barbarism. As we examined the piece in a little more depth, however, I pointed out that what Swift was mocking was not the conditions that inspired foolish solutions, but rather those ideas themselves.

"You may write a straightforward paper that executes this prompt," I told my classes as we looked at the guidelines for the assignment, "and I'll be happy to read that approach. If you want to try something different, though, then I'll also be happy to read your satire."

I know that at this point, I have writers who want to play it safe and write a researched paper that they know how to control. As I told my kids, I'm perfectly fine with that. Yet, we are starting to come out of that black hole (a neat trick, in itself), and I also know that I have kids who are curious about taking a writing risk. All they needed yesterday was a little push.

We took a few minutes to brainstorm problems, starting with our school as a context and then moving to our town and finally to our nation. With each issue, we first defined the problem and then talked about feasible solutions. Then we had fun. We generated outlandish suggestions for fixing the situation, and each time, I reminded the kids that they were satirizing not the problem but the manner in which such matters are handled. There was laughter, there was possibility. More than anything, there was energy somehow escaping that event horizon of the dreaded third nine weeks.

One of my favorite Ralph Waldo Emerson lines says, "Nothing great was ever achieved without enthusiasm." As we concluded our discussion of the essay's demands, I had the feeling that something great is going to be coming my way. My pen will be ready!

I f anything helps to create enthusiasm, it's choice. It's hard to get jazzed about an assignment when it feels as if it's nothing more than a matter of following instructions step by step. But if we're given some room for creativity, we tend to find more energy. It's as if instead of being confined to one lane on a track, we're allowed to run whichever path we want, or, even better, in a different direction. How much enthusiasm your students generate will in some part be tied to your expectations as their teacher. If your delivery of the curriculum limits their creativity, they might give you a good effort, but it's unlikely that they'll get all that excited about your assignments.

In February and March, that dreary part of the year when we were all tired of winter and still a ways from vacation, when all of us were a little stale, I learned that options were fine, but even that bit of freedom sometimes failed to spark much passion from my students. They still felt as though they were writing just another paper, just going through the motions one more time. Introduction, body, conclusion. Thesis and support. Strong clincher, catchy title. You know what that means? Zzzzzzzzzz. . . .

My solution was to empower my students to determine their own success criteria for an assignment. I let them choose whether to continue refining their command of structure and their use of conventions or to go outside that lane and try something new. If they picked the latter, then they were no longer trying to match my notion of a polished essay. Throughout the year, I had guided them to an understanding of my vision of an exemplary paper. Most had difficulty early on seeing what I held in mind, but with each prompt, they made a certain amount of progress toward that end. Now, with this alternate assignment, there was no picture to match, no model to follow. If they experimented but still stayed within the confines of a standard essay format, then I evaluated their work on the basis of our rubric's familiar benchmarks. But if they produced a different form altogether, then I concentrated my feedback on their logic, their support of their reasoning, even the artistic nature of the writing. In choosing that path, they acknowledged that their pieces would not be assessed for grading purposes, but at that point in the year, some kids needed to recharge a bit more than they needed to raise their scores. They had earned enough credit in our marking system so that taking a paper off ended up making little or no difference to their overall grade. And while there were other kids who really needed the assignment in order to acquire more points, they decided to trade in that chance for the benefit of having some fun with their writing. It didn't matter to me one way or the other. I let them choose the outlet they desired.

For some kids, that exercise was an entertaining diversion. For others, it was a real boost, a rare chance to escape the paper mill that had ground them down for years. I wasn't certain that my kids who struggled with writing were going to suddenly improve because they tried a novel approach on one paper, but I did know that it couldn't hurt. For my part, I learned to let go and enjoy where my students took me. I did wonder, though, what had taken me so long to find the courage to step back and let them go off on their own.

I've told you before that in order to be a great teacher, you are going to have to be daring from time to time. You'll need the courage to try new approaches, to stand up for your students when you feel that the system is being unfair to them, to stand up for yourself when the powers that be seek to limit your creativity. When you find the nerve to take those stands, you'll also find that taking risks is a sure-fire way to enkindle your own enthusiasm, and that will help you satisfy at least one prerequisite for greatness.

What Steinbeck Said: Post #67
Tuesday, March 28, 2017
Equilibrium

I came home today and took a nap. Well-earned, by the way. The day was more of a performance than a facilitation, and it is rare that I do that. It was necessary because early in our reading of A Tale of Two Cities, *I find myself doing more of the lifting until the kids are more comfortable with Dickens' prose. We took a step today toward comprehending better as my kids posed questions about plot, mostly. Every time they did, I took the discussion in the direction of character. Dickens is marvelous in that sense because he uses physical description as a window to personality and to character traits. By the end of the period, we had a good grasp of who Jarvis Lorry and Miss Manette and Dr. Manette and Monsieur and Madame Defarge are at an introductory level.*

An efficient discussion all comes down to a matter of balance. I can't tell you how I know the optimum level of energy in the circle, but it's a feel that I have developed over the course of decades of leading it. Too little enthusiasm, and we don't put forth much effort to dig for answers. In a low-energy discussion, kids fall into the inertia of rest, seemingly choosing to let their classmates carry the conversation. The problem is that if most of the students take that route, then the talk goes nowhere. Too much enthusiasm, and we have trouble focusing. In a high-energy discussion, kids are subject to the inertia of motion, and ideas bounce around the circle like excited electrons. That can be fun, but it's hard to find coherence in that event.

My role in each discussion is to strive for equilibrium, that balance that promotes an easy flow of questions and answers, facts and opinions, humor and serious contemplation. I, in effect, become the stabilizer. When the energy is high, I stay quiet, looking for opportunities to probe, to push, but also letting my students run with the analysis. When the energy is low, I animate myself. I get out of my seat and go into the center of the circle, the better to gesture, to dance, to urge my students into more active participation. I become less of a listener and more of an actor.

When did I perform today? In supplementing my students' understanding of what goes on in Chapters Three through Six, I looked for analogies, for word analyses that helped them see the delicious touches that Dickens infuses into his narratives. I raised my own energy level as a way of providing my kids with a sense of importance, with an optimism that tells them that they can do more than just read A Tale of Two Cities; *beyond that, they can find the treasures that the author buries along the way. Doing that three times in the course of the day didn't seem tiring to me at the time, but when I walked in the front door of our home, a weariness washed over me. A good tired, but a tired nonetheless.*

The nap? The nap was wonderful. . . .

256

A s I look back on my college days, particularly my classes in the English Education program, I see the combination of perspectives that my professors presented to me. It was the early 1970's, a cutting-edge time in language arts instruction, and I found no shortage of chances to learn about the nuts and bolts of an effective classroom or the esoteric theories of reading and writing skill acquisition. I was granted many opportunities to visit local schools to observe and to test my young instructional legs long before I even began student teaching, and I was privileged to meet a number of experts in the field who inspired me to adopt a progressive approach to my practice when I eventually hung out my shingle in a public school.

Despite my wonderful education and training, the one aspect of teaching that my professors could not instill in me was the knowledge of how to develop a feel in the classroom. How could they? How do you teach someone to whistle? To apply the proper pressure on a car's accelerator or its brake pedal? To sink a twelve-foot putt that breaks six inches from left-to-right? The touch required for each of those actions is only developed with practice and experience. Sure, I can model for you. I can give you feedback on your performance and answer your questions, but in the end, in order to perform well, you have to develop your own sense of what it takes to achieve the task.

How can a teacher preparation program show an undergraduate just how much energy to apply in a class discussion? How can a textbook tell a teacher when to suggest corrections on a student's essay and when to ignore its errors and write encouragement instead? How can a principal tell her staff when to insist on silence during independent reading in the classroom and when to appear unaware that two kids in the back of the room are whispering out a problem with each other? Each of those instances involves decisions based on intuition, and I don't recall seeing that topic listed the last time I looked at a college of education course description. Maybe that's because it's an intangible feature of teaching, not a plug and play. It's a matter of balance, and finding that equilibrium in any given class period is complicated by the fact that a teacher has fifteen or twenty or even thirty moving parts to consider when making an instructional move. There is no checklist that will ensure that those decisions will work, no recipe that will guarantee success if it is followed faithfully. That must be frustrating for those who evaluate teaching performance. They can see and hear that something special is happening in a classroom, but because they can't quantify that success, they know that they can't help other teachers replicate a great one's mastery of the moment.

What's even more exasperating is that the feel is not simply a function of experience. If it was, then every veteran teacher would have the knack for making just the right moves to keep the flow going in a lesson. Desire to acquire that touch certainly plays a part in its development, but perhaps—and I know that this is scary to some—it's more of a faculty, an innate talent, than it is a facility, a practiced skill. Even if that is the case, all is not lost. Sure, it would be great if every teacher was a virtuoso of lesson execution, but rather than spending time and effort to help folks acquire talents they weren't born with, administrators could devote their supervision to guiding all of their teachers to master what they do have an aptitude for. Not everyone in the choir is going to sing a solo. The key to leading a great school lies in being able to help all of the singers develop their voices, and beyond that, to blend in harmony. There will always be gifted people who take the lead, but complementary parts work so much better than strained voices pushed out of their comfort zones.

How the faculty functions is not going to be your direct concern, at least not early in your career. In time, you might take on the responsibility of bringing your staff together in pursuit of a common school goal or set of goals. You may serve as department chair or a building leadership team member, or you might just work behind the scenes to inspire your colleagues to try things, to do that little extra to make a lasting impact on the lives of their students. In the meantime, though, you can tend to your own garden. Go into your classroom each and every day looking for ways to improve as a professional. Watch your students more intently, listen to them more attentively. More than anything, get in touch with how they are feeling as they come into your room each period. The earlier in your practice that you begin doing those things, the more you will be able to accelerate your progress toward becoming a remarkably intuitive teacher.

What Steinbeck Said: Post #68
Thursday, March 30, 2017
Spittin' In

*S*ometimes when I read to my classes, I feel like a little boy given a chance to shine: bright-eyed and intense but eager. That was the case today as we shared the first two chapters of Book the Second of A Tale of Two Cities. There were voices to distinguish, brilliant understatement to highlight, and subtle wordplay to examine. How could anyone read Dickens out loud and not be in love with the author?

Today our reading dealt mostly with the character of Jerry Cruncher, the gravel-voiced odd-job man for Tellson's Bank. We had been introduced to him as a messenger in the novel's second chapter, but today, we saw him in three different settings and in three different lights. At home, he is a belligerent and abusive husband, cruelly chastising his wife for praying against his financial interests. As I read his rants, I effected a loud and obnoxious tone. This was quite a challenge over the course of three class periods, but my voice survived. At the bank, he plays a more servile role, sharing a post with his twelve-year-old son, awaiting direction for serving the bank. Finally, he takes a message to Mr. Lorry at the Old Bailey, the courthouse. Here his language is more amiable as he chats up a fellow observer of the Darnay trial. In all three contexts, I got to practice my best cockney accent and help my kids develop an understanding of this surprisingly complex character.

Beyond my reading, we had a little fun with language today. Young Jerry is described as "the expressed image" of his father. I took a timeout to discuss a familiar phrase with my classes.

"When you see a young boy who looks just like his father, you say that he is the—"

"Spitting image!" shouted most of the class. I wrote those words on the board.

"Exactly," I said, "and by saying that, you are a part of the ninety-nine percent of folks who would say just that."

I turned and faced the circle. "And you and the rest of that ninety-nine percent would be wrong."

At this point in the year, my kids are not surprised by such pronouncements. They just wait for the rest of the point to be revealed.

"What the expression really says is that young Jerry looks like his father," and I wrote "image" on the board. *"And he shares his father's blood, his spit."* I wrote "spit" to the left of "image."

"Therefore, the boy is the spit and *image of his father."* The circle erupted in *"ahs."*

"Of course, we don't enunciate all three words clearly, do we? We tend to say 'spittin' image,' but that's the story of that phrase." As it turns out, according to **grammartist.com**, the idiom is Biblical in its origin, referring to the saliva and mud that God uses to form Adam in his image. Ah, indeed. My tangent here was not designed to enlighten my kids about the novel. Rather, it was to further create our class culture, our appreciation of language. That's always worth a minute or two.

As much fun as I have had performing this book for my kids this past two weeks, I look forward to returning from spring break and sitting in on student-led discussions. They have a pretty good base now, and while some of my kids will forever labor to make sense of the novel, many of us will understand it, and together we will all have enough comprehension to dig deeply into characters, into motivations, into themes and symbols. Oh, and I will still read aloud from time to time. That's good for me!

As I told you earlier, every so often I would invoke my inner Robin Williams when I felt my class needed a little boost, though I was careful to avoid mimicking his character from *Dead Poets Society*. If I expected my students to forswear clichés in their writing, then I most definitely wanted to avoid doing a John Keating impression. Still, I held that characterization close to my heart sometimes when I sought to engage my students' attention, and when I read aloud to them, I imagined another Williams standup bit in which he invites his audience to come inside his comedic mind. In three frantic, kinetic moments, he provides a running mental commentary on his stage performance, including the panic he feels when his material seems to be bombing with the patrons. I must say that I rarely felt any agitation when I was reading and pausing to share my thoughts with my students—on the contrary, I relished those moments—but the notion of making public my thoughts and associations while reading was not unlike what the comic does in opening the door to his inner sanctum.

I don't remember ever listening to my college professors read anything more than a line or two as quotation, and I recall just a few times when my high school teachers read aloud to our class, perhaps from a text that we did not have copies of to read for ourselves. Sometime after the early elementary grades, it seemed either inappropriate for my teachers to read to us, or maybe they just didn't want to take away the class time to do so. Grownups read to themselves, the message seemed to be.

Nonsense.

We all like to listen to the human voice, love to listen to stories whether in conversation with a friend or alone with our headphones and an audio book. Why do we assume that as students grow older, they no longer want to hear their teachers read to them? Is it because the teachers don't enjoy reading aloud? Their administrators feel that it inhibits students from developing their own skills? Think about it. We seem OK with other circumstances where people show us how to do things by explaining the process as they go. Why do you think *Food Network* is so popular? Rachel Ray and Bobby Flay don't just cook with the camera on. They tell us why they're doing each step, and they pass along tips from time to time so that we can be more likely be successful when we step into our own kitchens.

That's what Williams did when he gave us a glimpse of what he thought and felt standing before the microphone. That was me when I stopped at certain points and either told my students what I was thinking or how I was dealing with difficult passages, when I swiveled out of my desk in the circle and hopped to the board to illustrate something like the spit and image example. I wanted to stimulate some of my kids to try thinking in a different way and assure others that it was okay to think in ways different from their classmates. There were more kids in the first group, but the longer I taught, the more fascinated I was by those in the second. They were the ones prone to becoming bored or discouraged, the ones who had so much to teach us all if only they could find a way to express their unconventional thinking. In some ways, they were budding Robins. I hoped that by sharing with my kids the way that my brained worked, I just might bring more performers to our stage.

I'm not suggesting that you turn your classroom into a comedy club, though if you have a humorous bent, then by all means let it flow. Rather, from time to time, open your heart to your students and share with them your secrets about teaching. Sure, there will always be moments that you'll want to preserve the mystical quality of your instruction, will want to keep your kids guessing as to what you're thinking as you guide them, but there will also come those lessons when you'll better serve your classes by breaking down the process not only into its steps but also into your rationale behind each move. When you do that, you'll create an academic intimacy with your students, and when they feel a part of that connection, they will also understand that what is transpiring within the walls of that particular classroom is not happening anywhere else in the building, maybe not anywhere in the world. When that happens, the lamp of learning will burn incredibly bright.

What Steinbeck Said: Post #69
Monday, April 10, 2017
A Perfect Storm

T his will be an eventful week. We came back from spring break today, and one look at the calendar at our faculty meeting reminded us all of the confluence of a number of major activities. As a younger teacher (say, last year), I would have felt a slight surge of panic when I realized that we have ACT testing, senior project presentations, a deadline for local scholarship applications, and a special visit from U.S. Senator Mike Enzi. Nearly all of those directly affect my students, and on top of all that, someone had the bright idea to hold a discussion on five chapters of A Tale of Two Cities *and collect an essay, both on Wednesday. Idiot!*

Well, that same dimwit did have the sense to schedule a study period for his students today. We started by talking about what happened over vacation, and we did our Word of the Day. *For the rest of our class time, I gave my kids the options to read their chapters or write their papers or even to work on their scholarship paperwork. Of course, I realized that most of them had done little of any of that before today, but it was a good faith gesture on my part.*

With this storm of due dates swirling around us, I chose to remain calm in the middle of it all. I took the time to visit with all of my kids to see if they had questions on the reading or the writing. Some did, and while many said they didn't, I knew that it was more of a function of being unprepared than it was of being ahead of the game. Because I know it to be a game, I simply played along. That meant being patient when some students were more interested in conversation than studying, but, after all, they hadn't seen each other in over a week, and they had so much to share. I gave them gentle reminders that we needed a quiet atmosphere, but I accepted the winds that rose from time to time as part of the classroom's weather for the day. I'm fascinated by the prospects for my teaching the next eight weeks. In most ways, it will be no different than it always has been. On the other hand, I can see myself being even more patient than is my custom as these final days of my career pass by. I will do what I can to encourage my kids to do their best, but more than ever, I see my energy being invested in love and understanding. Storms can be scary, and this week may turn out to be a bit overwhelming for some of us, but once the clouds pass, the coming weeks should see fair skies. In the meantime, my overcoat is buttoned!

In between reading over the above post and writing this reflection, Teresa and I watched a 2014 TED Talk delivered by Evelyn Glennie, a virtuoso percussionist who lost her hearing at the age of twelve. Undeterred by what most of us would consider a disqualifying condition for a musician, Glennie developed the ability to hear with her entire body and went on to achieve true greatness in the musical world. Well, let me amend that. In the world. Period.

That TED talk reminds all of us as teachers that not only must we never close a door to a student's opportunity, but we must also ardently advocate for students to find doors to open for themselves. With all good intentions, I sometimes tried to save my kids some grief by suggesting that they might as well move on to some other endeavor rather than risk frustration over what seemed destined to be a failure. It may have meant recommending that they try reading a book a little easier than the one they brought back to class from the library or discouraging them from applying to a prestigious college without possessing the requisite credentials. In effect, I played the role of training wheels on the bicycles my students were learning to ride, an umbrella to shield them from the rain that fell on them as they struggled to refine their skills. When I at last decided to stop protecting my kids and let them ride on their own, ready with Band-Aids when they lost control of their bikes, when I allowed them to find joy in the rain, to splash in every puddle, knowing that they could come back to me and get a dry towel, it was then that I was treated to some remarkable vicarious discoveries. Every time my students learned something and applied it in their own ways, I learned as well. More than that, I shared in the energy that they generated with their creativity, and again and again I drew on that power source to sustain me when the teaching wasn't easy.

Returning from spring break and running into a formidable number of tasks was just as difficult for me as it was my students, and there were years when I floundered a bit, not knowing how to help myself let alone my kids. Perhaps it was nothing more than the liberation of my impending retirement, but as Glennie demonstrates in her talk, a drummer can't play smoothly and at a great tempo with a death grip on her sticks. The hands, the wrists, the arms, heck, the whole body, must be supple and relaxed, allowed to bounce and to flow in order to play at a high level. You are going to find that teaching is no different. Tension will do nothing to help you keep a steady beat in the classroom. Instead, it will usually prevent you from being able to accurately interpret the needs of your students on a particular day, a specific context. As you learn to relax and to find the flow, you will be much more effective in helping your students. You will be able to wait to feel the beat that the day has created before you lean into your teaching. It will be more than what you see as the class period evolves, more than what you hear is happening among your students in their interactions with you and with their classmates. It will also be what you feel, the vibe that you learn to play in artistic ways. Is your toe tapping yet?

What Steinbeck Said: Post #70
Wednesday, April 12, 2017
Step by Step

*A*s I told you on Monday, we have found ourselves in a perfect storm this week in terms of activities and responsibilities, and as I planned for today's class, I decided to help my students navigate the flood that we were sure to find when we arrived to discuss Chapters Three through Seven of A Tale of Two Cities. I knew that even those kids who had read their assignment would most likely be a bit fuzzy on the details because they have had other things on their minds, so I pulled out some old props to help my kids draw conclusions. Defining the space between us in the circle as "The Pool of Interpretation," I laid posters labeled Literal, Inferential, and Symbolic on the carpet. More than just a visual representation of different types of interpretation, they became destinations for individual students as we discussed the significance of plot points.*

I started by modeling the process. I stood on the Literal Rock and read the prosecuting attorney's hyperbolic praise of John Barsad and Roger Cly, two witnesses called to testify that they had seen Charles Darnay consorting with the French, exchanging documents, traveling back and forth between England and France. I then walked to the Inferential Rock and explained that here I could apply my knowledge and experiences to make a judgment about the facts that I had shared from the story. I questioned the prosecutor's honesty, and I deduced that he is employing a strategy of exaggerating the virtuousness of his witnesses to boost their impressions upon the jury. I then handed the koosh ball to a student, asking her to follow my lead. At that point, she had a chance to walk to

Inferential or to Symbolic and either draw an inference about the event or explain a symbolic analysis of it. That in turn gave the rest of the class a chance to add to the interpretation. When we finished that bit, my student then decided who would go next.

Some kids were a bit hesitant about taking their place in the pool, but everything worked out fine as we helped each other dive deeper, understand the evolving plot more fully. It was a delightful exercise because we found a way to build on each other's ideas. There were a number of surprising connections made, and we celebrated each one. This is the power of a class. There is time for independent studying in our classroom, there is time for team collaboration. Nothing, however, will ever exceed the beauty of twenty-four students coming to a stunning realization at the same time. What could have been a disaster of a discussion turned into an invigorating hour because we took a novel approach.

There is nothing like experience, is there?

I came up with the idea for the interpretative rocks when I was teaching freshmen who not only had difficulty in analyzing on different levels but who also seemed incapable of sitting and concentrating for any significant length of time. If I was going to keep those young ones interested, I had to think of something, and the something I came up with was based on my understanding of learning modes and styles. I knew that students who achieved most easily in school tended to be logical and sequential in their processing, usually preferred to learn visually and auditorily. Those students who found difficulty in the system were often more random and concrete in their approach and were more often than not kinesthetic in their preference for acquiring information. It wasn't that the lower-achieving kids couldn't learn. They were just a poor fit for the way school was done. They liked to move around when they learned, got more out of doing than they did from watching and listening. They might not have been great at prediction or extrapolation, but once they grasped a concept, they could work well with it.

And what is high school in a traditional sense? It's a sit-down-and-be-quiet, read-your-book-without-talking-to-anyone world that rewards obedience and perseverance. It punishes those who feel the need to move about, to be silly sometimes, who have a hard time completing one task in rapt concentration. Teachers at the elementary and middle levels have accounted for those needs for a long time, but the American high school has long been monolithic in its learning culture. Sure, we've experimented with bell schedules, we've grouped students into learning academies and honors tracks. We've provided advocacy classes, study halls, and incentive-based early-outs. And there are always teachers who make a great difference by exploring alternative classroom methods, but by and large, academic classes tend to be what they have been for decades. That included my classes. Especially in my work with the younger grades, I fought the inertia of conventional English course work. Reading. Writing. Discussion. We were working on language skills, and for some kids, that was a grind, no matter how much I tried to make class fun. I had to find ways beyond that if my kids were going to develop the ability to dig deeper, to make connections in their learning.

Placing the rock posters on the floor inside the circle was a simple move, but it paid off because it was more than just a novelty. It was more than letting kids get up and move around. It got down to the level of how some kids' brains worked. Moving from one spot to another helped them focus on the difference between the literal and inferential. It also helped those students who learned best visually because they could track a classmate stepping across the room, carrying an idea from one place to another and, in the process, transforming it. As the interpreter announced an inference, the kids who learned best by listening were given an opportunity to exercise their most effective mode of perception. For the cost of three sheets of tagboard, a few markers, and some laminating film, I created a tool that I could break out whenever I felt my kids needed a change of pace or a little help in discerning the differences among the three types of interpretations. As it turned out, my seniors enjoyed the rocks just as much as my freshmen and sophomores had. If nothing else, the change from the routine of our discussions aroused their awareness.

As my mentor Joel Suzuki once told me, "Success breeds success." The effectiveness of the rocks inspired me to continually search for similar

Eric Stemle

techniques to keep my classes fresh. I wanted my students to enter our room every day knowing that they would find comfort in the familiar but also delight in the unusual. You know what? I wanted to come into the room that way, too. On day one I told my students that the worst thing a school can do to its students is to bore them. The same applies to teachers, and a bored instructor is a deadly instrument, I assure you. The good news is that in your classroom, you will have a great deal of control over that situation. There will be no reason for you or your students to suffer tedium day after day, no matter what the content of your lessons. You are in charge of the method of delivery, and even if you don't fancy yourself an entertainer, you can maintain your kids' interest in the learning by showing your genuine interest in them. When they return the favor, you'll experience one of the great gifts of teaching: a captivated audience.

What Steinbeck Said: Post #71
Monday, April 17, 2017
Old Dogs and English Class

I had one of those moments of insight today, a burst of instructional creativity that helped me focus my students' reading comprehension. I wouldn't exactly characterize it as an invention born of necessity, but after a few minutes of discussion in my first class, continuing with a few details we didn't get to last week, I grew wary of the blank stares and averted eyes when I asked questions about the reading. This situation was far from unexpected. As I told you earlier, last week was a tough one for my students, a confluence of assignments and deadlines. Most weren't prepared to discuss last Wednesday, and from the looks of things today, they hadn't caught up over the weekend.

There wasn't much I could do about that this morning, and calling my kids out on their lack of readiness wasn't going to magically pop answers into their heads. Moving on to my second class, I decided to do what I could to help them be more successful going forward. As we finished our discussion, with slightly more participation than we had in the first, I gave my kids the remainder of the class, thirty minutes, to read our next assignment for Wednesday. I had done the same in my previous period, but this time, I added some structure.

"As you begin reading Chapter Eight," I told them, "you will see that Monsieur the Marquis is continuing his coach ride home. He's going to stop to question a man by the side of the road. In five minutes, I'm going to ask you what that man says he saw."

In precisely five minutes, I called the group's attention and repeated my question. One of my girls raised her hand to ask for the koosh.

"He said he saw a man hanging from the carriage." Many kids nodded, and I probed a bit, asking just what this hanging man looked like. The class pieced together a pretty fair description, and with that bit of mystery established, I gave my class another direction.

"The Marquis' carriage is going to stop again, and this time, a woman is going to make a request. In ten minutes, I'll ask you what that request is."

In ten minutes, I learned that the woman had requested a grave marking for her late husband. We discussed the Marquis' reply, and we decided that the man was a total jerk. There were less than ten minutes left in class, time for one last clue to find.

"Before the bell rings, I'm going to ask you the name of the Marquis' expected guest." Just before the class period ended, I posed that question, and most of the kids replied, "Charles."

"Wait," I said, eyes wide. "Do you mean to tell me that Charles Darnay, the beautiful man who is courting Lucie Manette, is the nephew of this despicable marquis?"

The class smiled together just as the bell rang.

I decided to modify my process just a bit for my last class. My directions were the same, but when it came time to answer my questions, I had my students check their responses with partners first. I noticed that after the first two discussions, kids continued to chat for a second about what they had read. Suddenly, we had established a communication channel regarding our reading, and what had been a rather desperate groping for meaning in my first class now seemed a little more manageable. When it came to the last question, I asked them

269

to watch for me to touch my nose and then say the name in unison. "Charles Darnay!" filled the room.

I may be an old dog, and this wasn't exactly a new trick, but I had to smile as my last class filed out to the hall. Why hadn't I thought to use that strategy before with these kids? I learned long ago that the answer to that question isn't important. Looking ahead is.

On to Wednesday!

For years I watched my older colleagues as they neared retirement. "Short-timers" they often called themselves. I didn't really pay much attention to them in the early days of my career, but as I passed fifty, I started to watch and to listen a little more. What I had observed then became critically important to me as I neared the end myself.

In the last year of their teaching, some of my friends went about their business as if nothing was imminent. We'd chat in the hall or after a meeting, and the subject of leaving never came up. Others made it quite clear that they were marking the days, and some of them used their one-foot-out-the-door status to their advantage by skipping meetings or foregoing required paperwork. "What are they going do, fire me?" asked one of my close friends.

As the school year entered spring, I took the same route I had always taken when I faced a transition in my life. I worked harder than ever. For one thing, I wanted to feel satisfied that I had done all that I could up to the final bell of the final day. For another, I didn't want anyone to whisper that I was slacking off. I knew that there would be folks keeping a close eye on me to see if I changed my spots before I left the jungle, and I wasn't about to give them a chance to say, "I knew it!" No, I would leave the profession working harder than anyone around me. That was my goal.

That approach applied to my day-to-day teaching decisions. I could have easily accepted the fact that my students weren't comprehending their reading and just let it go. I mean, what would it hurt in the long run if my kids didn't catch Dickens' description of that coach ride? What did it matter that they understood Darnay's family tree? In the long, long run, would it really matter that my students understood or remembered *A Tale of Two Cities*? Of course, it wouldn't, but that wasn't my concern on that April day. I cared more that in that last half hour of the class period, I could help my kids concentrate with purpose in their reading. Most importantly, I wanted to continue being a learner myself in my own classroom up to the last half hour of my career.

A fellow teacher gave me some advice in those waning days. "Be sure to find purpose in your life after you retire," he said "or you'll be dead within five years. That happened to my uncle."

I thanked him for his concern and assured him that my learning would continue day after day long after I left the building for the last time. I have kept that promise. Want to become a master teacher? Take that vow at the beginning of your career. Find purpose in what you do from day to day, but more importantly, discover the meaning that will inform your teaching practice. It will be more than loving children, more than making a difference. Promise yourself that when you reach the point in your life where I am now, that you'll be able to reflect on how you were an agent of change. You'll know that you served as an inspiration for your students, their parents, and your colleagues by your words and your example. Will you have some regrets? Of course! We all have scars. Will you know every instance in which you helped a young mind dream? A tender heart heal? Not a chance. But if you follow one of Stephen Covey's habits and start with the end in mind, you will always have a star to guide you, and in the end, you just mind find that you have been a star for others to follow as well.

What Steinbeck Said: Post #72
Wednesday, April 19, 2017
A 25-Desk Salute

T *his was one of those days when I just take a few deep breaths and accept whatever comes my way. A colleague and I spent the morning in my classroom, proctoring the ACT for a roomful of juniors. Unlike other norm-referenced tests such as our state assessment, the ACT is a difficult administrative challenge. Kids can't have electronic devices with them, can't have food or drink at their desks (even water), can't even have books to read if they finish a section early. All of those measures have understandable rationales, but in total, they create a restrictive environment for the kids. My friend and I did what we could to ease any tension that might arise from warnings that I was asked to read such as, "If you use a cell phone, you will be dismissed from the room, and your test will not be scored."*

As a proctor, I have a responsibility to carry out the test's directions to ensure consistency. As a teacher, I have a responsibility to care for my students, even if they are only in my charge for a few hours. I found balance today by being upbeat, by using humor (surprise!), and by showing as much empathy for the kids in my room as I do for the students I see on a regular basis. The result was an atmosphere marked by studious attention and an appreciation for the significance of the task. We all had a good idea of the importance of the morning, both to each student and to the school at large. More and more, educators are being measured by the numbers they produce. Less and less, we as teachers are being trusted to assess the learning of our students. That is a trust that I'm afraid we abdicated years ago under pressure from various entities, and now what our kids know and what our kids can do is determined by a non-profit corporation founded years ago in Iowa City. Now, no offense to the good people of the Hawkeye State, but somewhere along the line, we teachers lost credibility when it came to identifying what our students achieved in their learning.

As I leave the profession, my heart knows that no one understands the capabilities of my students more than they do. At the same time, there are things that I know about my kids' performance that even they themselves don't realize. Perhaps that's why I was proud of my eleventh-graders-for-a-day. They gave a fine effort, even though I know that they weren't thrilled to be sitting in rows for four hours. They were gracious to their proctors, appreciative of the sincere consideration that we gave them. Tomorrow, when they walk back into their classes, they will have an opportunity to learn and to show what they know to experienced teachers, not to a Scantron machine several states away. They will have many chances to demonstrate their learning using more than the tip of a

No. 2 pencil. I hope that every one of my kids from the ACT has a fabulous day in their exploration tomorrow.
They all deserve it.

All right, let's talk about standardized assessment, objective tests that are designed to determine student abilities and are based on published standards. When I was in high school, one such measure was the Iowa Test of Basic Skills, a battery that assessed student achievement for the purpose of improving instruction. The ITBS was a supplement to aid teachers in evaluating the effectiveness of their methods, a mirror held up to help them ascertain not only the capabilities of their students but also the efficacy of their own efforts. Of course, I wasn't in the profession in those days, but I never had the impression that my score on that assessment meant very much at all.

What did matter to me were my SAT numbers because those scores had an impact on my acceptance into universities. That was the purpose of the SAT and the ACT. They were built to predict how well a high school junior would some day fare in college classes. I never really thought about the exams once I started teaching. Oh, I hoped my students did well on their college boards for their sake, but their test scores didn't affect me directly. Somewhere along the line, the powers that be, primarily state legislatures and departments of education, decided that those college predictors would be provide a simple and convenient score that could be used to evaluate a high school's performance. Combined with the draconian punishments built into the No Child Left Behind legislation, the ACT and the SAT became the currency of school rankings. The only problem was that those tests were never intended to show how well high school students were learning, how well high school teachers were instructing.

That's all well and good, but the fact is that the college boards are now the measure by which the public evaluates schools. Faced with that reality, what can you do in your classroom? First, you can acknowledge that standardized testing is not going away. I could have complained about its irrelevancy to my day-to-day work with my students, but the fact remained that my administrators bought into the primacy of those assessments because their jobs basically depended on them. The school accreditation process has become data-driven, and that data is based for the most part on multiple choice assessments. How does that work for measuring language arts skills? They claim to evaluate writing, but in essence, all they measure is a student's ability to detect errors in conventions or to choose effective rhetorical techniques. They do absolutely nothing to show how a writer engages in the creative process, how she revises and tightens her prose. They ask questions to determine a reader's comprehension skills, but truly, they only measure how that reader answers those particular questions, not necessarily what he gleans from the passage. How do they measure speaking? Listening?

The bottom line is that nearly everything my students learned in our class was not measured by the college boards. Those tests could not determine creativity or improvement or symbolic interpretations. They could not weigh the confidence that my kids developed, the self-assurance that told them that they could not only survive taking on rigorous courses but could also thrive in those classes. They could not ascertain a student's wittiness or compassion for the troubles of classmates as they took on learning challenges. In essence, the numbers produced on those tests were meaningless when it came to helping people understand the power and the beauty of our everyday explorations as a class.

In the end, what can you do? Plenty. You can teach the most effective way that you know how. You can devote your time and energy to inspiring your students, to encouraging them, to honestly evaluating their strengths and their weaknesses, and you can push them to work harder than they have ever worked. The standardized test scores will take care of themselves. If they don't, at least your students will leave your classes having learned how to learn. How to believe in themselves. And that, my friend, is measured by the heart.

What Steinbeck Said: Post #73
Thursday, April 20, 2017
Do You Feel Me?

O h, but if you feel like lovin' me/if you've got the notion/I second that emotion." I doubt that Smokey Robinson was thinking of A Tale of Two Cities when he penned those lyrics, but his tune ran through my head as our class discussed a few more chapters of the novel. Love was all over the pages we read for today: Charles Darnay expressing his love for Lucie to Dr. Manette, Mr. Lorry lovingly protecting Lucie from the matrimonial designs of Mr. Stryver. Above all was the poignant conversation between Sydney Carton and Lucie where the man vows to give his life for her after acknowledging that he knows that she can never love him. Solid gold Victorian ethic, there.

As critical as love is to this portion of the novel, it was even more important to our class today. We have had problems comprehending Dickens' prose, and while our reading has primarily focused on character development to this point, today's discussion took a turn toward plot. That gave us a little more to chew on, and while it took my kids a few minutes to try a bite, we eventually opened a rather lively conversation on the pursuit of Miss Manette's heart. It was emotion that finally stirred our opinions, that brought out speculation as to what might happen soon in our story. Will Lucy choose Charles? Does post Sydney have any chance at all? Who deserves her more? This was no longer a dispassionate use of logic to analyze character motivation. Rather, my kids spoke with feeling in expressing their ideas.

The effect of emotion on our interpretations, of course, came as no surprise. We might enjoy learning about characters, and we might appreciate the artistry of the author, but when we find the opportunity to see the novel in light of our own experience, our own values, we tend to get a little more involved with each other as well.

For all of our technical training as teachers, for all of our work on lesson design and assessment and curricular alignment, the magic of the classroom still comes down to the emotional connection that students have with their classmates *and their teachers. All I did today was to encourage that connection. The fact that Dickens did as well made it all the more interesting.*

With all due respect to my colleagues in other disciplines, why would I teach anything else but English?

I am serious about that final question. I know that I chose to major in English because I was good at it, but when I began teaching it, I realized that there were a number of advantages to the subject. For one, unlike a course such as mathematics, there is no hard and fast sequence for teaching language arts content. There is no order of operations. Instead, I could focus on literary interpretation or writing structure, conventions or public speaking in any series or combination that I desired. It wasn't a matter of me being random, it was just that I had the freedom to design my units and lessons to suit my students' needs. If my classes stumbled sometimes as they tried writing funneled introductions, we could spend extra time in practice. If a particular reading selection was difficult, we could slow our pace or read more aloud together. It all came down to the particular issues that my students were experiencing. The other teachers in my department might have been executing the same unit as I was but could have been on an entirely different schedule, depending on their classes' demands and their own preferences. In the long run, all that mattered was that our students grew in their abilities.

Another factor that worked to my benefit was the sharing of opinions. A science class might engage in problem solving and prediction, but the focus of those classes is clearly on data collection and facts. Procedures in biology, chemistry, and physics classes are, again, step-by-step. English class discussions, on the other hand, can diverge in all sorts of directions, depending on the flow created by student participation and the directing of the teacher. In my classes, that sparked more freedom for taking chances and speculating, opened doors for differing perspectives as well as humor. In addition to my classroom duties, I served my district as an instructional facilitator, and in my travels, I was continually struck by how quiet math and science rooms were compared to English and social studies classes. Part of that may have been grounded in the personalities of the teachers, but the nature of the instruction also played an important role. My students did most of their reading and writing outside of class, leaving us more time for conversation and team learning. That was an environment I felt comfortable in.

We had a principal who once dropped in on one of our department meetings to see what we were working on. When he heard us discussing journal writing, he spoke up to warn us about the dangers of becoming emotionally involved with our classes. "You can find out things you really don't want to know about your students if you're not careful," he said. "I know you like to get all touchy-feely with your kids, but it's not worth it. Just teach them how to read and write."

With that command, he left. I was impressed that my colleagues and I, as loquacious and quick-witted as we all were, could hold our tongues until the door closed behind him. At the sound of the click, we burst into laughter at the thought of us no longer making connections with our students. Of course, we were going to continue to touch their hearts, just as they touched ours. Besides, we had all been around long enough to know that it would do us no good to argue with an administrator over such a matter. It was probably hard for him and some of the others to fully understand the nature of the English classroom because they had taught courses that were meaningful but concentrated on the acquisition of knowledge and skills. Our classes seemed to be focused more on *life*.

Does that mean that if you are a teacher of a discipline that delves more into understanding what has already been discovered, that you and your students will have to check your personalities at the door? Of course, not. Solving mathematical equations or executing chemistry labs can be team efforts as well as solo pursuits, and kids can certainly celebrate academic successes with great exuberance in any classroom setting. They'll do just that if you create a culture that encourages enthusiasm. It's up to you to decide how much emotion is welcome in your class. A quiet, sober room is most likely that way because that's the way the teacher wants it. I'm guessing that no matter what you teach, your students will be a lot like mine were, and a great majority of them will appreciate the freedom to express their emotions. In other words, they will enjoy bringing their whole selves through that door each day.

277

Eric Stemle

What Steinbeck Said: Post #74
Monday, April 24, 2017
Sodium Chloride, Anyone?

*T*oday was a little tough. I thought we had turned a corner last week, that more of my students were beginning to comprehend Dickens' writing. With that in mind, I decided to stretch their minds a bit by adding a layer of interpretation. We had focused on literal, inferential, and symbolic meaning, and with guidance and prodding, I had helped most of my kids in grasping the nature of each character, in tracing the novel's plot to this point in our study. Today, I took them into the realm of style, specifically, the author's use of understatement. Dickens is a master of such, and to miss his point when he writes euphemistically is to completely lose out on his humor.*

I prepared a couple of passages for us to explicate, and while each class did a pretty good job of piecing together the meaning of those descriptions, as I continued on with our discussion, I found myself more and more stuck on my literal stepping stone, trying hard to find more than a handful of readers who could tell me what had happened in each chapter. As a result, I either relied on those few students who seemed to have a grasp of the literal, or I filled in answers to my own questions. This went on for most of the first two periods before I finally made a plea for my kids to work a little harder for Wednesday's discussion.

Maybe it's the lateness of the senior year. Perhaps there is still a lot going on in my kids' lives besides school. Whatever the reason, polite as they were today, as well as they seemed to be listening, I felt as if I were teaching English as a second language. It comes down to effort, no matter what else is going on. If I am an effective student, and I don't understand something, I find a way to figure it out. I consult sources online, I talk with my classmates about it, I go to my teacher for help.

It might just be that I have somehow created this situation. In guiding my students from step to step, perhaps I have made them dependent on me to show them the way. It's clear to me that some of my kids come to class having not read or having not understood what they have read. I can't accept the former. The latter? I know what we're reading is difficult, but what are my kids doing to better comprehend? That's the issue as I see it tonight.

Will I see a better effort when we discuss again on Wednesday? I have no idea. For weeks, I have encouraged. Today, I challenged. At some point, it's not up to me. At some point, students have to take charge of their learning. If that's something we don't learn in high school, we are hit hard with it in college. You all know that I will continue to push and to coax and to show my faith in my students. In the end, I will find a way. As Madeline Hunter taught me years and years ago, "They say that you can lead a horse to water, but you can't make it drink.

"Ah, but you can salt the oats."

I hope to have more thirsty students soon.

How hard to push? That was a question I pondered all the way to the end of my career. Of course, I was concerned about helping my students meet their needs, but sometimes I wondered whether I wanted them to improve more than they did. They had other things on their minds, other classes to worry about. They also lacked an understanding of what lay ahead of them in the coming years of school. As for me, I usually had to weigh a number of factors in deciding how much to challenge them. One was a comparison between where I judged my students to be and where they "should" be. There were several ways to discern where that second point was. For one, I could lean on my experience with students from year to year, a sense that I had developed about where the successful ones were at a certain place in the year. Another way came from external sources such as a published curriculum. I could always look at the scope and sequence to determine at which level my students should be performing. I also had their future to consider. When I taught middle school students, I tried to keep their ninth grade teachers in mind. What would they expect my kids to be able to do when they entered high school? When I taught seniors, I put myself in the place of the professors my kids would someday have to satisfy. Were they on track to be ready for that work?

Even though that day in April was disappointing to me, and it wasn't about skill at all but rather the lack of effort from kids so close to leaving high school, I never wanted to lose the moment with them. How they studied and how they worked in their classes after mine was going to be up to them, and it would not really be a reflection on my teaching, but I must say that when I was younger, I felt that it truly was. I worried about my colleagues judging my teaching of my freshmen and sophomores by how well they did in their upper level classes. I imagined college instructors asking my graduates just which of their high school teachers was responsible for their lack of writing ability. That sort of thinking led me to a certain amount of frustration, some self-inflicted pressure. It wasn't so much about the welfare of my students; it was my reputation that was on the line. When I felt that my kids were bringing that down with their lack of dedication to learning, I grew impatient with them. Yet as I matured as a teacher, I worried less and less about what was going to happen after my students moved on. I worried less about how they were going to fare by the year's end. What I learned to do was to plan each night for a great next day. And I entered that classroom with a sincere belief that no matter what had happened the day before, no matter what happened the next, that day was going to be awesome. As I became a better teacher, I had much more influence over that outcome, and the faith that I had in my students and in myself made for a series of great days.

Faith and perseverance are two gifts that will sustain you to the very end. One will keep you going on days when the kids just didn't seem to have it. The other will instill in you the belief that each day dawns with the promise of incredible learning. Bumps in the road will trip you up if you trudge along with uncertainty haunting your every step, but you won't even notice them if your two gifts help you soar!

What Steinbeck Said: Post #75
Wednesday, April 26, 2017
Finding the Key

W e started today by listening to a theme. I pushed the Play *button on iTunes, and we all experienced thirty seconds of a familiar song on piano, Sarah Ainsworth, the soloist. I paused the piece and asked my class what they had heard.*

"'Twinkle, Twinkle Little Star,'" came the reply.

"Or?" I said.

"'A-B-C,'" said several kids in unison.

I nodded. "Or?"

One girl piped up, "'Mary Had a Little Lamb.'"

I grinned and sang that title for her. "Were you thinking of 'Baa, Baa Black Sheep'?"

"What else did you hear?"

We talked about Ainsworth's playing of the melody with her right hand and an accompaniment with her left. A few kids noticed some embellishments.

"Can anyone identify the composer?"

Nothing.

Perhaps some had a good idea, but no one was willing to hazard a guess. No biggie.

"All right, then. Here's the next part."

I played about thirty more seconds of Mozart's first variation on the theme, a rollicking part in which he switches the melody to the left hand and adds rapid ornamentation to the right. We discussed that change, and then proceeded to listen to variations that changed key, that switched rhythms.

The point?

"Mozart took one idea, a French folk song, and created eleven variations. Let's consider A Tale of Two Cities. *Can you share an idea that Dickens presents in several different ways?"*

One boy talked about "love," and the variations on that feeling that play out between Charles and Lucie, Lucie and Sydney, Lucie and her father. I went to the board and wrote the words eros, philia, *and* agape. *We discussed the Greek meanings of those different kinds of love (erotic, brotherly, love of God), and then I asked which of those types Lucie expressed. One of my girls brought up the idea of "prison" and gave examples of the physical prison that Dr. Manette suffered in as well as the emotional one that he for some reason associates with Charles. The prison that holds Carton's heart.*

At the end of the day, I reflected on the exercise, on the way it warmed us up for a discussion of four more chapters of the novel. While we could have simply started class by reviewing the reading, I decided to use metaphor to help my kids find one more way to connect with the author's work. I am grateful for the fact that each class period allows me to open a different door of interpretation for my students. With each comes a unique entry into our understanding of the book. My hope is that within the next few weeks, my kids will come to realize that, rather than relying on me to unlock another strategy, that they have the power to do so themselves. When that happens, they will enjoy special access to the world of literature for the rest of their lives.

A 2011 report from the U.S. Department of Education cited a study that claimed that nearly fifty percent of new teachers leave the profession within five years. That is most certainly an alarming statistic, and we must be careful not to assign any one factor as the sole cause of such a situation, but the fact remains that young people who at one time aspired to teach, to make a difference in others' lives, aren't staying with that aspiration very long. What is it that keeps some of us in the classroom for decades while others last a handful of years or less?

One possibility is resilience. If I could bestow upon you any one personal quality, it would be the ability to bounce back, to get back up after a stumble. Lord knows, you will do plenty of falling in your early years of teaching. The workload will at times be staggering, and there will be the continual testing that your students will impose on you because they'll know that you are inexperienced. That will just be a matter of power, though it won't be really anything personal for the kids. They will just like to see what they can get away with. For you, their novice teacher, however, it will be a time of exasperation.

How will you learn to persevere through those early hard times? It will help to have a mentor. Some districts provide them in a formal fashion, and some schools have a culture of looking out for one another. If you aren't blessed with either of those possibilities, then it will be critical that you advocate for yourself. Clearly, that isn't currently happening for a great number in the profession or the dropout rate would be a lot lower than it is. Isn't it a shame that schools are held responsible for their graduation numbers, but we rarely hear much about their teacher retention rates?

The purpose of this book is not to advise districts or their schools on how to handle their affairs. It is, however, to help you not only survive in the profession, but to thrive and excel in your practice. Perseverance or gumption or moxie— whatever you want to call it—is something that teachers of any level of experience need because, whether or not we want to admit it, there are times when we get discouraged, when we start to doubt ourselves. Even in the final weeks of my career, as adept as I was at handling difficult situations, I had moments when I had to give myself a pep talk. I had to dip into that well of confidence and drink of my self-esteem to ward off worries that I wasn't doing enough to inspire my students. Two days before the class I just described, I had needed that elixir. As you can see from the post, it did the trick in renewing my optimism that I could create vivid learning experiences for my students. Now, if only I could bottle that and offer it to you and all of the rest of my fellow teachers. . . .

Eric Stemle

What Steinbeck Said: Post #76
Friday, April 28, 2017
A Dickens Sampler

W *ith apologies to Mrs. Gump, class discussions are indeed like a box*
of chocolates. Some are smooth and creamy, while others can be
brittle. Some can be dark, and some are just plain nutty. Today's
piece was small because of our shortened Friday schedule, and as it turned out,
it took on the nature of a truffle: sweet and intense.

There were a number of topics to bite into in that half-hour. There was the
vigilantism of the rebels as they captured and murdered an old foe. There was the
arson of the Marquis' chateau and the indifference of the villagers to the crime.
Finally, there was the power of the loadstone rock, the magnetic forces that draw
Lorry and Darnay to Paris in a time of peril. Perhaps it was the fact that our
assignment covered but nineteen pages, or maybe it was the way we applied
those topics to our own lives, but the conversation was brisk. We savored each
minute and questioned and commented with enthusiasm. A teacher can see
engagement in a student's eyes, and I saw more of that gleam on Friday than I
have noticed for a while.

With this discussion, we ended our reading of Book the Second. On Tuesday,
we begin the final book, and as I told my class before the bell rang, the stage is
set for accelerated action. The novel's last fifteen chapters will soar to a climax,
and I sense that we are ready to climb with the characters. We know those
people, we understand their motivations. There are secrets about to be revealed,
plot twists soon to turn, emotion on the brink of being felt.

What a grand way to approach the end of the year, the last few class periods
of a career, the last few chocolates. Wish you all could join me at the bus stop!

I f resilience is a crucial quality for a teacher, then it is followed closely by
openness and agility. I could come to school with the world's best lesson
plan, a sure-fire activity that had worked time and time again, and as the
class period began, the feel just wasn't there. I don't know whether my students

284

---

were as sensitive to that vibe as I was, but even if they were, the onus was on me to lead them to a meaningful eighty-five minutes. Especially late in the year, with so few days left together, so few candies left in the box, the last thing I wanted to do was waste an opportunity for us to do something special together.

That's were those two qualities came in. First, while I entered our classroom every day with high expectations, with hope for a spectacular time with my students, I had to be open to the dynamic of that particular day. That meant that I had to be aware of the signals that each class was sending me. On some days, everyone seemed ready to go from the bell. On others, there were kids who were distracted or perhaps disinterested. I had no way of knowing what they would be thinking or feeling on a given day, and so I learned to observe their body language, their facial expressions, to look and to listen for clues. When we for the most part seemed ready to roll, I let my energy flow and got after it. But, when something was amiss, I had to be ready to switch gears or directions quickly.

That's what I mean about being agile. It's more than having a bag of tricks. It's the willingness to abandon or alter a plan by using years of experience to take the lesson a different direction. As a young teacher, I didn't possess a lot of strategies to draw from, and that led me to being more rigid in my execution of the plan. It was like knowing that I needed an adaptor for an appliance but, not having the proper one, trying to jam together what I had on hand, and the results weren't often pretty. It's a terrible feeling to stay the course when things aren't working, isn't it? As I got more experienced, with more of those tricks in that bag of mine, I found it much easier to try something on the spur of the moment, whether it was taking a few minutes to play a quick game to raise my class' spirits or pausing in my instruction to show my kids an idea from a different perspective.

When those moves worked, I felt great for the rest of the day. When they didn't, I relied on my resilience to get me through. It wasn't easy to let go of a lesson that I loved presenting, but in the end, it was the learning that mattered. Who cared how well I taught if my students didn't grow from the experience? That might be hard for you to deal with early on in your practice. It may be difficult to accept that your best intentions just aren't good enough, and it might take you a while to come to terms with the fact that you're not going to be a star every day in your classroom, even late into your career. Still, you will eventually become confident in your ability to make on-the-fly decisions, and you will also develop a deep reserve of resilience upon which you can draw when things don't run smoothly. Remember that in your dark, early days, OK?

What Steinbeck Said: Post #77
Tuesday, May 2, 2017
One, Some, All

*T*oday was a microcosm of my career in teaching. In the span of twelve hours, I worked directly with a single student, with three classes, and with our school board. In each instance, I served a constituency, each in a unique way, each with excitement for the chance to serve.

Before my first class arrived, one of my seniors dropped in to do a special book conference with me. She had just finished William Faulkner's The Sound and the Fury, *and she was excited to discuss her findings. We had chatted just two weeks ago about her challenges as she was making her way through the second of four sections of the novel. I had given her a bit of clarification and a little direction, but I was surprised when she showed up this morning, a smile beaming. Faulkner's masterpiece is avant-garde in its style and its structure, and my student had struggled with both at first, but as we talked about the author's choices and his possible intentions, it was clear that she had at last grasped some meaning from the piece. I asked her whether she had employed any online resources to help her through, and she smiled once more.*

"No, I really wanted to see what I could figure out for myself."

"So how did you do?"

She nodded. "I think I did pretty well." I had a good idea about what she was feeling at the moment, and because I figured she wouldn't tell me, I said it for both of us.

"I am so proud of you," I told her. "I've had two or three other students choose to read this book, and it always feels good when my students really challenge themselves. You did it!"

The report finished, we chatted for another ten minutes. She asked me about my early teaching, and I asked her about her college plans. We talked Bob Dylan and the Beatles and movies. It was one of those conversations that comes out of nowhere and leads somewhere rewarding.

My first class came in a few minutes later, and I read aloud Chapter One of Book the Third of A Tale of Two Cities. *This portion follows Charles Darnay in his return to France, and as he makes his way to Paris to have his name cleared as a worthy citizen, we as readers are as surprised as the character seems to be at learning of the changes that have come to his native land. I stopped from time to time to check for understanding, to give my students a chance to opine on Charles' prospects, his treatment at the hands of the patriots of the new republic. Along the way, we did a little history, a touch of geography, some linguistics, and the mechanics of mounting and dismounting a horse. I apologized for my less-than-stellar French accent when I read dialogue, but I had fun with the reading.*

I finished in each class just before the bell, and I gave each class a brief preview of their assignment for Thursday: "There will be blood, you all." If that doesn't inspire reading, what will?

Finally, tonight I spoke briefly at our board's monthly work session. The early part of the meeting was devoted to curriculum study reports, and I provided an update on the team that I have been leading. I explained our process, some decisions that we have made in order to more thoroughly examine materials and programs. Our work will carry over into next year, though it won't include me. Retirement will be as clean a break as I can make it, and though I wish I could have reported tonight that we were close to selecting an approach to adopt, I feel confident that we are where we need to be to do the job well.

I am a fortunate soul. Throughout my four decades in teaching, I have been blessed by students who delight in discovery, by classes that come together to learn and to teach each other, by school leaders such as our board of trustees who care deeply about the welfare of the children of our district. Whether I am working with one or with some or with all in the district, I am consistently afforded great opportunities to serve and to grow. It's a blessing for which I will always be grateful.

I t was natural for be to express gratitude as I moved into the last month of my teaching career. As I looked at the dwindling number of days, I found it easy to give thanks for all that I had been given. It was more than just those blessings that I discussed in the previous post. Sure, my ultimate focus was always on my students, and I loved being part of a faculty, a guild of sorts that was dedicated to the pursuit of learning, to serving young minds. I appreciated my educational leaders, those who guided and supervised me, who helped me find the resources I needed to create a most remarkable classroom.

More than all that, however, I felt grateful for the unique training that I received throughout my practice. I had colleagues who shared those experiences with me, but I never met anyone who was gifted with more chances to learn from world-class instructors in the education world than I was. It started simply enough when I was asked to join three other teachers in becoming trainers for a program called Teacher Expectations, Student Achievement (TESA). In paired teams, we taught the class to our peers over the course of a school year, and perhaps it was because that first experience went well that I was invited to do training in other professional development programs. Just as I was privileged to study TESA under its creator, Sam Kerman, I was also granted the honor to learn Cooperative Learning from Spencer Kagan, Choice Theory from William Glasser, Mastery Teaching from Madeline Hunter. Along those paths, I was introduced to wonderful instructors such as Laurie Kagan, Kathy Curtiss, Steven English, Nancy Buck, Lil Hosman, and Joel Suzuki. Working with just one of those names would have been career-changing. I was fortunate enough to learn from them and other outstanding practitioners and theorists.

Why me? Good question. Maybe I was just the willing one, the guy who was always up for traveling to a conference or for spending my summer vacation learning. Perhaps my administrators, the ones who approved my training, who secured funding for it, trusted that I would take everything that I learned and put it into action in my classroom. If that was so, then they were wise and perceptive because that is exactly what I did throughout my career. Not only did I take the concepts and principles from each training and apply it in my teaching, but I had a knack for creating a synthesis of all that I had absorbed. I took Hunter's ideas on lesson design and the nature of human learning and layered them over my use of Kagan's cooperative learning principles. I designed my classroom based on Glasser's theory of how we behave and combined that understanding with Kerman's perspective on equity. The result was a beautiful mosaic held together by my love for my students, my dream for their success, my fervent hope that they would love to learn as much as I did.

I may have been lucky to have so many opportunities thrown my way, but I also took advantage of those experiences, and I worked hard to honor each of my mentors, to earn my place by creating a whole that ended up being greater than any one of its parts. I say that in all humility. I was fortunate to teach in districts that believed in me, that gave me a chance to grow in a way that I never dreamed I could when I walked into my first education class at Michigan State. But I also took the talents that I was given and invested them, making more of what I received.

As a teacher, you will have many challenges, but you will also have much for which you can be grateful. It is critical that you not wait till the sun is setting on your career to give thanks for your opportunities. By recognizing the doors that are waiting for you to open, you can take yourself on a learning journey far beyond what you traveled in your undergraduate training. It might be daunting to take on new learning with all of the challenges that the profession throws your way, but if you are truly going to serve your students and to a broader extent your community, it will be imperative that you find those entrances, that you throw them open and step through them with courage and the belief that you can always be a better teacher, a better person. I had the good sense to open all sorts of doors. For that, I will be forever grateful.

Eric Stemle

What Steinbeck Said: Post #78
Thursday, May 4, 2017
The Finishing Touch

S ometimes I look at my plans for a discussion, and I wonder whether the questions and topics that I have prepared will be sufficient to carry us through the class period. What if my kids don't have much to say? What if we reach the end of my notes and there are still ten minutes to go in class? A well-run classroom flows smoothly from bell to bell, and any loose time at the end seems not only wasted to me, but seems also to send a message to my students that I haven't prepared properly. If that happens with any frequency, I know that my classes will lose a little confidence in me as an instructor. That may seem to be a bit of a harsh self-assessment, but forty years of teaching informs that feeling.

Last night, as I was writing out my lesson plan in my notebook, totally cognizant of the fact that I would never use those notes again, I was struck by an impression that most of what I was highlighting was literal in nature. I wasn't coming up with a lot of prompts for deep interpretation, and I didn't have much to inspire opinion. I decided that the four chapters that we were to discuss today are designed as a setup for the action to follow in the remaining ten chapters of the novel. That's not exactly the most exciting content to explore, but it is necessary if we're going to create a context for the fast-moving events that are soon to come.

What to do? I had slated an hour for discussion, but an hour of "what happened" didn't thrill me. Not knowing how my students would treat the material, I entered class today with the tools that have always served me well: my passion for literature, my sense of humor, and my love for my students. It's amazing what one can do with those three elements. You know what? Each class was fun, and in each discussion, my kids did find a way to interpret, did find a voice for their opinions. We squeezed out a bit of symbolism as well.

It all comes down to touch, to feel. To having an ear for the flow of a discussion and an eye for the visual signals students give us. It's about pruning and weeding and replanting from time to time. A teacher's senses are refined over the course of a career. They aren't found in an education textbook or a curriculum map. Rather, they evolve from the realm of intuition, they develop with patience and insight and faith.

My teaching has a month to go. After all this time, I'm still finding my way around the garden. . . .

We have talked a lot about teaching intuitively. By now you know that I was never one to seek out a path of instruction laid by others, and while I gleaned whatever I could from my colleagues and my mentors and my research, my classroom was uniquely me. Part of that was surely based on my belief that I was responsible for helping my students meet their needs, and that often meant choosing the road not taken in order to find the best route. Another part was simple. I didn't want to be like anyone else. I sought my own voice, and I was perfectly fine with owning my successes and my failures in order to sing my own tune.

When I was a boy, I was a quiet singer. Of course, that wasn't true when I was protected by the roar of the shower or was riding my bike alone through the neighborhoods, but when I was with people, I rarely sang loud enough for most folks to hear me. It was totally a matter of not trusting that others would approve of my voice, and because I lacked confidence in the tonal quality of my vocals, I sang softly in church or at parties when the gang belted out tunes. I even kept it down when we sang "Happy Birthday" as a family. And it wasn't just being reticent to sing out; I was terrified of reaching my falsetto. Any song that got within walking distance of my head voice gave me the shivers, and so I rumbled an octave below, comfortable with scratching out the lowest notes in favor of screeching out the high ones.

It wasn't until I met Teresa, a talented and trained vocalist, that I began singing with more energy. I still didn't feel confident that I was a good singer, but I wanted to honor my love's faith in me. I sang out in church, trying to match her ringing tones, I messed around singing with my colleagues at school, even stepping onstage at assemblies to croon. Yet, I would listen to soloists, not professionals but regular folks like me, and I would envy their gorgeous voices, the ease with which they worked their way through a tune. I knew that I could never approach their gifts, but I continued to harmonize and to sing with enthusiasm among my friends.

The change came when I was asked to substitute as a cantor at church. I had sung with a small ensemble for a number of years, and that had helped me feel a little surer of myself, but as I stood alone before the microphone, eyes scanning the congregation in front of me, I felt more nervous than I had in years. I'm not sure that I got through that initial performance without my voice trembling, and I can't promise you that I stayed on pitch, but somehow I and my fellow parishioners survived, and over the subsequent weeks and months and years, I developed a more cultured tone. With Teresa's help, I learned to breathe properly, to round out my vowels, to anticipate the notes. In time, I heard a sound coming out of me that at the very least would not offend the sensibilities of my friends in the pews. From there, my confidence grew. I learned to trust myself to relax and to let the music flow from me rather than try to force it out. In time, I became one of those performers who others complimented by saying, "Gee, I wish I could sing like you," something I never thought I would hear about myself.

Like all teachers, you will be a singer of sorts. No doubt. You will anticipate. You will breathe. You will let your lessons flow, and when you do them well, you will inspire. Do you want to know why the discussion I talked about in the last post was a success? Because, despite my doubts, I relied on my experience, and I sat down in the circle that day trusting that together, my students and I would find a way. I had a strong belief that if the flow of conversation lagged, or if our sharing was superficial and nonproductive, then I would figure out how to change the situation. More importantly, I had faith in my students. With the great majority of our class time behind us, I trusted that they could lead me in an effective way. That trust was spectacularly rewarded.

And that's the name of that tune.

What Steinbeck Said: Post #79
Monday, May 8, 2017
Bringing Forth the Light

A *good class discussion involves all of its participants. Of course, in a large class, it's difficult for every student to partake with the group conversation simply due to time restraints, but an effective facilitator finds ways to engage everyone's attention and to provide opportunities for sharing. Today I used a number of strategies to accomplish those two goals. I'm not sure that I managed to hold everyone's attention, and I'm not positive that everyone expressed thoughts and feelings on our reading assignment, but I employed as many tricks as I knew how in order to help my kids dig deep into some truly eventful chapters.*

As with each of our discussions of A Tale of Two Cities, *I knew that I had to balance my own summarizing with my students' recap of the reading. I prepared a list of events from each chapter and interspersed questions that called for kids to voice their opinions about the ethics of a situation, to talk about their personal preferences. For instance, is it acceptable that Jerry Cruncher is a grave robber if his avocation results in him outing a spy and giving Sydney Carton leverage that might help the once again imprisoned Charles Darnay? Many kids said that the information gained wasn't worth the heinous nature of Jerry's crime. I then asked the class if they would accept a full-ride scholarship if they learned that its benefactor was a meth dealer.*

"Absolutely!" one girl said.

"Why not?" asked another.

"So, you'd take drug money to go to college?"

Lots of kids nodded. "But you don't think Carton should use the information he receives from a criminal?"

Here was a question that all students could answer, whether or not they had read the assignment. Another question that I posed dealt with Miss Pross and her loyalty to King George III. Pross disdains the liberty craved by the French, and so I asked my kids whether they would rather be poor citizens of a republic or wealthy subjects of a monarchy. This conversation provided a split of opinion. We kicked the idea around for a couple of minutes, and the kids did a good job of supporting their choices. Again, because anyone could answer that question, I used another strategy and called on specific students rather than letting them call for the koosh. That technique let the class know that all were expected to contribute, though I used that tool judiciously. If I call on students to answer a text-related question, I take a chance of embarrassing those who haven't read. Of course, if I do that on a consistent basis, I might encourage at least some of the kids to be better prepared, but in the long run, when my quiet kids have some success in sharing, they are more likely to read closely for later discussions.

Teaching is not cooking from a recipe, it's not paint-by-number. Sometimes, whether I like it or not, I have to explain what has happened in the chapter in order to give kids a chance to interpret its content. Sometimes I have to call on certain students in order to raise the energy level of the entire classroom, for nothing drains the circle's enthusiasm like the sound of two or three voices dominating the talk. Often, I ask kids to talk with partners so that everyone has a chance to say something. I don't know for sure that they've all taken advantage of that opportunity, but it's another window to engagement. Sometimes I inject humor, perhaps some verbal slapstick, in order to get the class laughing, thus increasing our vitality for a few minutes at a time. There are many paints on my palette.

Teaching is an art as well as a science. The latter is stressed in our college training, the former comes with experience. As my career has evolved, I have found myself more often wielding a brush than employing a screwdriver, more often singing an interpretation with my kids than solving it as an equation. Today was more of a dance than a distillation because, while I very much respect my students' minds, I am in love with their hearts. Therein lies learning's flame.

I n these early days of my retirement, I have been reminded from time to time about what mattered most to my students. Whether it is an e-mail or a Facebook message from one away at school who wants to let me know how she is doing in college, or a chance meeting with a parent who wants to tell me how his son is doing in industry, the message is pretty much always the same. They appreciate what I taught about reading, about writing, about presenting, but more, much more than that, they want me to know that they are thankful that I taught them to love those things.

One evening, a student who I taught late in my career sent me a message about a basketball game we were both watching, her college against mine. When the action ended, we continued our chat, and she told me that she had switched her major and was planning to attend law school. That news thrilled me to no end because I knew that she was a gifted writer and an uncommonly talented analyst. When I reminded her of that, she gave me credit, but I knew in my heart that I didn't make that gold, I just found it in the stream. She had developed skills long before she met me. Then she reminded me that it wasn't the technical aspects of interpreting and composing that had made the difference for her. Rather, it was the *love* of writing that I had instilled in her.

How did that happen? For one, I made it clear that essays just didn't flow from our fingers. Good writing requires effort and perseverance. Great writing requires those plus a little inspiration. I focused on the third element, and the other two followed. My kids knew that they had to work hard to become good or maybe even great at writing. I helped them by showing them models and helping them plan their routes to getting there, but in the end, it was my comments on their papers and in our conversations that seemed to make the most impact.

Kids don't respond well to what they consider empty praise. A few "good job" remarks on their papers don't do much to motivate them to work harder, to become more creative in their thinking and their phrasing. Because I saw myself as more of a co-creator than an evaluator, I filled the margins of my writers' papers with my questions and my celebrations. I pushed them to be anything but ordinary, to not settle for being competent. I used exclamation points (only one at a time, thank you) and smiley faces. I used wit and encouragement. I squeezed as many inked words as I could fit into the margins of their papers, and then I typed lengthy comments to staple to the back. I wanted my students to see just how thankful I was for their efforts in drafting, revising, and editing, in owning their work and in sharing it with me. I believed that if I took time to carefully read and

295

thoughtfully mark their essays, then they would do their best to match my efforts by putting in even more of their own.

One of my principals was in our room observing my teaching once on a day that I returned essays to my class. In our follow-up conference, he shook his head as he recounted what he had witnessed. "I have never seen anything like that," he said. "I swear, your kids were trembling with anticipation as you walked around passing back their papers. And it wasn't like they were nervous. They were excited to see what you had written to them. I asked a few why, and they said the marks on the rubric weren't the most important part. It was the comments they looked forward to seeing. One girl told me that the best days in your class for her were when you returned her papers. I can't remember ever seeing that before."

I smiled because my principal had discovered a secret that my students and I had known for a long time. They continually improved in writing because, somehow, I inspired them to love it. And they loved it not because they enjoyed getting good grades or because they feared getting bad ones. They loved it, as they loved all aspects of our class, because it was a bond between them and me. That's what brought me into the room each day with joyful expectations and a light heart. That's what continues after all of my students have now moved on, after I myself have left the classroom. Those feelings live on.

So, that becomes a challenge for you as you begin your career. How will you find a way to help your students not just acquire knowledge and skills but develop a love for that knowledge, those skills? Information can be forgotten. Ability can diminish with time and a lack of use. If the poets are right, however, love can last forever. The first obvious step toward influencing that feeling in your kids will be revealing your own love for your subject. When your students see that you chose to enter the profession not just because you liked summers off but because you have a passion for your discipline and you feel a true calling for sharing that feeling with others, when they come to understand that, for you, this is a vocation and not merely an occupation, then they will be empowered to follow. A beloved spiritual asks the question, "How can I keep from singing?" When you open your heart to your kids, they might just ask themselves, "How can I keep from loving to learn in this class?"

What Steinbeck Said: Post #80
Wednesday, May 10, 2017
Bye and Bye

*I*t was 1967. I was a freshman in Mrs. Moriarity's English class at East Lansing High School. Or was it 1968, and I was a sophomore in Mrs. Howey's room? Ah, the memory clouds a bit. Maybe it was both classes! In any event, after eight years of Catholic schooling, of rigid rows, some with desks actually attached to each other, I found myself sitting in a circle. Goodness. I could see the faces of all my classmates when they spoke, and more importantly, I could see their faces when I said something. It took some getting used to, but eventually I came to enjoy the setup. It was fun to make rolling eye contact with my friends when something off the wall was said, and if I had been the winking type, I'm sure I could have communicated that way as well.

Fast forward to my own teaching career. For the first dozen years or so, I taught in those parochial rows. If kids wanted to see each other, they had to crane their necks or twist in their seats. Of course, my seventh graders at Lincoln Middle School didn't mind that at all, but I felt comfortable in a setup designed for my convenience, especially when it came to classroom management.

In 1988, I moved across town to Green River High School. There I walked into one of the classrooms and saw that circle once more. It belonged to our longtime department chair, and her Twelfth Grade College Prep English class was legendary. Every day, her seniors would start class by moving their desks into the circle. It was ritual, that circle, part of the special nature of that class environment, something that her other classes weren't privileged to know. Eating lunch together with our colleagues in the English office, I marveled at the daily stories she told us about her College Prep discussions, but when I went back to the ninth graders in my classroom, I thanked God for my secure rows.

Until one day.

I stopped by to talk to our chair before school started and found her pushing her desks into their familiar arrangement.

"Don't you have freshmen first hour?" I asked her.

297

"Yep." She finished the transformation and turned to me so I could see that wonderful twinkle.

"Somebody told me yesterday that my circle was fine for seniors, but I could never pull it off with freshmen. Well, Eric Stemle, if there's one thing I love, it's being able to prove somebody wrong about me."

I decided right then that I would adopt a circular approach to my teaching from then on. I rushed back to my room and built my own circle. Did it work well immediately with my students? Oh, not at all. Chaos, in fact. After a while, however, we found our groove. Ever since that day, my students have sat in a circle.

Why a circle? There are many reasons. As I learned in high school, we can communicate more easily. As I learned as a teacher, it promotes an egalitarian environment. There is no teacher standing above students because I take my own seat among my kids to discuss. There is no front of the room, there is no back of the room. There is just us.

We don't call them discussions *in our class. We call them* circles. *That's the* way it has been for nearly thirty years.

Until today.

Today was the final circle for my seniors, and it was the final circle of my career. On Friday and next Tuesday, I will read aloud the last two chapters of A Tale of Two Cities. We'll talk a bit about the reading as we go, but today was the last time that we read outside of class and prepared to share with each other. And you know what? Each class had a glorious discussion. As the kids were at last pulling together all of Dickens' threads, so, too, were they putting the finishing touches on our class tapestries. I've seen our circle through many analogies over the years, but today, I realized that all this time, it has been one giant loom, and each of us a weaver.

Mrs. Moriarity? Mrs. Howey? Wherever you are out there, I want you to know that I have carried on your method. In my heart, I know that somewhere else out there, at least a few of my former students have carried our tradition into their own classrooms. Even as my weaving ended today, the circle is unbroken.

I don't know how you will eventually arrange your seating, and in the long run, it won't really matter all that much how you do. I have seen amazing classrooms set in rows, tables, team pods, and in one case, a spiral. You will find a way that is comfortable for you, and if you feel good about it, your classes will adjust. Over the course of your career, you'll probably experiment with a number of setups, but it's important that whatever you choose is grounded not only in utility but also in finding a structure that allows your students to function most effectively as a class.

As for our room, as the days of that last May passed more and more quickly, my sentimental nature came fully to the fore. I have always been one to commemorate milestones and anniversaries, to mark countdowns to events (as I write this, one month from today is Christmas!), to observe rituals. It is my way of celebrating life. I love to place happenings in a framework to help me understand how far I've come and how far I have to go.

When I realized that I had come to the final literary discussion of my career, I tried not to put too much pressure on myself or on my students. I certainly let them know that this was the last time we would bring our individual reading to the circle, and I also let it slip that it was the last I would ever lead, but my kids were good. They knew that without me telling them. Still, as I grabbed my copy of *A Tale of Two Cities* and my notebook with thoughts and questions written in it and found an open desk, I felt a subtle tingle. I was excited, not really nervous. Still, I was curious as to how we would handle the next forty-five minutes together.

As I said in the post, each class' discussion was remarkable. They had come so far in their ability to interpret, so far in being able to riff off of each other's ideas. On that day they quickly fell into a great rhythm and composed a wonderful conversation. Part of each dialogue's success surely stemmed from their preparation. They had learned to read Dickens well, and they came to class ready with points to share and questions to pose. Once the koosh ball started flying around the room, they immersed themselves in the zone, taking the class analysis deeper and deeper with each topic, with every contribution. Me? I sat silent for most of the day, simply shining with pride for what my kids were

299

doing.

If we indeed stand on the shoulders of giants, then those circles on that last day owed their brilliance in part to what I had learned from students over the course of four decades of conducting discussions. I progressed from my early days of following a script of questions that elicited one or two responses to posing open-ended questions to incorporating sidebar conversations to student-led discussions, and through it all I listened to what my kids were teaching me about what they needed in order to get the most out of the circle. As my classes became more adept at interpreting and sharing over the years, they inspired me to step away from telling my side of stories and to lead them in their own discoveries. That became my mission, to share strategies and encourage them to play with them, to reveal the secrets that I had discovered for myself. Perhaps the biggest of those was that when my students soared in a discussion, I learned, too.

Sometimes over the years I would be so touched by something said in the circle that I would simply call for the koosh and hold it for a few seconds so that we could all appreciate the moment. I would nod at the speaker, smile and maybe wink, but then I would scan the circle, and I would fix my eyes on each student there before thanking them all. For it wasn't me who had created that interpretation, and it wasn't even the kid who had uttered it. It was all of us, and it had taken all of the year to that point to get us ready for that particular revelation.

Put that on a standardized test.

What Steinbeck Said: Post #81
Friday, May 12, 2017
You're Just Going to Have to Wait

*A*nother short instructional day. With our new Friday schedule that *provides study time for those students who have fallen behind on their* *assignments, regular classes are trimmed by thirty minutes. Today, that* *meant that I would get close to reading aloud the entirety of Chapter Fourteen of*

A Tale of Two Cities, *but I knew that I didn't have time to complete it. My hope was that we would experience a major event in the plot before we had to leave for the weekend.*

To quote something I read long ago, we came thisclose.

The last two chapters of the novel bring closure to the stories of its hero, Sydney Carton, and its antihero, Thérèse Defarge. The latter's tale is highlighted in the penultimate chapter, and we traced her movements from a council with three of her supporters that confirms her decision to exterminate all of Charles Darnay's family to her arrival at the family's dwelling where she finds no one at home but Miss Pross. The governess has stayed behind with Jerry Cruncher in order to better facilitate the escape of the family's coach, and as Cruncher leaves to secure their own carriage, Pross is startled by the sudden appearance of Madame Defarge.

There then ensues a confrontation between the small but wiry woman who warns her foe that she will be more than a worthy adversary because "I am Englishwoman," and the powerful French force who Dickens describes as a "tigress." The author sets a battle between a tough but nurturing protector and a revolutionary who carries a revolver hidden between her breasts and a dagger hidden in the waist of her robe. In effect, Dickens has weaponized the two parts of Defarge's anatomy that distinguish her as a woman. This is a family servant versus a warrior, and at the beginning of their fight, each character hurls insults in her own language, unintelligible to the other. It is a darkly humorous moment that brought chuckles from my students, but before we could read the climax of the exchange, the dismissal bell pierced the room.

I love a good cliffhanger as much as anyone, but this was a premature slipping off the edge. As my kids grabbed their backpacks, I reminded them not to read until we returned for our next class. That means that we'll all be holding on by our fingernails until Tuesday. They have a sense that something dramatic is about to happen, but we're still a few paragraphs short of the payoff.

On Tuesday, I'll do a bit of a review, and I'll try to recreate the tension that we felt in our reading today. Once I feel that we're ready, I'll continue my reading to the class. Within a minute or two, we'll all learn that. . . .

I didn't have a lot of peeves when I taught, but certainly one was walking down the hall with maybe five minutes to go in a class period and seeing students lined up at a classroom door as if they were waiting for a bus. I'm sure that some of those kids saw themselves as prisoners waiting for a cell block gate to open, but in any event, the message from that room seemed to be that learning had ended before the bell.

One of the ideas that I took away from a week-long class with Madeline Hunter was that "time is the currency of education. Spend it wisely." I had not even reached the tenth year of my teaching when I heard those words, but they stayed with me the rest of my career. When I welcomed my students that next fall, I was ready to implement as many time-saving measures as I could. I found ways to efficiently pass out and collect materials, I prepared my chalkboard with directions before class started so that I didn't have to take time to write as I spoke to my kids. Of course, that move also helped me with my seventh grade classes because I could talk to them while I looked their way. Trust me, that was a great deterrent to all sorts of misbehavior. I also began using what Dr. Hunter called "sponge activities." It could take my middle school classes a minute or two just to take out their books, and not only were my students not learning during those odd minutes, but they were also tempted to chat. A sponge activity soaked up that lost time and replaced it with an occasion to sharpen our thinking. While my kids were getting themselves ready for a lesson, I would pose riddles or ask them to spell aloud or solve a multiplication problem, anything to keep them thinking and not mind-wandering. It was a lot easier to teach my students when their heads were with me and not roaming elsewhere.

Years later, teaching at the high school level, I squeezed every possible second out of our class time. My first word came within the echo of the tardy bell, and my aim was to say my last at the split second of the one that dismissed us. I didn't always achieve that goal, depending on what we were doing at the end of class, but even when we were finishing up work in teams or taking a few minutes to read silently, I made sure that the last thing that everyone heard before we left was my voice or that of a classmate. In the rare event that we were doing independent work and the kids put away their things to stand near the door, I would ask them in the most fatherly manner I could muster to return to their seats, even if that meant that they sat a few seconds after the bell. It was a matter of establishing a culture that said, "As long as we're together, for every second that we're together, we will be engaged in learning."

Eventually, a directive came from our administration that we were all to teach "from bell to bell." That brought a little grumbling from the faculty, and some of my colleagues asked how they could take attendance and teach at the same time. What were they supposed to do when the lesson was over and there was still some time left in the class? What was the big problem with a couple of minutes, anyway? I stayed out of those discussions and kept pushing myself to keep up the pace throughout each period. I had long before figured out that I could take attendance while my students were working with the *Word of the Day* in their notebooks or doing their *ARO* reading. If I needed to sponge up a few extra minutes at the end of the period, I could review key concepts or help kids make connections from that lesson to the unit at large. I wanted them to be focused on something productive throughout our eighty-five minutes, and while I could not guarantee that they weren't daydreaming or sneaking a look at their phones during independent learning time, those departures never occurred because I had sanctioned them. It was important that I did everything I could to spend my currency wisely. It was important that my students realized that, too.

In your classroom, just exactly what you choose to do to with your time will not be as crucial as the message you send to your students about its importance. Answering riddles and doing mental math certainly weren't part of my language arts curriculum, but those little activities continually reminded my kids that every second was critical in our class. It's not like I worked my students to death, kept their minds running ceaselessly from bell to bell. There was plenty of time for us all to breathe and to relax and to enjoy each other. What was absent was "free time," that dreaded void that was not only unproductive but culture-diluting as well. If you let your classes develop the notion that there are dead spots in your lesson plans, that it's not vital for them to make the most of their time and their resources, then they just might also start thinking that you yourself don't believe there's all that much to learn in your course. Or that you only care that they learn enough to get by. If that happens, why should your kids give you their undivided attention? Their best effort? I guess the more important thing is, why would you ever want to make those questions even possible?

What Steinbeck Said: Post #82
Tuesday, May 16, 2017
Last Call

T *he "last" tour continued today. Last week we celebrated my last circle discussion. Today, I conducted my last guided reading as we finished our study of* A Tale of Two Cities. *It would have been an emotional day any other year—Dickens gets me every time—but as I performed today, I kept in mind that this was the last time I would ever read an author's words to my students, the last time I would ever take on the inflection of characters. Would ever share interpretations with my kids in the middle of our reading.*

We began by finishing our reading of Chapter Fourteen and its confrontation between Madame Defarge and Miss Pross. Though this is a gravely serious conflict, one which ends in the former's death, Dickens does present some comic relief in the form of the latter's proud proclamation that she is an Englishwoman. The kids get a kick out of the lead-up to Defarge's shocking demise, and we stopped to talk a bit about the ramifications of her passing. Above all, it signifies the end of any threat to Lucie and her family as they make their way out of France. That chapter put to rest, we turned to the novel's final one. In a scant five pages, Dickens pulls the story together in a heartfelt denouement. The writing is exquisite, and as I carefully and lovingly read those last few pages, I had a great sense that my kids were picking up on allusions and on the completion of what had been long foreshadowed. Nonetheless, I knew we had to do a little processing after I finished my reading.

As I had done at the conclusion of Of Mice and Men, *I turned off the lights and gave my students a few minutes to get in touch with their hearts regarding our experience of the previous half hour. I then invited them to share thoughts and feelings with partners before asking whether anyone wanted to say anything to the whole class. A few volunteered, but all in all, they were a somber group. I felt like a police officer interviewing a family after a tragedy.*

"I'm sorry to put you through this," I told my kids, "but it's my duty as an English teacher to get the interpretation out." We smiled.

Lights back on, we looked at the author's craft one last time. Dickens presents the tumbrils as plows creating furrows through the populace that lines the street. We looked at that metaphor in terms of the planting of the seeds of freedom from this new form of oppression, of the blood sacrifice that would consecrate the ground. We considered the symbolism of the Twenty-third Psalm. *Finally, we discussed Dickens' original naming of his hero: Dick Carton. Pairing that with Charles Darnay, I wrote the two men's initials on the board: DC—CD.*

"They're a mirror image!" one girl shouted.

"Dickens' name is in each character, at least part of it," said another. Is there no end to the intricacy of this work?

Tonight, far away from my students, alone with Teresa and the cats, I reflected upon my years of reading aloud to my kids. Upon the voices I have sought to animate through my interpretation of their pitch and rhythm. Charlie Gordon. Tom Joad. Montresor and Fortunato. Jean Louise and Jem and Atticus. Lennie Small and George Milton. Romeo and Mercutio and Tybalt. Prospero and Caliban. Odysseus. Marc Antony. Tessie Hutchinson and Mrs. Delacroix. Pip and Estella and Magwitch. John and Lorraine and the Pigman. The Stage Manager and Emily Webb. Snowball and Boxer and Napoleon. Norman Maclean.

I closed my eyes and heard those voices singing softly in the classrooms that inhabit the school that is the memory of my career. They sang of journeys and adventures, of rivers and seas, of small towns and majestic empires, of conflicts and sorrows and triumphs. More than anything, they told the story of the magic that happens when one teacher opens a book and reads its words aloud to a circle of minds enchanted.

It has been my honor to be that teacher to so many of you over the years. Thank you for listening, for opening your hearts as well as your ears. Thank you for your laughter, your tears, and your imaginations. Together, we paid homage to some incredible authors, didn't we?

For the record, the final words I read today belong to Sydney Carton: "It is a far, far better thing that I do than I have ever done; it is a far, far better rest I go to than I have ever known."

Could I find any finer line to end upon?

Over the years, I was privileged to portray the lives of so many immortal characters. There is a profound understanding that we acquire when we perform their words, an intimacy that we create with our audience. Perhaps it is the primacy of the human voice, our love of hearing a tale well-told. There's nothing quite like curling up in a comfortable chair with a cup of tea and a favorite book, but there is little that is more inspiring than to be mesmerized by a dramatic reading. It was an honor to take that stage, and I savored every opportunity that I granted myself to add voice to an author's great words. I held that responsibility in the highest regard, and that meant that I had to prepare myself before each reading. I had to do more than just know the words. I had to appreciate their context. When I read description, I wanted it to flow, to paint pictures in my students' minds. When I read dialogue, I wanted to assume the essence of the characters, to know not only their motivations but also their inflections and the tempo of their speech. In the end, as much as my kids may have enjoyed listening as they read along with me, I was the one who truly benefited. I was the one who felt transformed as an instrument of a writer I had never met.

That was certainly one of the benefits of developing a sense of class with my students. While they all had many chances to learn independently in their reading and especially in their writing, the most important factor in their development as readers and writers and speakers was the work we all did together. That was a dynamic that I never wavered on to the last day of my teaching. I resisted the trend toward individualized learning and computer-driven instruction. It wasn't that I didn't employ both to some extent, but I knew that rather than continually changing tracks in search of the best route to teaching success, I devoted my efforts to making my train the most efficient and entertaining ride there was.

In the end, the I choice I had was to either improve the system or improve myself. I chose the latter, even while my school and my district focused on the former. I figured that no matter what techniques I used, no matter which curriculum I executed, my success as a teacher was grounded in the environment that I fostered, in the love and the nurturing that I gave to my students. How I did those things was as unique as I am as a person, and it is up to you to discover how to create a classroom that puts the needs of students first and the demands of data second. That will be by no means an easy undertaking, but if your children are going to blossom into remarkable adults, you will need to provide the proper soil and conditions for that blooming. It's all a matter of understanding how a garden grows.

What Steinbeck Said: Post #83
Thursday, May 18, 2017
Into the Feelings

*W*hen I taught Freshman English, we would follow our study of Romeo and Juliet with a viewing of West Side Story. This, of course, brought groans from some of my boys, who found the balletic efforts of the Sharks and Jets to be beyond the pale for any self-respecting gang member. It took me several years to discover an explanation that somewhat satisfied that complaint, and that story became the opening of my lesson today as I gave my students a little background on the nature of musical theater.

I opened by showing my seniors the first few minutes of the film, pausing as the sauntering Jets gradually broke into pirouettes. "At this point," I told my kids, "my freshmen would say, 'That's stupid.' I tried to explain that it was art, that it was the essence of the musical, but they weren't buying it. A few years later, I discovered a quote from Leonard Bernstein, who called singing 'speech elevated.' Wow." I pointed to the frozen image of the Jets in mid-dance and then continued. "That got me thinking. Is it just possible that dance is 'walking elevated'?"

I went on to suggest that song and dance give us a window into the emotions of .the performers. In the reality of the world of the play, characters are walking and talking, but we are privy to their feelings as expressed by their interactions with the music. To answer my freshman, I explained that, naturally, it would be odd to see people breaking out into song, into dance, but when we watch West Side Story, *we are not watching reality. We are observing art.*

With that story as a foundation, we began our viewing of the Broadway musical Into the Woods, *book by James Lapine, music and lyrics by Stephen Sondheim. It was a piece that I had shared with my* Senior Humanities *classes years ago in Green River, and I told my students today that this winter when I decided to retire, I also opted to return to the play.*

"This show is about following our hearts, about leaving what is comfortable to go out into the world to find our desires. It's something that all of you are about to do, and something that I am about to do as well."

Over the course of three class periods, we will be tracing the weaving of several fairy tale characters, and as we interpret their motivations, we will be cautioned to be "careful the things [we] do" because "children will listen," that we can help each other in our life journeys because "no one is alone."

Into the Woods *is clever and light, philosophical and dark. It is a wonderful way to remind my students of the layered integration of thought and form and art that we have created for the past nine months. As class ended today, we left the Baker and his wife about to sing "It Takes Two." That hopeful song will inspire the couple to complete their mission to satisfy the Witch's demands and in turn be blessed with a child. From there, well, life is nothing if not unpredictable in the woods.*

Make a smoothie in your blender. Put in whichever ingredients you want, sweet or green. Let's say you put in frozen yogurt, maybe blueberries, strawberries, and pineapple and push the button, swirling flavors and textures into a cold, delicious concoction. You pour yourself some, save the remainder in the fridge for later, and sit for a couple of minutes to enjoy the goodness you have created. All of those ingredients, inseparable in the glass have now become energy to enable your body and your mind to create for the next short while.

The smoothie that was my lifelong education held more parts than I can ever recount. The berries, the banana, so easy to taste, were the classes that changed my thinking, the mentors who inspired me with ideas and encouragement. The almonds or the coconut or the seeds that might have added a more subtle taste, were the lessons I learned through my reading and my own investigations. A spoonful of honey was the sweetness of my imagination, tying together all of the other flavors and textures. And the drinking? Well, that might seem an easy answer. The consummation of all of my education and training was the act of my teaching, but that assumes that once I put down the glass, I was done learning. Nothing could be falser.

Each day that brought me into the classroom, that found me in my living room planning and grading, was fueled by that energy carried in my smoothie, but it seemed that the blender jar never went dry. Throughout my years of teaching, I kept learning. All of the information that I absorbed about my students and how to communicate with them became ingredients for the mix, and I as continued to add my experiences to the blender and to partake of that wonderful drink, I found more power with which to carry out my lessons, my units, my practice in total. It was a wonderful cycle of learning, creating, sharing, and learning from that sharing.

Because I continued to learn while I taught, I continually sought ways of improving my instruction, and more than that, I worked to anticipate my students' questions, to be ready with analogies to help them better understand troublesome concepts. My application of the Bernstein quote was an example. For years, my students complained about the unrealistic portrayals of life by those characters, but I never had much of an answer for them. It was not until I came across the "speech elevated" comment that my mind made a connection by taking a sip of my smoothie and finding the answer. It was a few months before I could share it with my freshmen during our viewing of *West Side Story*, but as I moved to the center of the circle to demonstrate speaking rising to song, walking elevated to dance, I finally got the idea across successfully.

Though I'm sure my idea wasn't original, no one had ever explained me to why musical characters sang and danced beyond being a simple matter of entertainment. It surely wasn't part of my undergraduate courses. None of my friends ever sat down at lunch and said, "Hey, did you know that Broadway musical characters aren't in reality singing and dancing?" Rather, the insight was an amalgamation of years of filling that blender and drinking of my experience. How sweet is that?

Of course, what you mix in your blender will depend on your preferences and your experiences. As I'm sure you realize by this point in our time together, there is no recipe except what you decide to put together to inform your teaching. You didn't learn all of those ingredients and their amounts in your education courses, and you didn't learn them from reading this book. Rather, as you make your way through your professional career, you will experiment with all of that mixing, and if you're fortunate, you'll hit upon a winner before too long. Just don't be satisfied with drinking the same glass day after day. There are always more delightful flavors to discover!

What Steinbeck Said: Post #84
Monday, May 22, 2017
Stay with Me

*I*n her Broadway role as the Witch in Into the Woods, *Bernadette Peters sings a poignant lament to her daughter, Rapunzel. "Stay With Me" follows the mother's discovery that the girl has allowed a prince to climb her hair up into her tower. The Witch acknowledges that Rapunzel finds her old, ugly, and embarrassing. Despite her daughter's denial and her expressed desire to "see the world," the hag begs her child to stay.*

Who out there could love you more than I?
What's out there that I cannot supply?

Stay with me.
Stay with me, the world is dark and wild,
Stay a child while you can be a child
With me.

As we watched that song today, I paused the film and looked out at my class of seniors, children no more with less than two weeks to go before graduation.

"If your mothers have not sung this song to you yet, they will," I said to knowing smiles. "They're already feeling it in their hearts."

I am sharing Into the Woods *with my kids for a number of reasons. One is to expose them to a musical and dramatic form that has more sophistication than they are used to seeing. Sondheim's melodies are often surprising to the ear. His lyrics are intricate and also unexpected in their rhythms. Lapine's book is witty and complex in its structure. Then there is the marvelous cast, headlined by Peters and Joanna Gleason. Here at the end of the year, after all of our literary interpretation, after all of our creating in both writing and presentation, this play serves for us as a dynamic culmination. It is superb in its integration of fairy tale characters and plots, and if there's one feature that has long distinguished my teaching, it's my ability to help my students create connections. My classes have learned how to look for layers, and this piece is a fun way for them to test their mettle.*

Of course, you know it's more than that. My primary reason for showing this musical is because its themes are perfect for young people about to head out into the world. By the time our viewing ends on Wednesday, my kids will know that "No One is Alone." They'll be told again and again that we must help each other in times of need, that people make mistakes and yet there is always someone there to help us make things right.

In any other year, I would echo the Witch and ask my students to stay with me. To come back in the fall so that we could continue this wondrous journey together. Ah, but here I am, leaving along with them, ready to see the world in a whole new way.

You know, it just hit me. More than anything, I'm sharing Into the Woods *with myself. And it's almost time for the curtain.*

My original plan for retirement included one more year of teaching. It certainly wasn't a concrete decision, but Teresa and I had discussed possibilities, and while we knew that we could teach until we had reached the brink of age sixty-five, we also knew that we could exit the year before that and still be in the same financial situation. When folks asked me how close I was to leaving, my standard response was, "We're going to teach one or two more years, more likely two than one." That was the truth as I knew it in my heart, so much so, that I began laying down some plans for the 2017-2018 school year. I had a motif in mind, a year-long study of Beethoven's Ninth Symphony. I would play a movement at the end of each nine-week marking period, devoting time to showing my students what the composer was presenting in each section and how the work's building development paralleled our course of study and our growth as learners. That approach was going to require me to do a lot of learning on my own, and I figured that I would employ my wife as my musical tutor to help me make the abstract a little more accessible for my kids. It was going to be a challenge for all of us, but I was really looking forward to playing that fourth movement with my classes right before we reached our own final measure.

Beyond that theme, I was planning on opening the vault that contained all of the literature that I had ever shared with my students and pulling out my favorite pieces for that final year, sort of a greatest hits farewell tour. To that end, I purchased three class sets of *A River Runs Through It*, a jewel that I knew would provide my seniors with all sorts of life lessons to discuss as we prepared to go out into the world beyond high school. When the books arrived, I placed them on a shelf, waiting to number them at a later date. As it turned out, that task fell to my successor, another lover of Maclean's memoir. I'm happy that they eventually found their way to his students.

As I have mentioned it a number of times, it should come as no surprise that another work I contemplated returning to was *The Grapes of Wrath*. I have had a love affair with Steinbeck's writing going back decades, and I adore the experimental nature of that novel as well as its deep character development.

Because I devoted so much time to examining our selections, and because the masterpiece was longer than most of the other books or plays that I used, placing it once again in my literature rotation would have meant dropping a few pieces that I had used for a long time, but that would be a necessary sacrifice if I was going to be true to my greatest hits theme.

If there was another favorite to bring back, it would have been *The Martian Chronicles*. There was always something about Ray Bradbury's writing that touched my imagination, and I always thoroughly enjoyed sharing his wit with my students. A bonus was the episodic structure of the book, basically a string of chronologically-connected short stories that made it convenient to incorporate into a series of lessons, made it easy to read a few chapters at a time without interrupting the book's movement. More than anything, Bradbury's blend of science fiction and fantasy would have thrown open the doors of our fancy, something my students needed to experience when the stress of senior year became overwhelming. Besides, they were about to go out and do a little exploring of their own, so why not learn a little from the old guy before they blasted off?

Perhaps I would have dusted off a couple of videos from years past, maybe *The Red Balloon* or *The Dot and the Line*, short films that allowed for all sorts of interpretation. All in all, that extra year would have been a sentimental journey for me at least, but I found over the years that my kids often picked up on my vibes pretty well. They may not have understood the significance of my choices for that last go-around, but they would have at the very least grasped the notion that I was sharing my favorites with them. How much more of an honor could I bestow upon them than that?

313

Eric Stemle

I *love this day each spring. At the end of the last class before our final exam, I gather my students on the Flatland, that space inside our circle, and for twenty minutes or so, we reflect on our experience together over the course of the year. In the center of our circle I place the cup of M&M's that has symbolically represented our class since late August. Then we talk.*

"What are you going to remember about our class?" I ask them as a start. Then I wait to toss the same koosh ball that we used on the first day of class, a token that I only bring out for special occasions. Today was as special as it gets.

It came as no surprise that the kids were shy at first. I'm guessing that no one was quite sure how to begin. In each class, a hand eventually went up, and we were off and reminiscing. We talked about the family feel to our class, about the depth to which we interpreted, about our growth as writers. The kids were affectionate in their comments about me, and while I loved them for it, I really wanted to hear what they thought about us. After a while, we started to recall funny moments from the year, and laughing together one last last time felt so good.

At the end of our talk, I moved from student to student, holding out the chalice so that each could take out an M&M.

"Please don't eat yours yet," I told them. "Remember, they're supposed to melt in your mouths, not in your hands." When everyone was served, I passed around the circle a letter that I had written to the class. As it is every year, it was a love letter to my darlings. In it I reminded them of what they had accomplished, advised them about their futures. When I finished, we considered our M&M's.

"On our first day together, I explained that your M&M represents you as an individual, and we talked about the colorful candy shell that each of us can see. Back in August, all we really knew about each other was that shell. But as time went on, we discovered that next sweet layer, and we all know by now that at our core, we are all a little nutty."

My kids have heard this before, but they still smiled. Generous folks.

"Resting in this cup," I said, holding up the now-empty vessel, "our M&M's have been silent witnesses to each of our days together. As if through osmosis, every thing that happened, every word that was uttered, is now encapsulated in this little piece. Ready to taste our experience?

"One, two, three."

We popped our M&M's in our mouths and savored the sweetness. More smiles.

"Thank you, my friends," I said as the bell rang, and we all climbed to our feet.

Friday is Senior Skip Day. A few of my kids will come to class, and we'll work together in preparation for their final exams. Most will be off somewhere else besides school. We'll all be back together next Wednesday to write one last essay. We will need every minute of the exam period to complete that task, and so today was our last time to sit together, to share our thoughts and feelings, to be a class.

It was also to be the last time I'll ever sit within such a circle. That's why my voice caught just a little as I read the last paragraph, as I told my students that I loved them. I read a little faster than I would have liked, but that inexorable 3:10 bell was about to ring, and if my kids weren't already salivating at the thought of consuming an M&M, that dismissal sound would most certainly do the trick. I wanted to finish before we all started drooling.

To all of you who have sat with me in a circle on the floor, who have shared that candy communion to end a school year, I extend that cup to you one final time. We are a remarkable extended family, and over the decades we have gone far beyond a tiny classroom to make a difference in our communities, to in our own ways change the world. My friends, that's all I ever expected you to do.

I f anything defined me as a teacher, it was my ability to develop a sense of class with my students. Each of those classes was one manifestation of a culture that grew and refined itself over the years so that when my new students arrived that first day each fall, they brought with them an expectation born of conversations with their brother and sisters, their parents, their older friends who had all experienced English class with Mr. Stemle. And I brought with me a welcome from all of those thousands of young hearts who had helped me become who I was at that moment as a teacher, from all of those whose spirits, in some part, remained secure in the corners of the classroom. On that last day on the floor with my seniors sitting cross-legged in a tighter circle, their energy hovered above us, angels blessing me one final time.

You won't build a class in a week. You won't build a culture in decade. It will take a long while for your students to become comfortable enough to allow themselves to open their emotions to their classmates, to their teacher, to the learning itself. For some of them, it will take even longer to accept the fact that love exists in the classroom. They may be used to classes where praise and good will are given conditionally, where they feel that they must earn a place in their teacher's heart. I began each class in August by loving all of my students unconditionally, and while I always had a few kids who seemed to try to test that affection, my heart never wavered. I knew that even those who seemed distant, sometimes even hostile, were still trying to figure themselves out, and they might not have had the ability yet to figure out who I was in their lives. They were learning, practicing on their way to growing up. What they needed from me was what I gave them as best I could. Love and understanding.

By the time we sat together that one last time, my kids knew that I loved them. And I knew that they loved me. That's why we were able to accomplish as much as we did, and that's why we all developed more confidence in our abilities to lead and to work together. That's why the feeling was palpable across the Flatland as we held our M&M's, ready to consume the experience in one final sharing. For each class, it wasn't something that could have happened in September or October. For me, it wasn't something that could have happened in my early years of teaching. I was just grateful that it eventually happened at all.

Spreading

A s the school year came to a close, the garden in profuse bloom was an
extraordinary place to be. My students and I had risen and bloomed as
single flowers, but just as importantly, together we had made our
classroom a special place of rare beauty. Each class had developed its own
character, and yet what all shared was a spirit that enabled us to learn together, to
teach each other, to celebrate the miracle of a classroom that began within the
soil some nine months before and was now a fragrant and vibrant environment.
Learning had flowered and spread, and as new seeds had blown away on the
wind, much more learning would now continue wherever my students landed
after they left our school. For me, that final garden would be housed in my heart
along with all of the others seasons of growing and learning, but it would be the
last time I would ever enjoy the process of planting and tending and growing
along with my students. Looking ahead to my precious last days with my
students and my colleagues, I felt a wondrous sense of peace and fulfillment. It
was time to bask in just a few more hours of sunlight.

Eric Stemle

What Steinbeck Said: Post #86
Friday, May 26, 2017
For Love

*T*oday was the last day of my classes before next week's final exam. *Traditionally, I have used our last period together to say goodbye, to tie together our experience. Along with reflecting and the sharing of our M&M's as we did on Wednesday, we've often observed a variety of symbolic gestures to signify the end.*

For a number of years, I asked my kids to think about one way that they could be remembered as members of our school. I gave them all Dixie cups filled with water and asked them to sit in a circle on the floor, much as we did two days ago. In the center of the circle, I placed a glass pitcher, and as students rose to announce their legacies, they poured the contents of their cups into that container. At first, the water level seemed woefully insignificant, but by the time the last had shared, the pitcher was filled to the brim. I had used it to fill the cups, but I didn't bother to tell my kids that.

"Take a look at the pitcher," I told them. "Can you see where your cup of water is?" Of course, none of us could. That's the essence of what it is to be a class. We all contribute in our own ways, but in the end, the parts are indistinguishable in terms of the whole.

Another final day activity has been our viewing of "The Firebird Suite" from Fantasia 2000. As we watched the film's gorgeous representation of the finale of Stravinsky's ballet, I asked my kids to interpret the piece in relation to our class time together. Each year, they would work together to build analogies, and they inevitably focused on the flame of their learning, the stressful periods of the year where they felt they had burned out. Invariably, they saw me as the stag who carried them to safety. At the end, with the music's resolution, they saw the beauty of their shared experience. I have always loved that activity, not just for the stirring music, but also because it has given my students a chance to strut their interpretative skills at the end of the year.

My lesson plan for today as I wrote it at the beginning of the year was to include the legacy pitcher, "The Firebird," reflections on the year, and the sharing of our M&M's. That plan changed last week when I announced our upcoming schedule, and one of my students raised her hand.

"Mr. Stemle, did you know that next Friday is Senior Skip Day?"

A heart-sinking moment. You'd have to look a long time to find a more sentimental guy than me, and I immediately realized that we weren't going to have a full goodbye. I was upset, and while I usually try to hide that from my students, at that moment, I spoke from my heart.

"Well," I said, looking down, "that saddens me. You all do what you want that day. I'll be here."

We went on with our next activity, but I noticed the girl who had spoken whispering with a few of her classmates. They knew how I felt. They also knew that they wouldn't be coming to class today.

My first thought was to proceed as planned, to do my farewell activities with those who showed up today, but that would have been less about my kids and more about me exercising my German stubbornness. A few days later, I decided to squeeze in our goodbye on Wednesday after we finished watching Into the Woods, *and that's exactly what we did. We didn't have time for everything that I had planned, but at least we got to express our appreciation for each other.*

Today? A total of twelve students came to my three classes. I welcomed them, I sang to them a few lines from "What I Did for Love" from A Chorus Line, *I shared a* Word of the Day *with them, and I gave them time to study.*

Oh, yes. And I loved them. I loved them for coming on a day when most of their classmates were off doing something else. I loved them for working hard on a Friday in late May. I loved them because that's what teachers do.

I wish my other students could have heard the music of Marvin Hamlisch and Ed Kleban as I performed it for my small group today. I intended it for everyone to hear and to consider it as an expression of Sydney Carton's feelings, but it was much more for all of the time and effort that we have devoted to learning as a class:

319

Kiss the day goodbye
And point me toward tomorrow,
We did what we had to do;
Won't forget, can't regret
What I did for love.

Some of my students may have some regrets as they look back on our time together. We always wish that we would have worked a little harder, would have gotten to know a few classmates a little better. As for me, I have only a heart filled with fondness, a mind filled with memories of a good year, a final year.

I wouldn't have skipped that for anything.

In 2003, I was named the Wyoming Teacher of the Year. My selection brought recognition to me and to my school, and in the course of that year, I attended a number of honorary functions, including a trip to the White House and a week at Space Camp in Huntsville, Alabama. I also represented the Wyoming Education Association in a variety of ways, including a commercial that aired on the few television stations found in our sparsely-populated state. It was a special year, and throughout it all, I did my best to share my love of my profession with a variety of audiences.

A couple of years later I ran into a dear friend from our days in Green River. We had taught together at the high school and had each moved on to a different district. In our GRHS days there were times when we would seek each other out to relieve stress. It began when he showed up in my office one day during his planning period and pulled up a chair next to mine.

"I came to be with you," he said.

"Cool," I said. "What's up."

"I'm having one of those days," he said. "I decided that the best thing I could do was go find someone I love and I know loves me and just be with that person for a few minutes. My wife's not in the building, so here I am."

We spent the next twenty minutes laughing and goofing. He smiled and stood, gave me a hug and went back to his room. We never did talk about what was bothering him, but it was enough to forget about everything and just hang out. About three weeks later, I was having my own one-of-those days, and I headed down to see my buddy.

"I came to be with you," I told him when I came through the door.

"Outstanding!" he said and immediately walked over and picked up his guitar. We sang for fifteen minutes or so, and he let me sing melodies while he harmonized. I left healed.

We talked about that remedy when we saw each other in 2005, and then my old friend gave me an affectionate look. "I never got a chance to congratulate you on being Teacher of the Year."

"That's all right," I said.

"Oh, I know it is. That's what you are. But what I wanted to tell you was that I really appreciated that you didn't make the award about you. I saw you on TV, and it was so typical of you. You made it all about the kids. Not everyone does that, you know."

Of all the kind words and praise that I received surrounding my selection, that statement from a close friend meant the most to me. It said that he got it, he understood me perfectly.

I could have thrown a fit when I found out that my seniors were deserting me on what I had planned to be a farewell. In any other year, that would have been disheartening. In this final year, it was devastating. I had looked forward to that precious moment with my kids for weeks, well, months. It was to be a perfect culmination not only of our time together but for all of my time in teaching. Even though I conveyed my disappointment to my class upon hearing that my plans had been dashed, I did it as quietly and peacefully as I could. It wasn't about me. It was about the kids. The last thing I wanted to do was to introduce guilt into the equation. I didn't want my students to feel bad for skipping out on a classroom tradition, and I certainly didn't want to feel guilty if some kids opted out of a school tradition to be with me. The wise decision in my mind was to make the best of the situation and enjoy the day with whoever did show up.

Of course, that's exactly what I did. It wasn't about me. The school clearly supported the skip day as a time-honored ritual, and me objecting wasn't going to change anything for the positive. While my work-around wasn't all that I wanted, it was what happened. All I could really control was how I played it on that day, and I played it just fine, thank you, with a cheerful heart and a clear conscience. After all, that's how I tried to approach every other day, so why not that one?

It should come as no surprise that you will have days like that. There will be times when you look forward to a class and come to school only to hear of a last-minute schedule change for an assembly. There will be technical glitches, students called away to the office, or something as simple as kids just not feeling like participating in what you had planned. That's when it will be good to remember that the school doesn't exist for teachers but rather for the students. When things don't go quite right, keep your kids clearly in your focus. What can you do at that point to make their experience that day worthwhile? The answer might not be what you want for that period, but if it serves your children, then it is the right course of action. And if that becomes your guiding principle, then you'll find that over time, those decisions will serve you, too.

What Steinbeck Said: Post #87
Wednesday, May 31, 2017
Seasons of Teaching

F *ive hundred twenty-five thousand six hundred students. . . .*
Well, not exactly. Pretty close to five-thousand, though. Grades seven through university. Six schools, including a summer writing course at my alma mater. As close as I can guess, over twenty-thousand essays read and marked, grades recorded.

How do you measure a career?

Today was my last day of classes. Most of it was spent collecting exams and books and letters written to me. We brought a few things full circle. Our opening quote was from Oscar Hammerstein, Jr.: "So long, farewell, auf Wiedersehen, goodbye!" On August 29, our first day of class, I had greeted my students with another lyric from The Sound of Music: *"Let's start at the very beginning, that's a very good place to start." Our first* Word of the Day *had been* sanguine *("optimistic"), and we echoed that today with* buoyant *("cheerful and optimistic"). We're all about structure and balance in Room 218.*

The rest of our time together was spent creating one last essay, one final interpretation. The prompt asked my kids to show how one character in A Tale of Two Cities *influences three other characters. To begin the unit, we had sat in the Flatland inside our circle, making connections with each other and tossing a ball of yarn that eventually formed an intricate web of shared experiences.*

Today was less about all of us and more about my relationship with each student. As my kids came to my desk to turn in their papers, I shook their hands as always, told them how much I appreciated them. Each conversation was brief but personal, and I adored the look I saw in each student's eyes. We have built something pretty remarkable in the past nine months, and we feel good about it. Are we a bit wistful? I suppose, but the emotion that I sensed more than any other today was satisfaction.

Someone asked me the other day whether retirement felt bittersweet. I told him that when I was thirty, I ran a marathon. I trained hard for the race, and I ran as well as I could. When I finished, I was spent, but I had an incredible feeling of accomplishment. It had been a great experience to run through the streets of Denver, to be encouraged by fellow competitors and onlookers, but as I reached the end, I felt so happy to be done. In no way did I feel the need to run an additional ten miles.

That's how I feel tonight.

How do you measure a career? In students taught—in papers graded. In bus rides—in literary discussions. In colleagues—in mentors. In film—in poetry.

How about love?

Of course. What else could it be? When I think of all the aspects that have blended to create my practice, it all comes back to love. Love of language, of writing and nuance. Love of literature, of symbol and story. Love of discovery, of serendipity, of twenty-five minds becoming one class.

Love of young people. Period.

In Rent, *Jonathan Larson looks at what makes up the span of one year.*

Tonight, I do that forty-one times. I'm sure that over the course of the coming days and weeks and months, even years, I will remember other lovely facets of my experience as a teacher. For the next few hours, however, I have my current students to think about.

Back to the essays!

I was a renter for forty-one years. In that time, I set up shop in fifteen classrooms, including a high school auditorium in order to accommodate my forty-three students in an independent reading class (the counselors just couldn't say no on that one) and one next to a middle school cafeteria (try teaching there during a lunch period sometime). I occupied some of my rentals for just one class period a day when, due to school overcrowding, I was designated as a "floater" who taught in colleagues' rooms during their planning periods. Somedays, a teacher remained in the room to write lesson plans or grade papers, and I enjoyed the extra audience because it was fun to interact with a friend regarding my teaching in real time. Of course, I had no hand in decorating those rooms where I was a visitor every day, and it was difficult to cart my materials through bustling hallways on the way from one room to another, but I enjoyed the variety as well as the challenge. During those floating years, I was assigned an office so that I had a place to store things and to meet with students. It was also my home base on days when I was doing instructional coaching. Some years, I even shared that office space with another teacher.

By far, the place that I spent the most time in my career was Room 218 of Evanston High School, my home at school for the last eighteen years of my practice. It became a shelter for me, my students, and my fellow teachers, and we all felt a certain comfort in knowing that there was a consistent climate in that space, whether it was being used for classes or after-school help or faculty meetings. Folks respected the culture that I created over the years, and they knew that while it was a room that often buzzed with energy, it was also a calm environment. It was a place that always welcomed its visitors with affection and good humor.

Even Room 218 was a rental, however. I knew that I was no more than a temporary occupant who used materials that belonged to the school and not to me. The desks were the school's, the books and the video materials were the school's. The posters on the wall were made by me and by my students, but even then, they were created with paper and markers paid for by the school. Eighteen years may seem a long time, but in the grand scheme of the history of EHS, my students and I were still transients, sojourning for a short while before moving on.

Looking back on my days in Room 218 and in all of the venues in which I taught, one thing is clear. I didn't rent my students' hearts. OK, maybe it was a rent-to-own arrangement, but though all of those classrooms continue to be used for teaching and learning, all except those in a Green River building that was torn down years ago, the desks and chairs are now warmed by other bodies, the air perfumed by the breath of other people. It never was about the classrooms, though, was it? It wasn't about the buildings, the grounds, the gymnasiums, the ball fields, and the teachers' lounges, all of those spaces that my students and colleagues and I haunted for so many years. It was all about the heart.

Ernest Hemingway called Paris, "a moveable feast." Playing on the idea that some religious holidays, such as Easter, fall on different days of the year, he remarked in his memoir that if you are fortunate to visit the city as a young man, then you will take that experience with you wherever you go. That well describes my experience as a teacher, as a coach, as a staff developer. In the end, it didn't matter where I taught or coached or counseled. It mattered who was with me. It was the experience that I carried with me from classroom to classroom, from arena to arena, and as I reflect on my career, it is the love that I shared with my students, my players, and my faculty partners that I carry wherever my retirement takes me. Hemingway was right. Teaching will stay with me the rest of my life.

Eric Stemle

What Steinbeck Said: Post #Last
Tuesday, June 6, 2017
Suitable for Framing

I t began with a lie. It was winter of 1973, and I bounded up the stairs of Morrill Hall to a meeting with an advisor from the Department of English. I was about to switch my major from journalism with the intent of becoming a famous writer.

"So, you are thinking of majoring in English?" I can still see the professor's face, her glasses and her upswept hair, but I long ago forgot her name. She was cordial if not exactly encouraging.

"Yes, ma'am. I want to be a writer."

"A writer." A wry smile for a second or two. "What do you want to write, Mr. Stemle?"

"Novels, mostly."

"I see. Have you thought about what occupation you'll have along with your writing?"

Didn't see that coming. "Well, I was thinking that writing would be *my occupation.*"

The smile returned, a bit broader this time, accompanied by a slight shake of her head. "You just can't write," she said. "Even great novelists have other sources of income. Saul Bellow had a job when he started. John Barth has a job. You just can't write."

I was stuck. It had never occurred to me that great writers had to earn money on the side, and I was going to be one of the great ones, right? Hadn't my teachers had always praised my writing?

"What sort of jobs can I get with an English degree?" I said.

"Oh, there are all sorts of possibilities," the professor said. "You can work in communications, go to law school. Teach." She leaned just a bit across her desk. "Have you thought about teaching?"

"Sure," I said. "I could teach."

She leaned back in her chair and swiveled toward the window. "You can't

326

just teach," she said with a touch of exasperation. "You have to want to teach."

Here is where I lied. Straight-faced. "I want to teach," I said with as much conviction as I could muster. "I really do."

Best fib I have ever told.

I never did become a famous writer. But in time, I realized that I had become an artist. As I explained in my first post, this blog's title comes from the words of John Steinbeck: "I have come to believe that a great teacher is a great artist and that there are as few as there are other great artists. Teaching might even be the greatest of the arts since the medium is the human mind and spirit."

As I reflect on my career, I do see it as a slowly-evolving piece of art. From the thumbnail of my education courses at Michigan State to the charcoal sketch that was my student teaching, my formative years taught me that I really did want to teach. From the background painted in oils in my early teaching in Arizona and Michigan to the foreground that emerged as I truly learned to teach in Green River, Wyoming, I came in time to realize the gift that teaching was to me. It was in Evanston that the final details were applied to the piece, the finishing touch to what had become a beautiful practice.

I thought about this process this morning, my last day as a teacher. My classroom was cleaner that it was when I moved in, and all I had left to do was turn the lights out one last time and walk that long hallway down to the school's back door. I saw no one on that final passage—it was just me and my thoughts and feelings. They were grateful thoughts, they were feelings of satisfaction, of a teaching life well-lived. Thanks to all of you who have shared this experience with me. You have brought me more blessings than I could have ever dreamed when I told that lie nearly forty-five years ago. How could I have known?

When an artist completes a painting, the last touch is the signature, but it's not my name that is written in the corner of this piece. This portrait of the artist as a teaching man is signed by each of you who have ever graced my classroom. It is all of you who have created this work.

I am forever in your debt, and I remain, as always, your servant.

Love,

Eric

N early three years have passed since my final day of teaching, the day that I left the garden for good and for the last time walked down the upper hall of the school I had called home for nearly two decades. It was a solitary stroll, for it had taken me a while to pack my car, to make sure that everything was in place as I left, and if there were any other teachers in the building in that early afternoon, they didn't step outside their room to wave goodbye. That was OK. I had spent the morning moving from classroom to classroom saying personal farewells, sharing hugs and sometimes tears. Over the years, I had missed so many of my friends when they left school for the last time because I was either too busy cleaning up when they slipped out, or they had decided to go quietly into the good night without going through any of that emotional stuff. Well, that was hardly me. I had spent my career arranging closure at the end of every year for my students, and I was determined to at last find my own on that final day.

Now it has come to you, my friend. I think I can call you that after talking to you over the course of these pages. I came into the profession a joyful optimist, and despite dire predictions for the eventual demise of the public school system, I still believe in the goodness of those who dedicate their lives to teaching. I still believe that magic happens when a teacher looks into a child's eyes and shares and shows. And I believe that if you are willing to give your time, your spirit, and your heart to your students, then you will help them change their lives and the lives of countless others. I look forward to living in that world.

Acknowledgments

My first thought was that this book was forty years in the making. That was basically the arc of my teaching career, but as I thought some more, I realized that there were things that informed my teaching that came into my life long before I stood before my first class. There were all of the teachers who loved me for who I was, even when that me wasn't the most motivated of students. There were classmates who inspired me, coaches and teammates who pushed me and challenged me, friends who supported me, and family who shaped a boy into the man I eventually became. I thank all of them for the part they played in helping me to become a teacher.

Of course, I am indebted to my students, my co-creators who shared their energy with me and gave me much more than they'll ever know. When deadline stress and committee work got to be more than I thought I could handle, it was my classroom family that lifted me, that helped me forget my nagging thoughts and enjoy my time together with them. You all were a blessing to me year after year after year.

I am also thankful for my colleagues, both those who taught with me and those who led me in their various school capacities. It was their camaraderie and their continual desire to learn that spurred me to try new approaches, to reach out to other minds to better understand our challenging profession. I loved being a member of a faculty that pulled together to effect change, even in turbulent times. On a more personal level, I am grateful for my fellow writers who supported and guided me as this book took form. Thank you to Anjoli, Bren, Elissa, Jen, Lynn, Rachel, and Tyler, who listened in living rooms as I read aloud; to Mary, who inspired and encouraged me from afar. Each provided me with thoughtful responses, and each sincerely championed my efforts. As my consultants, they helped me find a sense of purpose in writing to a larger audience.

Finally, I owe more than I can say to my family. To my parents, Terry and Ed, for their faith that I would someday make a difference in the world; my sister Laura who shares a passion for language that always makes me smile; to my brothers Chris and Drew who passed too soon but taught me the value of patience and perseverance. To our son Paul, who inspires his students to embrace possibility in his classroom every day and who designed the cover art for this book; our daughter Ellen who has woven a beautiful teaching tapestry in her own classroom and who coaches her fellow teachers as well; and our son-in-law Dustin, who reminds me a lot of a young teacher from years ago who dedicated his efforts to awakening minds that waited like sleeping seeds in the belief that they would eventually blossom. Finally, to my wife Teresa, simply the best teacher I ever had the honor to watch perform magic. A quiet master who taught children that music lives inside of them and showed them how to bring it forth.

I have been blessed by them all.

Made in the USA
Coppell, TX
09 July 2020

30331069R00198